MW01505035

# Unspeakable
# Things

# Unspeakable Things

### SILENCE, SHAME, AND THE
### STORIES WE CHOOSE TO BELIEVE

---

## BROOKE NEVILS

VIKING

VIKING
An imprint of Penguin Random House LLC
1745 Broadway, New York, NY 10019
penguinrandomhouse.com

VIKING and VIKING ship colophon are registered trademarks of
Penguin Random House LLC.

Poem on page 198 from the collection of the author.

*Designed by Christina Nguyen*

ISBN 9781984880185 (hardcover)
ISBN 9781984880192 (ebook)

Printed in the United States of America
1   3   5   7   9   10   8   6   4   2

The authorized representative in the EU for product safety and compliance
is Penguin Random House Ireland, Morrison Chambers, 32 Nassau Street,
Dublin D02 YH68, Ireland, https://eu-contact.penguin.ie.

*For my children*

Fear makes us afraid of the dark and shame makes us afraid of the light.

———

HARRIET LERNER

# CONTENTS

# Author's Note

He-said/she-said stories are nightmares—to tell, to hear, and to live. No little girl dreams of growing up to write *this* book. This kind of story makes us want to throw up our hands and turn away. Just by listening, it feels as though we're getting dragged into someone else's ugly, irreconcilable conflict. In a way, that's true. With every he-said/she-said story comes an unspoken demand to choose a side, to believe one person over another when the truth may well be unknowable, and when being wrong either way feels unconscionable. In other words, every he-said/she-said story feels like a trap. Living one feels much the same way.

The real trap, though, is repeating the past rather than questioning it. My purpose here is not to demand that you believe my side of the story without question, but instead to ask that you question all sides of your own beliefs about sexual harassment and assault. For years now, I've been doing just that.

Had I wanted to ask these questions in my former career as a news producer, I would have asked a booker to convince a sexual assault victim to share *their* story on camera. It was always someone else's story—their pain, their shame, their vulnerability—that I would use to lay bare the stakes of these issues in the most human of terms. In this book, I have chosen instead to offer my own.

It's fair to ask whether I, or any reporter, can objectively cover issues that have affected them so personally, and telling your own story is treacherous territory for any journalist. But since so many of us, unfortunately, have personal experiences with sexual harassment and assault, I believe it is more honest for me as a reporter to acknowledge mine openly. Readers may decide for themselves the degree to which these real-world experiences bias my perspective as a journalist, but, frankly, given the pervasiveness of sexual harassment and assault, I question whether any journalist who does not live in a vacuum can ever offer a truly unbiased perspective. Even the term "he-said/she-said" reflects the good but sometimes counterproductive intentions of journalists: It describes the conventional reporting practice of giving equal weight to both sides of a conflicting story, theoretically preserving fairness and impartiality.

In practice, the scales are often far from balanced. In the case of my he-said/she-said, the "he" in question is a household name who wielded one of the most powerful media platforms in the world for twenty years as anchor of NBC's *Today*. I, on the other hand, am just a name, singularly defined by my small role in Matt Lauer's downfall. Since it's human nature to trust what we know and suspect what we don't, Matt's voice—familiar to and trusted by millions upon millions of American television viewers for decades—will always carry more weight than mine. Nevertheless, I have included Matt's side of the story here at length, and this book contains no new allegations beyond those I reported in detail to NBC in November 2017 and those since made public by *The New York Times*, *Variety*, *The Washington Post*, investigative reporter Ronan Farrow, and NBC's internal investigation. As such, Matt has had ample opportunity to address all allegations against him in the time and manner of his choosing. As of publication, he has done so in a series of statements, three interviews, an open letter, and a 4,800-word opinion piece. I refer to these directly throughout and include his open letter in its entirety. All remain available online and I encourage readers to consider them independently. Matt's words provide a more thorough portrait of his character, motives, and credibility than I ever could. I have not reached out to him for additional comment. Furthermore, as of publication, Matt has not been charged with or convicted of any crime and denies all abusive or coercive sexual conduct and nonconsensual sex with any woman at any time.

While this book unreservedly represents my perspective, I include my own narrative here as I would any other primary source with direct knowledge of events and I trust readers to decide how much weight to afford it in their final analysis. As I explore in detail in later chapters, human memory is often fallible despite our best intentions. I have verified or corroborated my own memory when able, but in a story so intensely personal, emotional, and at times acrimonious, the perspectives of all individuals cannot be represented directly. To protect the privacy of others, I describe peripheral events sparingly and have named only public figures. When recounting allegations against Matt beyond my own, I refer to victims exclusively by their job titles to keep the focus on the extreme disparities in power. The terms "sexual assault" and "rape" have specific legal definitions that vary by state; unless specified, I use them here colloquially. Areas of speculation or uncertainty are acknowledged, and reporting is otherwise sourced. Direct quotes are taken from interviews, documents, and published works, and this book has been professionally fact-checked by a third party for accuracy. Unless specifically attributed, the conclusions drawn and arguments made are my own and should be considered my opinions.

I cannot express the depth of my admiration and gratitude for the work, insights, and generosity of the experts who contributed to the reporting of this book. Many regularly testify in court, work directly with law enforcement and parole boards, or provide training on victim and offender behavior so investigators can more effectively address sex crimes. These experts include clinical and forensic psychiatrist Barbara Ziv, MD (who testified for the prosecution in the Bill Cosby and one of the Harvey Weinstein trials); clinical and forensic psychologist Veronique Valliere, PhD; clinical and forensic psychologist Dawn Hughes, PhD; and psychologist and director of research for End Violence Against Women International Kimberly Lonsway, PhD. Similarly, memory expert Elizabeth Loftus, PhD, a professor at the University of California, Irvine, *also* consulted or testified in both the Cosby and Weinstein trials, but for the defense. To further address issues of memory relative to sexual assault, alcohol, and trauma, I spoke with Heather Flowe, PhD, a professor at the University of Birmingham in the United Kingdom and a coeditor of *Alcohol and Remembering Rape*; Aaron White, PhD, a leading expert on alcohol-induced memory loss and a senior scientific adviser at the National Institute on Alcohol Abuse and Alcoholism at the National Institutes of Health; and Richard J. McNally, PhD, a professor of clinical psychology at Harvard University, a preeminent scholar in the study of traumatic memory, and the author of *Remembering Trauma.*

Also interviewed are Jennifer Freyd, PhD, a professor emeritus at the University of Oregon who studies the psychology of sexual violence and betrayal trauma; Louise Godbold, the executive director of the nonprofit Echo, which provides training on trauma and resilience; Bruce Perry, MD, PhD, a psychiatrist and neuroscientist and the coauthor, with Oprah Winfrey, of *What Happened to You?: Conversations on Trauma, Resilience, and Healing*; Barbara Rothbaum, PhD, a professor at Emory University, the coauthor, with Edna Foa, PhD, of the seminal *Treating the Trauma of Rape*, and a leading authority on the treatment of post-traumatic stress disorder; Jo-Ann Rojas, LCSW, a sexual violence counselor of more than twenty-five years and a licensed training supervisor at RAINN (Rape, Abuse & Incest National Network); Joyce Short, the author of three books on sexual assault and the leader of a coalition advocating for the inclusion of a legal definition of consent in penal codes; sexual harassment investigator Fran Sepler, who has conducted more than a thousand independent fact-findings into sexual harassment and misconduct; attorney Lynn Hecht Schafran, a senior vice president, a senior staff attorney, and the former director of the national judicial education program at Legal Momentum, the first and longest-serving legal advocacy organization for women in the United States; attorney Tammy Marzigliano, a partner and the cochair of the Whistleblower and Retaliation Practice Group at leading employment law firm Outten & Golden; and Helen Benedict, a professor at the Columbia Journalism School and the author of *Virgin or Vamp*, the groundbreaking 1992 book exploring the media's unconscious perpetuation of rape myths. I spoke to the clinical psychologist and bestselling author Harriet Lerner, PhD, about shame and to Hope Edelman, the author of *Motherless Daughters*, about the profound nature of grief.

No expert was asked to evaluate or comment on my story specifically, and all have participated only to educate and inform on their respective areas of expertise, not to validate or corroborate my allegations. I am grateful to each and every one of them for their time and trust.

As devastating as these events were for me, they also undeniably impacted the lives of many people I loved. Having been wronged does not make me right by default, and to those I hurt— including by my choice to tell this story—I am truly sorry. It is my hope that this book may give others the resources to do better.

# Introduction

I n 1987, a Manhattan jury unanimously convicted two teenage boys in the murder of an elderly tourist in Midtown. Their verdict was in no small part due to the testimony of four eyewitnesses who placed the boys at the scene. Even though she had no doubt she'd done the right thing by voting to convict, one juror later found herself avoiding any part of the city that reminded her of the trial. For years, she avoided walking down the block where the victim was murdered. She avoided the courthouse on Centre Street. Eventually she told *The New Yorker* that she entirely avoided discussing her experience serving on the jury, for "she did not like to talk about things that upset her."

All this *before* she learned, thirty-seven years after voting to convict, that three of the prosecution eyewitnesses had lied on the stand. The two boys, now in their fifties, were innocent.

Here had been a young woman who made only the all-too-human mistake of accepting as truth the sworn testimony of liars. Simply by believing, she became party to a miscarriage of justice that would haunt her long after the convictions were vacated and the two innocent men freed.

Her story has stayed with me because it reminds me of the natural temptation to avoid the most painful parts of the past, for it is only human to avoid what is painful. It stays with me because it reminds me that to believe anyone, ever, is to take a terrifying leap of faith. Mostly it stays with me because it serves as a chilling reminder that we all have parts of the past we want to bury and forget and, until we confront them, they haunt us.

I was haunted by my past for a long time. Some secrets are too dangerous to tell, and yet too dangerous to keep. What then? There are no easy answers, but if I've learned anything in the years since those secrets—the most horrific episode of my life—became front-page news during the frenzy of MeToo, it's that too many people have their own long-buried stories they feel they cannot tell. The public airing of my private pain has turned out to be the most unexpected of gifts, for it leaves me no choice but to be vulnerable among friends and strangers alike. Over the years, they have responded not with judgment but relief to have found someone who will listen and understand. From that, I've learned that the more we talk about painful chapters of the past, the less painful they become.

I won't pretend, though, that I didn't learn that lesson the hard way. If you think a woman would have to be out of her mind to want to talk about any of this, you're not totally wrong. When I decided to write this book, I actually *was* in a psych ward. Granted, the choice was much easier back then, when I was not a married mother of two living a life I cherish but a shell-shocked woman who felt she had very little left to lose. I was thirty-four years old and I'd just walked away from everything I'd ever achieved, with zero prospects of another job as a news producer in a shrinking media bubble filled with powerful friends of the *Today* anchor I'd "gotten fired." At that extremely low point in my life, telling this story was not so much a choice but what felt like my last hope to offer anything meaningful to a world that had left me feeling utterly powerless, ashamed, and alone.

The only path I'd ever imagined for myself—my endless quest to make it as a journalist in New York, the naive ambition of a St. Louis high schooler obsessed with *The West Wing*, Nora Ephron, and Joan Didion—had imploded and then vanished before my eyes. In truth, since the 2014 Sochi Olympics four years earlier, that quest had become less about climbing a notoriously steep career ladder than it was about simply surviving at all. My job at NBC News was not just one part of my life but its organizing principle. I'd met nearly everyone I knew in New York through working at 30 Rock and NBC felt like family, the place where I thought I would always belong. For years I'd been living paycheck to paycheck in tiny, rented apartments, drowning in credit card debt and student loans, my feet paddling furiously beneath the surface to keep that all-consuming quest alive. It was more than the way I earned my living. It was my life, my identity, my purpose; I believed I was part of something important and that without it, I would be nothing and have nothing.

That was why, when I woke up one morning in Sochi with my underwear and sheets caked with blood, my first thought was *This must have been a misunderstanding*. This was not necessarily because that made any sense, but because it was the only acceptable conclusion I could reach without my whole life falling apart. The night before had been a blur but not an incomprehensible one. My longtime boss and mentor, Meredith Vieira, had just become the first woman in history to anchor primetime Olympic coverage, and we'd met for a glass of wine in our hotel bar to celebrate. We'd been there for a while when her former *Today* coanchor, Matt Lauer, happened to walk in. We waved him over and I patted the seat next to me for him to join us. Nothing would ever be the same again.

Three and a half years later, at the height of MeToo, I made a confidential complaint to NBC News human resources about what had happened later that night. After hours of drinking together in the hotel bar, Matt summoned me—an intoxicated subordinate employee—to his corporate hotel room, where he engaged in what he characterizes as an "extramarital but consensual sexual encounter." For me, however—the intoxicated subordinate employee in question—characterizing what happened that night has never been so simple. Consent? Under *those* circumstances? Not simple at all. It's taken me more than a decade to fully come to terms with what happened in that hotel room and the months that followed.

But for three long, self-destructive years between Sochi and MeToo, I refused to acknowledge any of it, even to myself. It is only human, after all, to avoid what is painful. But it is also incredibly dangerous: In a slowly devolving, chaotic attempt to bury, normalize, and rationalize what happened, I lost who I was and the person I might have become. That the anchor of *Today*, who I'd watched on TV and admired and trusted since I was ten years old, could ever have done anything wrong was not something my brain could begin to fathom back then. In those days at NBC, Matt Lauer could seemingly do no wrong. As *Today*'s longest-serving anchor, the network had given him the biggest contract in the sixty-year history of morning television, paying him a reported $25 million a year. I was a nobody from nowhere—the nerdy assistant whose literal job was to keep the on-air talent happy. I earned less in a year than Matt earned in a day and had no contract at all. Since it was my job as a talent assistant to fix talent-related problems, any problem with the talent could only have been my fault. Nothing else made sense. So I blamed myself, lied to everyone in my life, drank constantly, and became a different person, one I didn't know and couldn't stand.

To be sexually harassed is to have your value reduced to your body at the cost of your ability to earn a living. To come to terms with any form of sexual assault is to reckon with a traumatic loss of control over your body and life. To blame yourself after experiencing either—or both—is an attempt to regain some of that lost control retroactively, for the fastest way to reassert control is to convince yourself you never lost it in the first place. For that to be true, whatever happened must be all your fault, even if that makes you a fool or a bad person. It may even require returning to your abuser to prove to yourself that it was your choice all along. At least then, you are not a victim but once again the master of your own fate. But the illusion of control comes at a cost. The truth of what happened must be put in a box and buried. Shame takes its place.

In a purely practical sense, it worked: I kept my job and life went on. But when you bury a secret, it takes root. It grows and grows until eventually all of life, and whatever person you've become, feels grounded in lies. Because NBC *was* my life, my whole existence soon felt like a lie. When I made the complaint to NBC three years later, it was not because I thought anything would come of it—this was Matt Lauer, after all—but because I could no longer bear to be complicit in the secret. NBC could believe me or not, but at least I would have some small hope of being able to live with myself again. And by making an on-the-record complaint to my employer rather than going to the press or filing a lawsuit, I'd made Sochi a private issue between me and my employer. I saw it as hermetically sealed off from the rest of the world forever, like medical records and nuclear codes. It was the most discreet option for everyone involved. I would put it behind me and move on.

But that's not the way it worked out.

The day after I made my complaint, Matt was questioned by NBC and fired by NBC News chairman Andrew Lack later that night. After his firing was announced the next morning— Wednesday, November 29, 2017—*The New York Times* and *Variety* published a slew of other allegations against Matt, and by that afternoon my complaint was being characterized alongside them in the *Times* and *Vanity Fair.* The next day, an investigative reporter was texting my personal cell phone. Eventually a tabloid began calling my coworkers at 30 Rock, apparently asking whether they were aware that I was Matt's "mistress who'd gotten him fired." After that, I made it a few more months before taking a leave of absence that would ultimately prove permanent. I'd started at NBC giving studio tours for ten dollars an hour, and it had taken a full decade to work my way up to salaried primetime news producer. Now that life was gone, and so was the future it once held. Weeks later, I found myself in a psych ward, where the mere idea of writing this book would give me the sense of purpose I needed to keep going and start again.

But even then, I was not so out of my mind that I didn't know how the world—or at least the media—would see me for writing it. I'd be cast as a shameless fame seeker looking to cash in by writing a salacious tell-all about the disgraced celebrity whose career I'd had the audacity to ruin. At that point, though, I hardly cared. In the ten months since I'd made my confidential complaint, I'd refused every interview request, citing my desire to remain anonymous and move on with my life. Reporters would typically respond that I could help countless other women if only I'd speak out, which made me feel cowardly and selfish for wanting privacy to heal. It didn't matter whether I kept silent or shouted from the rooftops. I'd be blamed either way. There was no winning.

But the decision to write this book was about more than having a voice in the public narrative of what happened to my body. What

I really wanted was answers. What happened to my life? To my career? How could any of this have happened to *me*? I was no delicate flower. I drank Scotch and told dirty jokes and swore like a sailor. You don't get to be a network news producer by being terrified of men and running to HR all the time.

No—I'd turned the other cheek, put my head down, done the work, and dealt with whatever I had to, like every other woman I knew. Then suddenly MeToo came along and now I was complicit, a part of the problem. First I'd been a fool for falling for it, then again for putting up with it, and finally for waiting so long to report it. I wasn't tough for putting my head down and getting back to work; I was weak for caring about keeping my job, paying my bills, and not losing my health insurance. Apparently I'd done everything wrong, yet now I was supposed to use a hashtag and call myself a survivor. I didn't feel at all like a survivor. I felt like an idiot, set up to fail from the beginning.

MeToo was a long-overdue reckoning that asked a lot of unsettling questions it ultimately left unanswered. The changes it sparked were so sudden and sweeping that they ignored the uncertainty that many of us felt and still feel. Its wake left a growing divide between those who "got it" because we'd lived it and those who didn't because they hadn't. I lived it—at the very center of it—but *still* didn't get it. How was I supposed to have stopped what I had never seen coming? Why had it taken me years to even begin to understand Sochi, or even my own response to it, which defied everything I thought I knew about both myself *and* sexual harassment and assault? The questions I most needed answered were the ones everyone either seemed too afraid to ask or was pretending to have understood all along. Why the hell do victims—myself included—go back to their abusers? Why do they lie to cover it up instead of reporting it? If yes can mean no (and, by the way, since when?), how is anyone supposed to know when yes means yes?

Yet, again and again, I was told that everything that happened in 2014, from Sochi to its messy aftermath back in New York—all of which had felt so utterly incomprehensible and insane that I thought the problem could only have been me—was "textbook." Whichever textbook that was, I'd never heard of it and I'd certainly never read it. Why would I? I knew what sexual harassment was; I'd done the online trainings. I knew what sexual assault was; I'd heard the "yes means yes and no means no" speech back in high school. But I didn't know what I didn't know, and that nearly everything I thought I knew about sexual harassment and assault was wrong.

Though perpetrators and victims of sexual abuse often conform to well-documented patterns of behavior, we rarely recognize those patterns because they look nothing like how we think abusers and victims "should" act. Worse still, many of these textbook behaviors tend to be the very same characteristics that we see as red flags, causing us to doubt the credibility of sexual harassment and assault allegations. Even as a shell-shocked woman wearing sticky socks in a psych ward, this seemed patently insane.

I was a nerd. A journalist. I'd thought I was a feminist, but my understanding of sexual harassment, assault, consent, and victim and perpetrator behavior was based almost entirely on a set of false assumptions and stereotypes that have startlingly little to do with reality. Black-and-white, quid pro quo sexual harassment cases and violent, stereotypical sexual assaults are rare. It's the messy gray area that is the norm.

From going back to their abusers to lying to normalize the abuse, victims can react in seemingly counterintuitive ways that, once understood, are not counterintuitive at all but very common survival responses to sexual trauma. Yet instead of helping those victims who desperately need support, we doubt them because their reactions aren't what we think a "real" victim's would be. We blame them for their innate survival responses—and allow them to blame themselves—while their abusers avoid blame altogether.

Journalists play a role in this, too, often unconsciously perpetuating stereotypes about sexual harassment and assault when we should be unraveling them. Before MeToo, I was no different. While reporting this book, I saw again and again how I'd unknowingly reinforced these tropes in my own work because I'd believed them myself. Those unquestioned beliefs not only impacted how I saw and helped shape stories but also rendered invisible the many "messy" stories of "unsympathetic" victims I never bothered to explore because they didn't fit the stereotypical mold. This book is an earnest effort to ask the questions now that I should have asked earlier in my career, when the answers could have helped others and fundamentally changed the course of my life.

Matt is but one example of a much larger, systemic problem. The only thing particularly remarkable about my story is his extraordinary fame and power as anchor of *Today*, but in a way, even that is not so remarkable. In 2016, more than a year before MeToo, the United States Equal Employment Opportunity Commission (EEOC) specifically described and cautioned against the dangers of serial "superstar" harassers. These are employees perceived to be of such high value that they are virtually irreplaceable and answer to practically no one, which emboldens them to abuse less powerful colleagues they see as expendable. The long string of then-unreported allegations against Matt—which, by the time I was in the psych ward, had been revealed by NBC's internal investigation to go back as far as 1996, when I was in *fifth grade*—bear an undeniable resemblance to the pattern of behavior the EEOC's report describes. It was Matt, not me, who chose to set himself out as a personal and professional role model as anchor of *Today*, and it was in that capacity that he chose to engage in predatory sexual behavior toward subordinates. This story serves as a powerful example of how these abuses can happen, even in the most highly scrutinized of workplaces.

But after years of frank conversations with experts and those struggling to come to terms with their own experiences, I know that it is possible for two people to leave the same interaction with wildly different understandings of what took place. In some he-said/she-said stories, neither party is lying but both believe the other is not telling the truth. To believe anyone is to take a leap of faith, but to believe ourselves? Is the truth of these events—not "his truth" or "her truth" but *the* truth—even knowable? When the past is a minefield of unanswerable questions, how can we heal?

There have been times in the years that I have been reporting and writing this book when it has felt like sheer insanity to walk away from a loving husband and two beautiful children to sit alone, hiding away, endlessly reliving this story. Every moment with my family is a precious piece of a life that I once believed I would never get to live. Yet I know that somewhere, others are trapped in the same impossible situation I once was, left with the same set of bad choices I once faced, believing they no longer deserve the futures that still lie ahead of them. To them, I would never say that the past can be fixed or changed, that justice is guaranteed, that life is fair, or that everything will be okay. I know all too well that it can't, it isn't, and all too likely, it won't. I *can* say that I know what it is to feel truly alone and ashamed, living a life that seems irredeemable, believing yourself to be worthless and unlovable.

Not one of these things—for any one of us—is ever true.

# Unspeakable
# Things

# Prologue

n January 2015, the United States Equal Employment Opportunity Commission (EEOC) created a task force to investigate
whether meaningful progress had been made in eliminating
workplace harassment in the thirty years since the Supreme Court
ruled it was prohibited under the Civil Rights Act. Eighteen months
of investigation later, the task force found that harassment remained
both widespread and rarely reported, and that prevention efforts
by employers were ineffective at best and counterproductive at
worst. Its report included an examination of workplace conduct
and behaviors that would potentially "set the stage for unlawful
harassment" if left unchecked, which included:

### THE CASE OF THE "SUPERSTAR" HARASSER
Excerpted from the REPORT OF THE CO-CHAIRS
OF THE EEOC SELECT TASK FORCE ON THE
STUDY OF HARASSMENT IN THE WORKPLACE,
JUNE 2016

. . . Employers may find themselves in a position where
the harasser is a workplace "superstar."

By superstar, think of the high-earning trader at an investment bank, the law firm partner who brings in lucrative clients, or the renowned professor or surgeon. Some of these individuals, as with any employee, may be as likely to engage in harassment as others. Often, however, superstars are privileged with higher income, better accommodations, and different expectations. That privilege can lead to a self-view that they are above the rules, which can foster mistreatment. Psychologists have detailed how power can make an individual feel uninhibited and thus more likely to engage in inappropriate behaviors. In short, superstar status can be a breeding ground for harassment.

When the superstar misbehaves, employers may perceive themselves in a quandary. They may be tempted to ignore the misconduct because, the thinking goes, losing the superstar would be too costly. They may wager that the likelihood or cost of a complaint of misbehavior is relatively low and outweighed by the superstar's productivity. Some employers may even use this type of rationale to cover or retaliate for a harasser.

Employers should avoid the trap of binary thinking that weighs the productivity of a harasser *solely* against the costs of his or her being reported. As a recent Harvard Business School study found, the profit consequences of so-called "toxic workers"—*specifically including* those who are "top performers"—is a net negative. Analyzing data on 11 global companies and 58,542 hourly workers, the researchers found that roughly one in 20 workers was fired for egregious company policy violations, such as sexual harassment. Avoiding these toxic workers, they found, can save a company more than twice as much as the increased output generated by a top performer. As a result, the study urged employers to "consider toxic and productivity outcomes together rather than relying on productivity alone as the criterion of a good hire." No matter who the harasser is, the negative effects of harassment can cause serious damage to a business.

Indeed, the reputational costs alone can have serious consequences, particularly where it is revealed that managers for years "looked the other way" at a so-called "superstar" harasser.

# ONE.

# Magic

*This Was* Today *at NBC*

Right at seven o'clock, my mother would put on the *Today* show. From kindergarten through high school, when I came downstairs for breakfast, I'd find her standing in the kitchen by the television, coffee in hand, listening intently to the news at the top of the show. My mother rarely stood still, but she would always stop what she was doing for a few minutes to watch *Today*. Children first see the world through their parents, and just by making a point to watch and listen to these faraway strangers on television every morning, my mom's morning ritual taught me something. *What these people say is important. I trust them, and so can you.*

One of those people, Meredith Vieira, the *Today* coanchor who would one day become my boss and mentor, often told a story about the first time she traveled with the show to broadcast live from the site of a major story. It was the mass shooting at Virginia Tech in April 2007, and she had only been a *Today* anchor for six months. She was attending a candlelight vigil when a young woman approached her.

"She told me that her parents lived far away," Meredith wrote in an essay ten years later. "She said that she had watched *Today* for years and had grown to see us as an extension of her family. And right now she needed a mom to hold her."

I was a senior in college that year. That young woman could just as easily have been me.

My generation will likely be the last to have that kind of emotional attachment to news anchors we grew up watching on television. Most of the kids in my neighborhood now have never heard of the *Today* show. They turn to their phones, not the television, for information and companionship and that warm, fuzzy feeling of familiarity I used to have while watching *Today*. We don't have a television in our kitchen. We don't have one in our house at all.

How can I ever explain to my children just how much the *Today* show once meant to me, how much it meant to my mother, the role that it played in our home every morning, and what a privilege it felt like to work there? The world has changed so much that I know they will never understand how a morning news show could have felt like real family to millions of us, and why.

Maybe that's for the best.

I worked at NBC for about a decade and at *Today* for only a small fraction of that, but even that short amount of time in proximity to the show's power changed the way I saw the world.

Imagine arriving at work every day to find that a crowd of hundreds is already there, standing in the darkness. It is so unnaturally early that, really, it's still the night before. Yet these smiling people have packed up their families and traveled across the country to be here, and now they are craning to get a glimpse inside the window of your workplace. They are excited to see you, waving with excitement, giddy to be seen and acknowledged, just because you work at *Today*.

Suddenly it no longer matters how tired or grouchy you are. Every day, in the rain and snow and God-awful sticky heat of the summer, that crowd shows up—or rather, a different version of it, every single day, each equally thrilled and giddy as the last. This is to say nothing of the crowd of millions watching at home, just as I used to do every morning before school. Of all the ways in the world to make a living, this is yours. Hundreds of strangers travel thousands of collective miles to stand for hours just to be seen in the background of what you do. More than that, you know that those very few seconds of being broadcast on *Today* will make them and their families very, very happy, and that they will never forget them.

I never stopped feeling gratitude for that smiling, waving crowd in all the years that I worked at NBC, but I see now that it didn't do much to make me a kinder, more empathetic person. It was mind-warping, imbuing even the most menial tasks with an addicting sense of urgency and importance. You tell yourself that if you don't get this coffee or track down the movie star stuck in traffic, then the show might not go on, and millions of people across America will wonder what the hell happened. Whatever your job—whether printing scripts or sitting in a windowless control room every morning while someone else puts your children on the bus to school—it *means something*. It matters. If, even for a moment, you don't think so, then plenty of people are out there waiting to take your place.

From the very beginning of my career at NBC, that was quite literally true. In 2008, when I started at the NBCUniversal Page Program, seven thousand applicants competed for about sixty jobs that required a college degree but paid only ten dollars an hour. Getting into the program was not so much an accomplishment but a lottery I still don't know how I won. The only connections I had in media were the ones I'd made myself, mailing unsolicited copies of my college newspaper articles to reporters I idolized. I didn't go to journalism school. I'd only interned at newspapers and magazines and knew absolutely nothing about television production. Yet there I was, with my foot in an extremely rarefied door. To walk through it every day felt like a dream.

What I couldn't possibly have understood when I watched *Today* on television as a child was the way that going to work at NBC in Rockefeller Center felt like going to work within history itself. Tucked away in Midtown Manhattan is a twenty-two-acre Art Deco city of its own, dubbed Radio City because the RCA Building at its center—known today as 30 Rock—was once a literal city of radio studios for America's first national broadcasting company, NBC. Radio City Music Hall, with its iconic neon marquee, opened in 1932; the observation deck now known as the Top of the Rock first opened in 1933; the Rainbow Room on 30 Rock's sixty-fifth floor opened in 1934; and the Rockefeller Center ice rink opened in 1936. It's all still there, and looks mostly the same. I've never forgotten how small and insignificant I felt the first time I went to Rockefeller Center with my mother, a TWA flight attendant, when she brought me along on one of her rare overnight trips to New York City back when I was in high school. Eight years later, when I started working there, I felt exactly the same way: small, insignificant, and utterly in awe.

This was a different NBC then, in the waning days of the final golden era of broadcasting. Netflix had just begun streaming, only the rich kids had iPhones, and people generally saw the news networks as nonpartisan. Tim Russert hosted *Meet the Press*. Brian Williams anchored *NBC Nightly News*. Dick Ebersol ran NBC Sports and Bob Costas was still its star. Jay Leno hosted *The Tonight Show* and Conan O'Brien hosted *Late Night*. Kristen Wiig, Jason Sudeikis, Amy Poehler, Bill Hader, and Fred Armisen were on *Saturday Night Live*, where, that fall, Tina Fey would moonlight as Sarah Palin. But the undisputed crown jewel of NBC News was

*Today*, which reached number one in the ratings in 1995 and was still there thirteen years later.* The show averaged an incredible six million viewers a day. As of 2025, that number is about half. Its hosts at the time—Matt Lauer, Meredith Vieira, Ann Curry, and Al Roker—were billed as "America's First Family." By the time it had been number one for fifteen years, the then NBCUniversal CEO, Jeff Zucker, estimated that *Today* had earned NBC $3 billion in pure profit. It, alongside CBS's *60 Minutes*, represented the pinnacle of news broadcasting's power and reach.

But when you spend your formative years orbiting power, you learn very quickly that your value is determined by your proximity to that power, and you soon lose any sense of your own gravity and worth. After six months in the page program, I was assigned to *Today*, where I brought the day's newspapers to the anchors and producers and then spent the rest of each morning in the greenroom, shepherding guests to the set for their segments. Early in 2009, I was hired to fill in for Meredith's assistant while she was on maternity leave. Then I became an associate researcher on the show's weekend edition, printing endless backup scripts that nobody ever read and checking the on-screen graphics for spelling errors. I produced a few segments, but much more memorably, my cat Oscar modeled a sweater on the weekday show, which led to an animal talent agent and a brief feline modeling career. Nothing drives home the sheer power of being on camera at *Today* better than the experience of cashing your cat's paycheck.

It was no surprise, then, that it was my relationship with the on-camera talent that made my career. After Meredith left *Today* and joined an NBC prime-time news magazine as a correspondent, I became her full-time talent assistant and associate producer, then

---

* "The Streak," as everyone called it, lasted 852 weeks, from December 1995 to April 2012.

a field producer and coordinating producer on her daytime talk show. It took nearly a decade, but all those years of hard work didn't make it feel any less like a fluke. Every day in that building, I wondered how it was possible that I was allowed to be there at all, let alone get paid for it.

That sense of vital importance, and meaning, and mattering, never went away, even on the most frustrating and stupid of days. Once I found myself scrubbing what I think was camel shit out of a dressing room carpet after a prank segment (no matter how exotic, live animals still poop at their own convenience), and even as I crouched on the floor with my wad of wet paper towels, that sense of importance and meaning and mattering was somehow still there, but now beyond all reasonable proportion to reality. We were *broadcasters*, I'd tell myself. Our work went out on public airwaves, which made us—at least according to the Federal Communications Commission—"public trustees, afforded their spectrum so that they may serve the needs and interests of their communities of license." Whether making a restaurant reservation or picking up dry cleaning or pandering to some idiotic reality show star, I was a public servant, working in the public interest. The chauffeured cars, international travel, five-star hotels, and six-figure hair, makeup, and wardrobe budgets were beside the point.

It was a rationalization for the ages, of course, but neither was it entirely untrue. There was always that crowd on the plaza outside of Studio 1A, and the tourists buzzing around 30 Rock, who'd see my NBC badge and ask excitedly if I knew any of the on-air talent. I did, I would tell them, and they were *wonderful*. Then I would watch as their faces lit up with the joy of genuine connection with the anchors they'd been welcoming into their homes for years. Every time that happened, I'd realize all over again what a miraculous thing it is in this world to feel like you know someone, that you can count on them to be there for you every single day, that they care about and speak to you, and make you feel like you matter. That connection meant something to those people, just as it had meant something to me when I watched *Today* as a kid. That connection to viewers—embodied by its anchors—is power, personified.

But the longer you internalize that you matter only because you are close to powerful people in powerful jobs, the smaller and more inconsequential you feel—as though without them, you wouldn't register in the world at all. Every day I would walk into work and look up at the 850-foot monument to broadcasting that is 30 Rockefeller Plaza, and I knew that on some level, nothing I could ever say or do in my career would really matter in the scope of NBC's long, illustrious history. I thought that was humility, but it wasn't. It was dangerous. My own lack of consequence became the permission structure I used to avoid being accountable for what I saw and did in that building, and all the times that I looked the other way.

———

IN MY FIRST COUPLE OF WEEKS as the *Today* greenroom page, a crew member told me about an incident with Matt. I don't remember the specifics anymore, but Matt had said something lewd about the breasts of a woman on set that day and people in the control room had apparently heard it through a live mic. At the time, I wondered if it was some social litmus test to see how I responded. Would I laugh, or was I some priss who was going to run off to HR? Apparently I was neither. The realization that America's Dad had used the word "tits" was gross—as though I was back in high school and I'd heard a teacher tell a dirty joke about one of the other girls in my class—but my first instinct was to pretend I'd never heard it, to wipe from my memory anything that would tarnish the golden image of Matt I had from so many years of watching him at home.

Yet at the same time, I felt strangely honored to have been initiated into the show's inner sanctum, where people were allowed to know gross, behind-the-scenes things about Matt Lauer. It meant I was trusted. It meant that I belonged. That any of Matt's lewd behavior could ever be directed at me never crossed my mind. The world of television is populated by charismatic, beautiful people who've all seemingly won the bone structure genetic lottery. I was tall and awkward, a gangly green bean with curly hair who laughed at her own weird jokes. At *Today*, I was wallpaper.

But only at *Today* could being the wallpaper be so exciting. Leonardo DiCaprio once stepped on my foot in the greenroom (he was very apologetic). I did the twist with Chubby Checker. I met Michael Phelps when he brought back eight gold medals from the Beijing Olympics. I was there for the *Today* Halloween show, which, back then, was still one of the more anticipated television events of the year. Meredith was Pinocchio, with a nose that really grew; Al was the Gingerbread Man; Ann was Cinderella; and Matt, comically enough, was Humpty Dumpty.

It was never said explicitly that protecting the talent was a part of the job. It was just professionalism: Off camera is meant to be a safe space where the talent, scrutinized by millions while on the air and in public, does not have to be "on" or scrutinized by anyone. A professional does not ask to take photos with the talent or get autographs or do anything else that a fan might do, like gawk at celebrities or get nervous around them. A professional does not write about the talent on social media or otherwise speak out of turn about them in public. A professional makes the talent look as good as possible at all times. That's the job.

But there's good reason for that. In news, the on-air talent is more than just a smiling face. They're the embodiment of the show's journalistic integrity. They are the public face of everyone's work. If the viewers decide they don't trust or like the on-air talent, they change the channel. To work off camera on a news show means your success is directly tied to the talent's. To protect them is to protect your own future, along with the integrity of your work. Everyone is on the same team; the talent are the most visible members of the team; to protect the talent is to protect the team.

And so what begins as teamwork can become something of an omertà, and then a cult of personality. Ordinary people become larger-than-life figures, the human equivalent of a rising tide that lifts all boats. It's not difficult to see how this can devolve from not needing to be "on" when off camera, to not needing to be nice to staffers who are paid to accommodate you, to behaving like a full-fledged prima donna.

I'd never been around celebrities before starting at NBC, but I soon noticed that people in the business talked about being "good with talent" as though it was an innate gift, like horse whispering or having perfect pitch. Some people, it seemed, embodied the perfect blend of deference and directness, and it turned out that I was one of them. The talent, meanwhile, were talked about as though they were odd hybrids between babies and circus animals. They had handlers and groomers, ate special diets, and required special transportation and enclosures, whether a dressing room with specific snacks or a suite at the Four Seasons. Most of the time they were lovely, but sometimes, if you made a wrong move in their presence, you'd get your head bitten off. By the end of my career, I'd been on the sets of films, Broadway shows, television dramas, talk shows, game shows, comedy shows, late-night shows, and every genre of news show, at nearly every network. On every one of them, the talent was discussed the same way.

I asked other staffers, all of whom started in the business as pages, production assistants, or interns around the same time that I did, about their experiences working with talent.

"It's like walking a tight rope while balancing a pot of boiling water on your head and smiling the whole time. Then you're constantly told, 'You're lucky to be here. Don't you know how many people would kill to have your job?'"

"If they weren't happy with you, you'd hear about it, but never from them directly. Soon you're scheduling things so the talent doesn't have to see anyone they don't like, and you just pray that you haven't become one of those people but nobody's told you."

"The talent is the face of the network. They're the money-maker, the product. From the president of the network down to the intern, we have to keep them happy. Nobody wants to rock the boat."

There are certain things that no one with that much relative importance and power can safely be told: *Actually, this was your fault. Actually, you are the one being unreasonable. It was a huge problem that you were late, since dozens of us could do nothing but stand around and wait for you.* Instead, those uncomfortable realities are simply absorbed by the staff. If the talent is late, it's because their car pickup wasn't scheduled early enough. If the talent is unprepared, it's because no one adequately prepared them. If the talent forgets someone's name, then they should have been reminded.

What does it do to a person's perception of reality—of basic human interaction—to spend their working life this way?

"When you're the star of the show, nobody can afford to correct your behavior," wrote actor and writer Tavi Gevinson in a telling 2022 piece in *The New Yorker*. "There's not even a penalty for being late. I've been embarrassed, on set, to learn that I don't know my lines as well as I think I do, then to notice that the director has no choice but to assure me that I'm killing it while anxiously checking the time. Equally disconcerting is being surrounded by hundreds of crew members and background actors who are instructed not to look at or talk to the cast, to only mime speaking when the camera is rolling. It is sort of your job, as a performer, to have Main Character Syndrome, and after years in such an environment, maybe the condition becomes permanently embedded."

After a fatal shooting on the set of the film *Rust*, longtime Hollywood armorer Thomas Pimentel told *The Atlantic*, in 2023, that one of the perils of show business was the near impossibility of correcting the behavior of the on-camera talent. "An armorer can come in and handle weapons, but good luck trying to speak up when you hand an A-list celebrity a pistol and he puts his finger on the trigger and he's not supposed to," he said. "I've been there: 'You can't say anything to them in front of the rest of the crew. It'll be embarrassing.'"

"Someone is responsible for what happened and I can't say who that is, but I know it's not me," actor Alec Baldwin, the A-list celebrity holding the gun at the time it discharged and fatally shot a woman on his film set, told ABC News.*

If walking past the crowd outside *Today* every morning for a few months while I worked in the greenroom could warp my sense of self-importance for years afterward, what would it do to someone who anchored the show for twenty years as that crowd screamed his name?

---

* Baldwin was charged with two counts of involuntary manslaughter in January 2023. Those charges were dropped in April 2023. He was indicted by a grand jury in January 2024, again on two counts of involuntary manslaughter. Those charges were dismissed with prejudice in July 2024. In a separate trial, attorneys of *Rust* armorer Hannah Gutierrez-Reed argued that it was difficult for a twenty-four-year-old armorer to "stand up" to Baldwin, especially when older, more experienced crew members did not; she was convicted of involuntary manslaughter in March 2024 and sentenced to eighteen months in prison, the maximum possible punishment.

BUT FOR EVERY ANCHOR monster and prima donna, there is talent so warm and magnetic that the on-air magic they create is not a performance but an authentic function of the person they really are.

I first met Meredith when I was the page at *Today*, and if getting into the page program felt like stumbling upon a winning lottery ticket, filling in as her assistant in 2009 seemed like an outright miracle. Despite two impossibly high-pressure jobs (at the time, she was hosting both *Today* on NBC and *Who Wants to Be a Millionaire* on ABC), Meredith was universally beloved, and she became a tireless mentor to and advocate for me. Since I had no family in New York, she often invited me to join her family at Thanksgiving and Christmas. Later, she sat in the waiting room of a hospital all day while I had surgery, then helped me up the three flights of stairs to my walk-up apartment. I stayed an assistant far longer than I should have because I loved her so much.

But I also stayed because, if I am being honest with myself, I knew that to work for the talent was to wield a small amount of the power I would never otherwise have myself. To do anything on Meredith's behalf was usually to make someone's day or help their charity or give them a potentially life-changing opportunity. It was to generate a fraction of the joy I saw on the plaza outside *Today* in the mornings when I walked into a room next to her. It was to feel that my work was as meaningful and important, like hers. To work for the talent was, more often than not, magical.

Some of that magic refracted back on me, even when I was no longer a talent assistant. One early spring afternoon later in my career, I ditched the noise and chaos of the newsroom to edit a script with a glass of wine at a sidewalk café. It was near Central Park and filled with delighted tourists, including a group of women who loudly discussed how sad it was that I was there alone, with my laptop and phones and wine, clearly married to my work and missing the best years of my life. Then they abruptly went silent. I heard a booming, familiar voice: *Haaaaaaaaayyyyyyyyy, Brookie!*

It was Hoda Kotb, then a *Today* anchor, tall and elegant and radiating charisma as she walked briskly by the café, leaning over to squeeze my shoulders without stopping. I smiled at her and went back to my script, but the women remained speechless, snapping photos of Hoda as she walked away. In an instant, I had gone from a figure of consummate pity to the envy of everyone there.

To work with the talent was to feel that way pretty much all the time.

———

DURING ITS 2018 INTERNAL INVESTIGATION into Matt's sexual misconduct, NBC interviewed sixty-eight current and former staffers about his behavior: "Most witnesses had positive things to say about Lauer's demeanor in the workplace. Lauer also was described as a very private person who acted as a friend and professional mentor to both men and women alike over decades at the *Today* show."

Had I never gone to Sochi, I would have described Matt the same way. When I filled in as Meredith's assistant while they were *Today* coanchors, my desk was in a small alcove outside their offices. Matt was intimidating and direct but kind enough to me. Most other producers I've spoken with since Matt's firing felt similarly, saying that he was always willing to give advice and that his feedback improved their work. I don't doubt the validity of any of those positive experiences with him, but neither do they invalidate the negative experiences of others. A person can behave with genuine kindness to one person and terrible cruelty to another; the two are not mutually exclusive. Just as there were countless women in

Hollywood who were abused by Harvey Weinstein, many more women worked with him who were not. People are complicated.

But it is also chillingly rational behavior. If an abuser overtly sexually harassed or assaulted every person they encountered, they wouldn't get away with it for long. But if they only abuse a few people—more pragmatically, if they choose those they know are likely to stay quiet or who wouldn't be believed anyway—then the vast majority of people who work with them will be legitimately shocked when the abuser's bad behavior is revealed. Even if they had an inkling that something was going on, out of a misplaced sense of politeness or deference, they'll probably look the other way because they assume it is none of their business. Sexual behavior is some of the most private behavior there is. To work with someone for two decades without knowing anything about their sexual proclivities or habits is *normal workplace behavior*; it doesn't automatically equate to complicity in what they do behind closed doors. Even an open secret is still, after all, a secret.

As for who knew what about Matt's sexual misconduct toward female subordinates, I can only speak for myself. I knew.

I knew, and I knew long before I went to Sochi. In the six months or so that I sat outside his office in 2009, I saw that while he had a close coterie of bookers and producers who adored him,* there were also a few female producers who seemed to avoid him. At the time, I didn't give it much thought. Staffers often waited until the talent was gone to relax and be themselves.

All the executive offices had the now-infamous buttons that allowed the person at the desk to close the door behind guests without having to get up. Once the door closed, people could be locked out but not locked inside. Matt used his button constantly, though

---

* One in this coterie, a booker who eventually became head of booking for all of NBC News, was also fired in 2017 in his own sexual misconduct scandal.

I didn't give this much thought at the time, either. I hadn't been in the work world long enough to understand how quickly the dynamic in a room changes once the door is closed, or how disconcerting it would have been to walk into Matt's office leaving the door deliberately open only to later hear it shut behind you.

But more to the point, I heard the myriad rumors about Matt hitting on and having sexual relationships with women who worked at the show. I was just far too immature and ignorant to understand their significance. To me, it was just gossip, another trade secret about the talent that made me feel important to know. On one level, it *was* just gossip, in that I didn't personally walk around the newsroom to each woman I'd heard discussed to ask them directly if the rumors were true. There was no concern for these women that I can remember—only resentment that they were seen as monopolizing Matt's attention for professional gain. Granted, when I'd been hit on at work, it had always been by men my own age in parallel jobs, and somehow I failed to see the distinction between that— which was just run-of-the-mill awkwardness—and getting hit on by your boss, which is sexual harassment.

Mainly, I wanted to belong, and so regardless of what I heard around the office, I just nodded eagerly in agreement and then adopted the prevailing way of thinking. Back then, the workplace was dominated by a generation of women who'd been dealing with sexual harassment their entire careers. It seemed that to them, sexual harassment was practically a rite of passage: If they'd had to put up with it for all these years, well, then, so did we. Powerful men having affairs with subordinates? That was just the way of the world. It was certainly never discussed as abuse. As a result, I didn't see the women who were rumored to have been ensnared by Matt as victims but as amateurs who hadn't been savvy or deft enough to find a way out of it. Matt was the talent, who could do no wrong. When a lion bites a lion tamer, you don't blame the lion. In the meantime, I felt honored and special to be trusted, thrilled that I knew a secret that the tabloids had been trying to nail down for years.

Then I think, if *I* heard about Matt in 2009—the naive fill-in assistant making fifteen dollars an hour—how much of a secret could it really have been?

"In 2006, when my first book was published, I was invited to go to New York to discuss it on the *Today* show," journalist and author Caitlin Flanagan wrote in *The Atlantic* in 2019. "While I was sitting in the studio's makeup room, something unusual happened. At the end of the row of chairs, sitting in the one closest to the wall, was a relatively new newswoman who was quietly reading through some notes. Suddenly Matt Lauer appeared at the door. He practically ran across the room to her, zeroing in on her and bantering with her as though they were the only two people around. His behavior was intense and odd because of its brazenness and because of the setting. She matched it in kind, and they laughed as though they were at a cocktail party, although I noticed that as soon as he left the room—the show was live, and he had to go to the plaza for an outdoor segment—she went immediately back to her work. Well, I guess those two are having an affair, I thought to myself. I wasn't particularly shocked; Lauer was known to have a rocky marriage. . . . NBC News management now claims that it had no idea whatsoever that Lauer had a problem with women until it received a lone harassment report in 2017 that led to his firing. But that is hard to countenance. I was in that studio for just twenty minutes before I observed Lauer behave oddly with a woman."

I witnessed that kind of behavior from Matt in the *Today* greenroom too many times to count, just in the three months that I was the show's page. What strikes me about it now is that it didn't even register to me as odd. If you were a relatively new newswoman at *Today*, generating chemistry with Matt was a highly marketable, monetizable skill. Part of the job for his coanchors was making him look likable on the air, whether laughing at his jokes, bantering with him between segments, or constantly ceding the spotlight without betraying the slightest hint of resentment. Catering to the ego of the network's prickly golden goose was not optional but a work requirement. Matt was the star of the show. Whatever he did was, by definition, exemplary. It couldn't be odd or troubling, because Matt was the one doing it.

Should I have been more thoughtful and less eager to belong? Obviously, yes. But like most people, I saw acceptable workplace behavior as whatever behavior was accepted in my workplace. Anything else I thought I knew about sexual harassment was limited to what I'd picked up as a child watching the news coverage of Anita Hill in 1991, or the sexual harassment and assault allegations against Bill Clinton by Juanita Broaddrick, Paula Jones, Kathleen Willey, and Monica Lewinsky. What was the key takeaway from those stories? That whatever happened to those women didn't matter all that much. Clarence Thomas was confirmed to the Supreme Court. Bill Clinton served two terms in the White House. Boys will be boys. Where had I watched those stories? On *Today*. Who had it been, more than a decade earlier, interrogating the then First Lady, Hillary Clinton, about the nature of her marriage and her husband's relationship with a White House intern, prompting her now-famous answer about a "vast right-wing conspiracy"? Matt Lauer.

By the time I began my career more than a decade later, sexual harassment was supposed to be a long-vanquished relic of the twentieth century, something the American workplace had already addressed and moved past. I did my mandatory online sexual harassment training. Like most of the talent assistants I knew, I actually did it twice—once for me, and once for the talent. I didn't see anything wrong with that, either. Why would the talent need sexual harassment training? They weren't the stereotypical creepy guys lurking in dark corners of the office, making gross comments.

They were charismatic superstars with million-dollar paydays and morals clauses in their contracts, their behavior evaluated mercilessly each week in the ratings. They had the highest-visibility, most scrutinized jobs in journalism, working in newsrooms where everyone's job was to expose abuses of power. The talent, I thought, would have been the last people to sexually harass anyone, not least because I didn't think anyone smart enough to make it to the top of such a cutthroat business would ever risk so much to do something so stupid.

I never considered the possibility that for anyone with enough power, there wouldn't be much risk involved.

# TWO

# A Breeding Ground for Harassment

*When Rules Don't Apply to Superstars*

I n the wake of Matt's firing, a parade of telling on-air moments began to resurface.

There was the interview with actress Anne Hathaway in which Matt gleefully referenced an explicit upskirt shot taken by a paparazzi photographer ("Seen a lot of you lately"; "What's the lesson learned from that, other than to keep smiling, which you always do?"). There was a leering interview with actress Sandra Bullock in which he repeatedly referenced a nude scene ("I have now seen you naked"; "I watched it last night. It's a lot of fun. Did I mention you have a nude scene?"), and another with a twenty-year-old Miley Cyrus ("I'm never going to go to a sporting game and see a foam finger again in the same way").

Under the MeToo spotlight, these were glaringly inappropriate—

yet I could remember when every single one aired, and I'd thought nothing of them. Gross as they were, they'd been aired live and then re-aired on national television, guided there by a team of hundreds of staffers I knew to be decent, hardworking people. Then they'd been watched by millions of viewers at home, and there was no overwhelming public outcry that I can remember. Standards of behavior change over time, obviously, but something feels insincere to me about recoiling in horror over these moments as though it hadn't taken a village to produce, televise, and popularize Matt Lauer. Had we all been watching without seeing, or had we just seen what we wanted to see, blinded by Matt's star power and success?

NBC's internal investigators confronted the same unsettling contradictions when they released their findings in 2018. They found "current and former NBC News and Today show leadership, News HR and others interviewed who were in positions of authority in the News Division to be credible in their denials of knowledge of Lauer's inappropriate sexual behavior in the workplace," but "also found credible the complainants' allegations about Lauer's inappropriate sexual behavior in the workplace, as well as other witnesses' statements about Lauer's sexual overtures and his sexual banter in the workplace." To translate, investigators believed the allegations of sexual harassment and misconduct against Matt but also that management hadn't known anything about it. "It was troubling, therefore, that no complaints appear to have been reported about Lauer's behavior through any channel, over a long a period of time," the investigators wrote in their final report.

In all those years, why had no one complained? I think the answer is circular: Matt's behavior was clearly a problem, but it could never be *seen* as problematic because it was Matt's behavior. It was okay because he did it, so he apparently kept doing it because it was okay. We were all watching but still didn't see.

Throughout the MeToo era, the toxic consequences of these workplace power dynamics echoed through the broadcast news business as superstar on-air talent and news executives left or were dismissed amid sexual harassment and misconduct scandals. At Fox News, there were Roger Ailes, Bill Shine, Bill O'Reilly, and Ed Henry; at ABC, there were Mark Halperin and Michael Corn; at CBS, there were Charlie Rose, Jeff Fager, and Les Moonves; at PBS, there was Tavis Smiley; and later, at CNN in 2021, there were Chris Cuomo and Jeff Zucker.* Nor was it a new problem. At *60 Minutes*, the most successful news show in American television history, reports of rampant sexual harassment by anchor Mike Wallace and creator Don Hewitt had first been reported back in 1991. An external investigation found that beginning in the nineties and as late as 2018, CBS continued to pay a former *60 Minutes* employee millions of dollars to settle claims that she was repeatedly sexually assaulted by Hewitt and that he had destroyed her career.

This blind spot wasn't unique to television, either. About a month before Gretchen Carlson filed her $20 million sexual harassment suit against Roger Ailes, the Equal Employment Opportunity Commission (EEOC) released a damning report—excerpted in the prologue of this book—that described it in eerily prescient

---

* Cuomo was suspended and then dismissed for breaching journalistic ethics by utilizing his position and resources at CNN to advise his brother, the then governor of New York, Andrew Cuomo, on weathering a sexual harassment scandal; after his suspension, CNN received an allegation of sexual misconduct against him, which he denied (he had previously been accused of groping a female colleague in 2005, for which he apologized). According to *The New York Times,* "it was not fully clear what role the allegation played in CNN's decision to dismiss Mr. Cuomo." Zucker, then president of CNN Worldwide, resigned after admitting to a sexual relationship with a subordinate in violation of CNN's code of conduct.

detail, warning employers of the threat posed by "superstar" employees who create "a breeding ground for harassment."*

"Those of us in the field—the geeks—we read that report and we know it and use it in our forensic work," says Dr. Dawn Hughes, a New York clinical and forensic psychologist who has performed hundreds of assessments for sexual abuse and harassment cases. "But nobody else was thinking about it until all these stories start breaking. Having been doing this for twenty-five years, I'd see more patients coming into my private practice and asking for help navigating these problems than I ever saw actually reporting them. That was clearly problematic. We've known this existed way before MeToo."

Workplace "superstars," the report explains, are individuals perceived to be of such high value that they are virtually irreplaceable and answer to practically no one. They make more money, have more privileges, and operate by a different set of rules. Their success gives them enormous power relative to everyone else, which emboldens them to abuse those they see as expendable.

These rainmaker types exist in a wide spectrum of workplaces, from academia to law, medicine to tech. Think of the star chef at a restaurant, the top partner at a law firm, the pioneering surgeon at a hospital, the vaunted professor, the legendary gymnastics coach, the CEO of a tech start-up. Wherever they are, superstars create a work environment primed for abuse and harassment because management is unwilling or unlikely to challenge their behavior and the superstars themselves "may believe that the general rules of the workplace do not apply to them."

In other words, the superstars with the most power get the most

---

* Perhaps because of its headline-grabbing title—*June 2016 Report of the Co-Chairs of the Select Task Force on the Study of Harassment in the Workplace*—the report received minimal press coverage.

freedom to abuse it, and then are the least likely to be held accountable.

———

FOR ALL OUR WATERCOOLER jokes about political correctness and the uptight behavior police from HR, sexual harassment remains a widespread problem that's very rarely reported. That's in no small part because—despite all the tedious, employer-mandated training—it's so poorly understood.

The EEOC's report found that anywhere between 25 percent and 85 percent of women have experienced sexual harassment. That range is so ridiculously broad because of the appalling difference between its actual legal definition and what most of us consider to *be* sexual harassment. When asked if they'd experienced "sexual harassment" without the term being defined, only about 25 percent of women consistently said yes. When asked whether they'd experienced specific behaviors—such as unwanted sexual attention or sexual coercion—60 percent to 75 percent said yes. That means as many as half the women who experience sexual harassment don't realize that their experiences qualify as sexual harassment and that, legally, they don't have to tolerate it.

Clearly the term "sexual harassment" is itself a problem. Everybody thinks they know what it means but hardly any of us can accurately define it. When so many workers can experience sexual harassment without realizing it, the term is not only functionally useless but actively counterproductive. If the term is so poorly understood that it isn't helping the workers it is meant to protect, then who *is* it helping? The organizations that are liable for protecting workers from sexual harassment, who then benefit when it goes unrecognized and unreported. That's employers.

Most workers primarily learn about sexual harassment from

their employer-provided training, yet the same employers who provide that training are then responsible for the harassment should their employees recognize and report it. The more confusion there is about what sexual harassment actually is, the less likely it is to be reported, and as long as it isn't reported, the company likely isn't going to be held liable for it. This obvious conflict of interest creates a powerful incentive for employers to make harassment training every bit as boring and pointless as we all know it to be, perfunctory at best and counterproductive at worst.

This is exactly what the EEOC task force found.

"Much of the training done over the last thirty years has not worked as a prevention tool," it wrote. "It's been too focused on simply avoiding legal liability."

"It's mostly lip service," says Tammy Marzigliano, partner and cochair of the Whistleblower and Retaliation Practice Group at leading employment law firm Outten & Golden, who often handles sexual harassment cases. "Very few cases that come our way look anything like the examples in a sexual harassment training. The vast majority of cases are messy and complicated and there are a lot of different variables. It's not, 'You have sex with me and I'll give you a promotion.' Those kinds of strict, quid pro quo cases are not the norm."

Nor are workers constantly running to HR with sexual harassment complaints. Quite the opposite. Reporting or formally addressing the behavior is by far the *least* common response to sexual harassment, according to the EEOC. Instead, victims respond by avoiding the harasser, denying or downplaying the problem, or trying to ignore, forget, or put up with it. Most workers will tolerate harassing behavior as long as they possibly can without having to deal with it. Who wants to get involved in a sexual harassment complaint? We just want to do our jobs, get paid, and go home. But by the time the harassment gets to the point when it's so bad that ignoring it is no longer an option, the victim has probably been tolerating it for so long that they blame themselves for putting up with it instead of nipping it in the bud—which makes it even less likely that they'll report it.

So what do we have to show for all these years of mandatory sexual harassment trainings? Practically nothing. We still respond to sexual harassment the same way we always have. We put our heads down and do the work. We turn the other cheek. We try not to be difficult, to make a big deal out of it, to cause more trouble than we believe we are worth. Whether we are choosing to tolerate it because we don't believe anything will be done about it or because nobody's ever told us we don't have to, tolerating harassment is overwhelmingly what we do.

"Part of the problem is that we need to get to young people earlier," says Marzigliano. "I've met with young people just entering the workforce, and my mind was blown on how many things that young people thought were okay in the workplace that were totally inappropriate. It was really shocking, because they felt like they had to have a certain tolerance for that behavior, and they don't."

I thought that tolerance was a sign of the celebrated female toughness required to survive in a male-dominated industry. So ingrained was this way of thinking that, on some level, I was even proud that I had been a good soldier and "handled" what happened in Sochi without complaining or making a fuss. But putting up with bad behavior is not a sign of our will to succeed or our right to a seat at the table. It's a fool's errand that undercuts us in the long run and makes harassment harder to report once it becomes truly intolerable. That same toughness that we celebrate at the beginning gets turned back on us at the end, making us look—and feel—like fools. However wrongly, it also makes it much easier for others to blame the victim for the harassing behavior, and for victims to blame themselves. If you didn't have a problem with it when it started, why do you suddenly have a problem with it now? Why did you allow it to escalate?

When we don't report abuse, we become complicit in it by modeling to others that unacceptable behavior is acceptable. When we finally *do* try to address the problem after putting up with it for so long, we aren't celebrated as team players or good soldiers. We're disbelieved and blamed.

In the meantime, the harasser's behavior continues unchecked. The longer it goes unaddressed, the more emboldened the harasser becomes. When that growing sense of invulnerability meets the actual invulnerability of a high-value performer whose behavior is never questioned, a superstar harasser emerges. If you behave badly once and nobody says anything, why stop there?

"In some ways, it's addictive behavior in that it requires a bigger and bigger hit to get the same sense of self-satisfaction that you really are free to do whatever you want," says workplace abuse investigator Fran Sepler. "What could be better proof of my worth than knowing that I can get away with pretty much anything I have the impulse to do?"

I first learned of Sepler's work through the voluminous endnotes of the EEOC report. She is a remarkable student of human behavior. Sepler began her career in the rape crisis movement ("Back when it was a movement, so that dates me") before working as a child sexual abuse specialist for the state of Minnesota, where she lives. She eventually shifted into developing workplace investigation techniques, sexual harassment training, and cultural assessments that identify areas of risk for bad workplace behavior. She has conducted more than a thousand independent fact-findings in her thirty years of doing this work. Some of those findings are borderline unbelievable.

"I dealt with a situation where a surgeon actually put people in his operating room in danger," Sepler says. "He threw a scalpel at somebody when he was angry. He pulled a central line out of a patient. He assaulted a nurse."

If he could get away with such outrageous behavior in an operating room, then it should come as no surprise that the surgeon was also sexually harassing young women, particularly those in allied medical fields that required less education and were lower paid. He chose victims that would be viewed as easier to replace than he was as a superstar surgeon, which made them more vulnerable to harassment.

"He would do everything from use diminutives with them to comment on whether their breasts looked perky on a particular day," Sepler says. "He grabbed asses under people's scrubs. He looked down a scrub nurse's pants one day. What finally got him was that he made the mistake of doing it with a thirty-year nurse who wasn't going to take anything from anyone, but he'd gotten away with it for years. None of them had come forward because they'd said to themselves, 'What's the point? He does this in the light of day.'"

Imagine being one of those scrub nurses. You've just been groped by the star surgeon at your hospital—a person you know has a volcanic temper, and perhaps the only surgeon who can perform a particular life-saving procedure. To stop the harassment would, at minimum, invite his wrath. But it would also likely stop that surgeon from performing those life-saving procedures, inviting blame and scrutiny from patients, colleagues, and administrators alike. Would you report it, or would you put up with it, as countless others in your hospital have been doing for years?

"The biggest reason people don't say anything," says Sepler, "is fear or futility. Either they are afraid it will splash back on them in terrible ways that will impact their career, or they don't think anything will be done about it, even if they do."

Sepler testified to the EEOC about a professor who, for years, had his foreign doctoral students "bathe his feet, clean his toilet and service his sexual needs" but was only reported to university officials when one of those former students had acquired her own superstar status—as tenured faculty at another university—and made a complaint. "Upon investigation," Sepler testified, "it became clear to me that school leaders knew what this professor was doing but he was the source of so much income and had acquired such superstar status that there was no will . . . to act."

If you're a foreign doctoral student being sexually exploited by your superstar professor, that professor is likely to be one of the sponsors on your visa and perhaps also the compelling factor in choosing your doctoral program. Get rid of the superstar professor who brings all the acclaim and funding to that program, and you lose not only your visa sponsor and your doctoral advisor but all the acclaim and funding that allowed you to pursue it in the first place. Your degree is devalued, along with everyone else's in the program—people who matter greatly to you, who are your close friends and future connections. Would you report the abuse, or would you do what all the other doctoral students are doing and put up with it?

"Having been involved in a lot of high-profile cases, it's so disheartening because the rainmaker has to continue to make rain, right?" says Hughes, the forensic psychologist who first told me about the EEOC report. "People are dependent on that, so it creates this whole subsystem that allows this to occur."

Consider Bill O'Reilly: Fox News paid out $13 million to five women over more than a decade to settle sexual harassment claims made against him, yet O'Reilly told *The New York Times* in 2017 that he "had never had one complaint filed against me by a coworker in any human resources department in forty-three years." What would have been the incentive to do so? *The O'Reilly Factor* was the highest-rated cable news show for fifteen years. It brought in $325 million of ad revenue during its last season alone, which made it the top revenue earner of any show on Fox News, CNN, or

MSNBC. Unlike *Today*, an expensive four-hour show with an ensemble cast, *The O'Reilly Factor* was just Bill O'Reilly sitting in front of a teleprompter for an hour. Thirteen million dollars in sexual harassment settlements was a relatively low price for Fox to pay to keep their star on the air. In 2017, O'Reilly personally paid $32 million to settle one sexual harassment suit, but he earned $37 million that year and so still came out ahead. Factor in the $25 million severance package O'Reilly received when he left Fox and he came out *way* ahead.

But according to Sepler, that math is misleading.

"Whenever I get a call from a corporate counsel saying, 'We have a high performer with some behavioral problems,'" she says, "I immediately say, 'Can somebody with behavior problems that are doing harm to others really be a high performer?' If you map that out over weeks or months or years, you're ultimately going to find a net negative."

A 2015 Harvard Business School study backs her conclusion. Analyzing data on eleven global companies, the study found that the overall profit consequences of a "toxic worker," specifically including those who were top performers, were indeed a net negative. Moreover, the study found that avoiding superstar harassers altogether could save companies more than twice as much as the increased output they generate.

"The reputational costs alone can have serious consequences, particularly where it is revealed that managers for years 'looked the other way' at a so-called 'superstar' harasser," warned the 2016 EEOC task force.

The O'Reilly case echoes this. Only when *The New York Times* publicly revealed the settlements and advertisers began to boycott *The O'Reilly Factor* were the reputational costs apparently high enough to outweigh O'Reilly's profits. Fox finally let him go.

How do these superstars amass such power?

They cast a lot of light, and that light can be blinding.

"Organizations rely on the productivity of these people as a significant source of not just revenue flow but reputational value, and continuing flows of demand for their product," says Sepler. "These folks have acolytes, who believe these people are virtual deities, and will do anything to follow and support them. They will often tolerate treatment that is harmful or derogatory or diminishing or even harassing, because they get to be bathed in the light as well."

TODAY WAS THE BIGGEST PROFIT DRIVER in morning television with its half a billion dollars a year in advertising revenues, three times more than that of *NBC Nightly News*. Matt was *Today*'s longest serving anchor. During his time at NBC, he outlasted the network's longtime corporate owner General Electric, four NBC News presidents (Andrew Lack, Neal Shapiro, Steve Capus, and Deborah Turness), five *Today* executive producers (Jeff Zucker, Michael Bass, Jonathan Wald, Tom Touchet, and Jim Bell), and three coanchors (Katie Couric, Meredith Vieira, and Ann Curry). With every departure, Matt's power at the network was consolidated. In 2012, he became the highest-paid anchor in the history of morning television, with a contract reported by *The New York Times* to be worth $25 million a year. *The Hollywood Reporter* named him the "most powerful face in news," suggesting that his "merry-go-round of female anchors" was "less critical than his stability."

The first female coanchor on that merry-go-round, Katie Couric, wrote in her 2021 memoir that she heard that *Today* turned "frattier" after she left.

". . . it was now Matt's show," Couric wrote. "He'd become cocky and reckless, which changed the tone of the place, the control-room guys opining loudly about the anatomy of female guests and staffers and openly playing the crude game Fuck, Marry, Kill. At a certain point, all the PAs [production assistants] seemed to be pretty young women; when passing out the rundown, one of them would plop in each guy's manspreading lap. By the time Ann Curry was at the big desk, Matt was the highest-paid anchor in TV history and the top dog in every sense."

At that point, *Today*'s ratings had already fallen behind *Good Morning America*'s. They fell even further when Curry was unceremoniously pushed off the show in June 2012 after fifteen years as a beloved member of the *Today* family and of what she later described as "professional torture" during her tenure as Matt's coanchor.

Even though Matt's dislike and animosity toward Curry had been fully visible to viewers on live television, then executive producer Jim Bell told *The Hollywood Reporter* that Matt "really should not bear any of the blame for that . . . Matt is probably the best guy to ever host morning television."

The then NBC News president, Steve Capus, echoed Bell's message, telling media columnist Howard Kurtz that Matt was being unfairly blamed: "[Matt] is one of, if not the best, morning show hosts in the history of that genre. We are lucky to have him."

Four months later, in March 2013, NBCUniversal CEO Steve Burke told Kurtz that Matt had even offered to leave amid the backlash over Curry's departure, but he'd told Matt that he was "the best person who's ever done this" and that "we'll get through this."

Around the same time, the *Times* reported that NBC news executives had expressed concern to *Today* staff that the show needed to work on "the anchor connection to the audience," while going to great pains to leave Matt's name unspoken. Two potential replacements, Sam Champion and Josh Elliott, were both poached from *Good Morning America*. Both departed the network within three years after receiving minimal airtime. Instead, new NBC News president Deborah Turness renewed Matt's contract for another two years in June 2014, telling the *Times* that "he's the best in the business, and there is nobody I would rather have in the anchor chair than Matt."

In 2016, Matt's contract was renewed for another two years—even after hosting an embarrassing "Commander-in-Chief" presidential forum in which his interview with then candidate Donald Trump was called "an embarrassment to journalism" by the *Times* columnist Nicholas Kristof and "a master class in bad interviewing" by the *Bloomberg* executive editor and Columbia Journalism School professor Bill Grueskin.

In 2017, *Vanity Fair* media reporter Sarah Ellison noted that for the past thirty years, *Today*'s audience had done nothing but decline, which made protecting the morning show's profits all the more important for NBC.

"Lauer's knack for survival gets to the heart of something fundamental about traditional TV news outlets, and morning television in particular," wrote Ellison. "NBC News has had to deliver four multi-million-dollar settlements to employees who have been separated from the *Today* show for one reason or another. Each move caused high anxiety inside the news division—and internally, an elevated sense of Lauer's importance to the bottom line. There's an investment concept known as the 'melting ice cube' syndrome—it describes assets that are likely to decline in value over the long term. If NBC News is the ice cube, then Lauer is the element that keeps it from melting away. In the process, the one thing perpetually preserved is Lauer himself."

"Matt was seen as indispensable," wrote Couric in her memoir. "Did that make him feel invincible? That level of fame and power, when you're surrounded by smiling yes-men and -women whose job it is to keep you happy and make you believe you can do no wrong, can lead to your downfall."

═══

MATT'S RISE AND SUBSEQUENT DOMINANCE as a morning news superstar was so meteoric and overwhelming that it could easily be mistaken for inevitable. Yet after his firing, a parallel timeline of Matt's time at NBC emerged—this one beginning in or around 1996, when Matt was *Today*'s newsreader and I was just wrapping up elementary school.

According to the NBC News internal investigation, this was the first reported instance of Matt sexually harassing a subordinate. A female staffer told her manager that Matt "placed his hand on her thigh and made a sexually suggestive comment. According to the complainant, her manager inquired about her well-being, and they agreed that, for a time, the complainant would not be assigned to projects that required travel with Lauer. The manager had a similar recollection of the conversation and stated that she does not recall reporting the interaction to anyone."

The NBC investigation reports another instance of "inappropriate sexual behavior in the workplace" by Matt in 2000. By then, he was the show's anchor, and the circumstances are not described in any further detail. (Because NBC's investigation was obligated to protect the privacy of the complainants, all incidents are characterized as "inappropriate sexual behavior in the workplace" regardless of the specific conduct.)

Also in 2000, in an incident reported by *Variety*, Matt made overt sexual advances on a twenty-four-year-old production assistant over an NBC News messaging system that resulted in a series of exploitative sexual encounters she later described as "an abuse of power." The subordinate, who was nearly twenty years Matt's junior, provided copies of the messages to *Variety* in 2017. One was prefaced with "I hope you won't drag me to personnel for saying this," suggesting Matt was already aware that the overtures were inappropriate and in violation of company policy.

The next year, in 2001, the pattern reportedly continued. The NBC News investigation reports another instance of inappropriate sexual behavior in the workplace involving the same female staffer harassed in the 1996 incident. The report does not describe it in any further detail. The *Times* reported an account from a former NBC employee that "Mr. Lauer had summoned her to his office in 2001, locked the door and sexually assaulted her," and that this former employee had provided the same complaint to NBC. These two accounts may or may not refer to the same instance. (As of publication, Matt has not been charged or convicted of any crime and denies all abusive or coercive sexual conduct and nonconsensual sex with any woman at any time.)

In 2004, according to Couric's memoir, "the scuttlebutt was that Matt had a fling at the Olympics with a production assistant." *Variety's* 2017 investigation indicated that this was part of a pattern, reporting that multiple independently corroborated accounts described how Matt "would invite women employed by NBC late at night to his hotel room while covering the Olympics in various cities over the years." During Matt's time at *Today*, NBC held the US broadcasting rights to ten Olympic Games between 1996 and 2016.*

---

* In June 2023, a former NBC production assistant at the 1996 Olympics sued a *Today* senior staffer for sexual assault under New York's Adult Survivors Act. Her suit alleged that she "observed a free-wheeling, unchecked culture in which married, older, and more senior NBC employees regularly targeted far younger women, such as Plaintiff, for sexual harassment and, in the case of Plaintiff, assault. This was an eye-opening experience for her, as she had never seen such blatant abuse of power."

Couric describes how the "fling" at the Athens Olympics in 2004—a full decade before the Sochi Olympics—was seemingly confirmed when a producer told her about sexually explicit messages she'd received from Matt that he had intended to send to the production assistant in question. The producer, who'd been with the network for more than thirty years, told *Rolling Stone* that discovering Matt's sexual misconduct with the production assistant was a professional "death knell." Along with former *Today* executive producer Tom Touchet and others, she told the magazine that "it was unspoken but understood that powerful men were making moves on underlings, who would then be committing career suicide to report them."

In 2007, another instance of "inappropriate sexual behavior in the workplace" occurred, according to the NBC News investigation.

In 2008, a now-infamous Friars Club roast of Matt, widely attended by NBC executives and on-air talent, included numerous oral and anal sex jokes and referred to Matt as the "Cock of the Rock." *Morning Joe* anchor Joe Scarborough would later describe walking out of the event in disgust: "The whole theme was that he does the show and then he has sex with people, with employees . . . so was this whispered about behind closed doors? No. It was shouted from the mountain tops and everybody laughed about it."

In 2012, a *Today* senior producer came to then anchor Curry and told her that Matt had "sexually harassed [her] physically" in his office and that she was afraid of losing her job, according to an account given by Curry to reporter Sarah Ellison. Curry said she then warned two members of NBC's management team that "they had a problem and they needed to keep an eye on [Matt] and how he deals with women." (NBC News investigators were unable to corroborate this warning to management, who Curry has declined to name.)

Also in 2012, according to investigative reporter Ronan Farrow, a female member of on-air talent left NBC after being propositioned by both Matt and a senior executive. Both men allegedly also made lewd remarks about the woman over open mics during broadcasts. After refusing their advances, she said she received fewer assignments, which prompted her to leave.

In 2013, then *New York Times* media reporter Brian Stelter wrote in his book *Top of the Morning: Inside the Cutthroat World of Morning TV* that "for what it's worth, some executives at NBC told me they believed the rumors [about Matt]," and that "maybe what's more important is that the executives didn't think Lauer's behavior, real or imagined, had hurt the show."

The next year, in 2014, another instance of "inappropriate sexual behavior in the workplace" is listed in the NBC investigation's report. Presumably this was my complaint.

Farrow reports that in 2017, a senior member of the *Today* team received a seven-figure payout in exchange for signing a nondisclosure agreement and that he later reviewed voicemails and texts from Matt that she'd seen as passes at her. "When he took her responses as a cold shoulder," wrote Farrow, "she felt he'd retaliated against her, spreading negative rumors in the office."

That year—at the height of MeToo, in 2017—*Variety* and *The New York Times* began investigating allegations of sexual harassment against Matt. I made my on-the-record complaint to NBC on November 27, and he was fired on November 28. On November 29, *Variety* reported that, based on more than ten accounts from current and former NBC employees, "despite being married, Lauer was fixated on women, especially their bodies and looks . . . He was known for making lewd comments verbally or over text messages. He once made a suggestive reference to a colleague's performance in bed and compared it to how she was able to complete her job, according to witnesses to the exchange. For Lauer, work and sex were intertwined."

In April 2018, Sarah Ellison reported in the *Washington Post* that thirty-five current and former NBC staffers said that of Matt's sexual relationships with junior staffers, some "were consensual and some were not." Twelve said that they had been sexually harassed and had not reported it. Three of those twelve described sexual advances by Matt: one said that he "exposed himself in his office and asked her to touch him, and a second said he had sex with her in the middle of the day in his office—alleged incidents that have not been previously reported."

In his 2019 book *Catch and Kill*, Ronan Farrow reported that he eventually learned of seven claims of sexual misconduct against Matt, but it's unclear which or how many of those overlap with the incidents above.

Of the sixty-eight staffers interviewed by NBC, "a number of individuals interviewed said that Lauer could be flirtatious, would frequently make jokes, some with sexual overtones, and would openly engage in sexually-oriented banter in the workplace. Several women also credibly described to the investigation team being the subject of what they believed was a sexual overture from Lauer in which he complimented them on their appearance in sexually suggestive ways. According to these women, Lauer did not pursue them further when they deflected or ignored the overture, and they did not experience any retaliation."

On the other hand, a former staffer told *People* in 2019 that "if you didn't find [Matt's] 'flirting' behavior charming . . . if you dared to say it was inappropriate or worst of all, asked him to please not say that again, then you were either dead to him, like you really became invisible, or worse, you were someone he'd talk about in negative terms. 'She's so uptight, she's not a team player, she's really uncooperative, she's got a terrible work ethic.' You were either able to be 'one of the guys' with him, or you were in jeopardy."

Couric reflected in her memoir that she "wrestle[s] with the tricky notion of agency. I kept asking myself, why didn't these women just tell Matt to take a hike? But the more I thought about it, the more I realized not everyone is built for that kind of confrontation. And maybe they aren't in a position to deal with the consequences of speaking up, which, for too many women, includes losing their jobs. And why should the onus be on women to navigate men's advances and not on men to stop making them?"

Why, indeed? While some women told NBC investigators that they felt they could safely deflect Matt's advances, others clearly felt they could not. Either way, none should ever have had to gamble their futures by being forced to choose between rejecting or placating the most powerful man at the network. To better understand the stakes of those gambles, let's take a closer look at how those scenarios play out.

Consider the 2010 alleged encounter between Matt and the *Today* senior producer, as described by Farrow in *Catch and Kill*. During a work cocktail party, Matt asked to see the senior producer in his office. According to her account, when she arrived, Matt invited her to sit next to him on the sofa and then exposed his erect penis. The senior producer tried to deflect by making a joke about not wanting to have sex in Matt's office, where "everyone else has done it." Matt ignored the deflection and doubled down, allegedly saying that he "knew she wanted it" and "that he figured she liked it dirty . . . by her account, he became angry, saying, '. . . you're a fucking tease. This is not good. You led me on.'" When Farrow apparently questioned Matt about the encounter, he "recalled making a joking lewd gesture but not exposing himself or propositioning her."*

Either way, Matt apparently did not talk to the senior producer

---

* Throughout *Catch and Kill*, Matt's version of events is indicated by "sources close to Lauer," but Farrow has since confirmed publicly that one of the sources was Matt himself.

for weeks, a situation so untenable that she began looking for other jobs. After receiving an offer from CNN, "several NBC News executives called her into their offices for meetings and delivered the same message. Each said that Lauer had insisted that she stay. 'I don't know what's going on between you and him,' one told her, 'but I need to keep him happy.'" Another no-win situation: If the senior producer left the network against the wishes of its superstar, she would make an enemy of one of the most powerful names in the business. At the same time, if she stayed to "keep him happy," what *else* might she have to do to keep him happy? What would be the consequences if she didn't?

The senior producer stayed, only to be fired later. After her allegations against Matt were reported publicly, Matt questioned both their credibility and Ann Curry's corroboration of them, characterizing both women as disgruntled ex-employees.

Or consider the experience of the on-air talent who left NBC in 2012, who told Farrow that she was sexually propositioned by both Matt and a senior executive, both of whom allegedly made lewd remarks about her over open mics during broadcasts. "I was like a hanging piece of meat. I would walk into work with a knot in my stomach. I would come home and cry," she told Farrow. Then, when she declined their advances, "I got punished . . . My career took a sharp nosedive."

On the opposite end of the power spectrum, consider the twenty-four-year-old production assistant that Matt, nearly twenty years her senior, "aggressively, almost obsessively" targeted over NBC's internal messaging system in 2000.

"I remember seeing her diligently handing out scripts and working late in the edit room," wrote Couric, who had gotten the production assistant her job at *Today*. "I was so proud of her."

After four years at the show, the production assistant was hired as a local anchor/reporter in her hometown. "Once [Matt] learned she had only a few weeks left at 30 Rock, he summoned her repeatedly to his dressing room, his office, a bathroom at the Staples Center in LA during the Democratic National Convention for wholly transactional sex. It nauseated me," wrote Couric.

When Matt first summoned her to his dressing room, the production assistant *also* tried to deflect the advance, responding over NBC's internal messaging system, "Matt, think about this first . . . you have a wife." Matt ignored the deflection and doubled down, repeating his request that she come to his dressing room. If she declined further, she'd risk antagonizing the anchor of *Today*, which no production assistant could afford to do. If she acquiesced, she would be putting herself into an even more precarious situation. It was roughly a five-minute walk from the newsroom to Matt's dressing room, but the production assistant told him she would be there in twenty minutes, perhaps stalling for time. Now Matt plays the talent card: "I can't stay that long, I have a car coming at 3:00." It was 2:42 p.m.

Reminding someone of a ticking clock is a ready means of increasing pressure and exerting control. A production assistant can neither say no to the talent nor make him wait. Left with only bad choices, she went to his dressing room. Her life would never be the same again.

"He got in his car and I had to go back to work, and now my life had completely changed," she later said. "The situation really took its toll on me. I changed physically. I changed emotionally. Fear crept into my life. I became unsure of myself. Any confidence I had was gone. For him, it was a conquest."

Consider how improbable a path that production assistant took to *Today* and a job on air in her hometown: She found the courage to write a letter to Katie Couric, took a Greyhound bus to New York, and then worked for four years at a menial job at *Today* to earn an on-air position back home. Her dreams were coming true.

But then, in her last few weeks at *Today*, she was sexually exploited by the show's anchor. When she got home to begin her dream job, a reporter from the *National Enquirer* was waiting in her driveway. When she asked Matt for help, he first blamed her ("Who did you tell?"), then simply ignored her. She was harassed by the *Enquirer* for years, eventually quit her job to join the army, and served two tours in Iraq. Another career derailed, another life altered, another human being shattered.

This was three years after Matt became anchor of *Today*, eight years before I started at NBC, and fourteen years before the Sochi Olympics.

# THREE.

# The Script

*The Media's Role in Normalizing Predatory Sexual Relationships
and Perpetuating False Tropes About Sexual Assault*

All that I should have known about sexual harassment and assault, I could have learned from my own reporting—if only I'd paid attention.

The real-world knowledge I needed wasn't in the cookie-cutter corporate training modules I took but right before my eyes, in the stories I worked on. In 2011, I'd gotten what I thought would be the big break of my journalism career—a job at *Rock Center with Brian Williams*, the first new primetime news magazine to be launched by a network since 1998. The show would only last about a year and a half, but it had a generous budget and had been staffed with some of the most experienced long-form producers in the business. Though I had no experience whatsoever in either newsmagazines or primetime, my relationship with the talent got me onto the staff in a dual role as associate producer and assistant. Dual roles always sound like extraordinary opportunities to learn how to be great at two things at the same time, but in reality, you just end up being mediocre at both things all the time. I was no exception.

My first story was an interview with Mimi Alford, a former Kennedy White House intern whose book, *Once Upon a Secret: My Affair with President John F. Kennedy and Its Aftermath*, would eerily foreshadow the issues raised six years later by MeToo.

Her story, like so many to come, began with a few drinks at work and an impressionable young woman's trust in a powerful man she admired. At the end of her fourth day at the White House, President Kennedy had an aide bring the nineteen-year-old intern to the residence to share a pitcher of daiquiris. There he offered her a private tour, which ended in the First Lady's bedroom with the loss of Alford's virginity. She told no one about their encounter, returned to her internship the next day as though it had never happened, and her involvement with Kennedy continued until his death. It took Alford decades to untangle and fully comprehend its impact on her life.

Our hour-long interview with her was introduced as "the story just published of an affair between a college student and President John F. Kennedy," and yet little about that sentence struck me as particularly troubling at the time. Today, I find it very troubling—beginning with the casual use of "affair" and the characterization of Alford as a college student rather than an employee. When we talk about an affair, our minds assume a familiar script: *It takes two to tango.* Two equally complicit partners abuse the trust of one or more innocent parties. The only victims involved are those betrayed. But when a president sexually exploits a teenage intern, it's much more than an abuse of trust. It's an abuse of power. In retrospect, characterizing that as an "affair" was about as accurate as describing the Cuban Missile Crisis as a naval traffic jam. The point is not about language policing but the distinction between sexual behavior that is simply inappropriate and sexual behavior that is potentially predatory. Still, we went on to refer to the workplace sexual encounters between a president and his teenage intern as an affair eleven separate times in our piece.

But what *other* word would we have used in 2012? It was post–Monica Lewinsky but pre-MeToo; it would have been anachronistic to describe it any other way. "Affair," after all, was the word *Alford* used, including in the subtitle of her book. Though she acknowledged that it "was not a romantic affair"—Kennedy never kissed her, and she always referred to him as Mr. President—Alford viewed what happened as more than purely transactional sex. I can understand why. As exploitative as the eighteen-month relationship plainly was, there was also an undeniable emotional component. Kennedy called her repeatedly at college, gave her gifts, and cried to her over the death of his infant son. Their relationship ended not because he'd cast her aside but because he was assassinated. These situations are rarely as black and white as we'd like them to be. It's not a binary choice between seeing them as meaningless exploitation or meaningful emotional connection. They can very well be both, and often are.

It was workplace investigator Fran Sepler who most forcefully drove this point home to me.

"I get worried when people speak in platitudes, like 'this is about power, not about sex,' because sometimes it's about both," she said. "The thread and texture of these things is very complex and pulls on lots and lots of different human desires and needs and fears and expectations . . . When you spend thirty years listening to these stories, you have to have respect for the complexity of how these things happen."

Despite the affection the president seemed to have had for Alford, he also coerced her into performing oral sex on a fifty-year-old White House aide while he watched. According to Alford, he once gave her amyl nitrite, then left her terrified and crying in a guest room at Bing Crosby's house in Palm Springs while he partied. When she thought she might be pregnant, Kennedy had an aide connect her with an abortionist.

"Did you feel at all, you know, like I'm being used here?" we asked Alford during our interview. "It's almost like you were a call girl to him."

"Oh, but I never felt that," Alford answered. "Now looking back, I can see that it's not a good place for a nineteen-year-old girl to be, in a relationship that's so imbalanced and with such a powerful person and an older man and at their beck and call. I see how sad it was, but that is not how I felt."

But just because a nineteen-year-old intern did not *feel* she was being exploited by the handsome, charismatic president of the United States does not mean that it can't still be true. Our understanding of the past changes with time, and manipulation and exploitation often only become clear in retrospect. Here we meet the first of many uncomfortable truths about predatory sexual behavior: It is not always obvious. If it were, it would be a lot harder to get away with it. People rarely realize they are being exploited in the moment, and once they do, most will go to great lengths to deny they've allowed someone to take advantage of them. Nobody wants to feel like a fool or be seen as one, and anyone can be awed and flattered by power. For most people, simply being asked to do something by a powerful person is flattering enough to do it. Instead of feeling put-upon, we feel honored to have been singled out and asked. As a result, there's little need for a powerful person to resort to overt threats. Their power speaks for itself, and is freighted with emotional significance that can blind us to the obvious.

In practice, this means that the president of the United States doesn't *need* to explicitly invoke the power of his office to get a teenage White House intern to comply with his sexual demands.

How many people on earth can defy the leader of the free world without fearing the consequences? When the power imbalance—however extreme—is couched in emotion, meaning, and flattery, it can take years for the less powerful person to recognize that, regardless of whether they realized it at the time, there was never really much choice.

Consider Monica Lewinsky, who wrote in *Vanity Fair* in 2014 that "sure, my boss took advantage of me, but I will always remain firm on this point: It was a consensual relationship. Any 'abuse' came in the aftermath, when I was made a scapegoat in order to protect his powerful position." After four years and the MeToo movement, Lewinsky saw things differently. "I now see how problematic it was that the two of us even got to a place where there was a question of consent," she wrote in 2018. "Instead, the road that led there was littered with inappropriate abuse of authority, station and privilege. (Full stop.) Now, at forty-four, I'm beginning (just beginning) to consider the implications of the power differentials that were so vast between a president and a White House intern. I'm beginning to entertain the notion that in such a circumstance the idea of consent might well be rendered moot."

―――――――

THIS MAKES THE "IDEA" of consent, then, considerably more complicated than "yes means yes" and "no means no." No always means no, but in any number of circumstances, saying yes does not necessarily equate to consent. If you agree to something because there's a gun to your head, have you really consented? If you agree to give someone your ATM code while drunk and they empty your account, have you consented to giving them your money? I might agree to go skydiving, but if you neglect to tell me that the parachute isn't part of the package, I haven't actually consented to suicide. Agreement and consent are not synonymous. Consent is its own separate thing.

Think of the times we specifically use the word "consent" rather than "agreement." We consent to medical treatment, to give blood, to participate in a clinical trial, to let our child go on a field trip, to jump out of a plane, to have sex. We consent rather than agree in these situations because each involves acknowledging and assuming some degree of risk. For any one to take place without our consent is not only wrong but potentially a crime. If you knock me out and slice my body open *with* my consent, it's surgery; without it, it's aggravated assault. To take my child on an overnight hockey trip without my consent is kidnapping. Sex without consent is not "nonconsensual sex" but sexual assault. Consent is specifically required when the stakes are so high that there can be no misunderstanding. It rises above regular old agreement in that it must be both informed and freely given: A person must fully understand the circumstances and terms of the agreement, and *also* be equally free to say yes or no.

This means that if something infringes on your ability to give or withhold consent—like a gun to your head, or a threat to your family or livelihood—it's no longer consent but submission. I might agree to do whatever you want because you have power over me, but I'm certainly not *consenting* to it. When one person has explicit power over another—a boss to an employee, a doctor to a patient, a teacher to a student, a prison guard to an inmate, a gunman to a hostage—that explicit power makes the less powerful person subordinate to the other, and a *sub*ordinate can only *sub*mit, not consent. Sexual relationships in those circumstances are off-limits for a very specific reason: By definition, they cannot be consensual because the disempowered person isn't totally free to say no to the person with the power advantage. Hence, the term "taking advantage." A more direct word would be exploitation.

So when we refer to a relationship between a more powerful person and a subordinate as an affair, we're describing an inherently exploitative situation as consensual. More than that, we're normalizing it as mere infidelity, conflating an abuse of trust with an abuse of power. When we talk about this in such absolute terms, I know it can sound absurd—especially in the context of everyday work life, where it's also a matter of degree. There's a vast difference between two employees with a slight disparity in seniority and the president of the United States and a White House intern. But what about a shift manager and a waitress?

It doesn't have to be so hard. Anyone who can get in trouble for insubordination—for not doing what you tell them to do—is your subordinate. If they're not entirely free to say no to you, then they are not entirely free to say yes—which means they cannot consent to your sexual advance. As your subordinate, they can only submit, and consent and submission are not the same thing. A more implicit example: If you have the power to help someone's career, than you also likely have the power to hurt it. A Hollywood mogul who can make someone a star can likely also keep them from becoming one by blacklisting them. In that case, even though an aspiring starlet may not be an employee, they still can't freely consent to the mogul's sexual advance because of the potential repercussions of refusing it.

Maybe your subordinate appears willing to say yes and you legitimately believe that they are. When the power imbalance is so overwhelming, it doesn't matter. Neither you, nor the employer who is legally and financially liable for your behavior, can take the risk that they are only submitting to you because they feel they have no choice. It's off-limits. It's just too big a risk.

When you think about it, sex is always a risk, every single time. It's never completely, absolutely safe. Whenever you have sex, you risk disease, pregnancy, and disappointment. You might physically hurt or be hurt by your partner. You risk that your partner might override your autonomy over your own body, or lie about past behaviors, contraception, using protection, their age, or anything else. Anytime you have sex, you're weighing and considering all these risks, and that includes whether your partner is consenting. At any point, consensual sex can still become sexual assault because consent can be revoked at any time. If you're drunk and your partner is drunk, is it automatically sexual assault because intoxication inhibits your ability to consent? No, but it's riskier than if you were both sober. If your partner doesn't explicitly give verbal affirmative consent, is it automatically sexual assault? No, but it's a bigger risk than if they did. Could you do everything right and then have your partner lie afterward and say they didn't consent? Yes, and that's another risk that you take whenever you choose to have sex.

Is sex with a subordinate always sexual assault because it cannot be consensual? No, of course not, but it's always sexual misconduct and it's always a huge, huge risk. Nobody should have to leave a job, be penalized at a job, or fear for that job because of anyone else's "inappropriate sexual behavior in the workplace." These are not "inappropriate relationships" or "affairs" but abuses of power. And putting a subordinate in the precarious position of having to risk their job by refusing an inappropriate sexual advance? That's an abuse of power, too. The reason these standards of behavior are so high is because they are for people *with power*, and power plays a role in every human interaction, whether we're consciously aware of it or not.

Comedian Louis C.K. was accused of sexual misconduct by five women in *The New York Times* in 2017. "These stories are true," he said in response to the allegations. "At the time, I said to myself that what I did was O.K. because I never showed a woman my dick without asking first, which is also true. But what I learned later in life, too late, is that when you have power over another person, asking them to look at your dick isn't a question. It's a predicament for them."

In a workplace, it's a predicament for everybody, not just the subordinate. If you're one of the other employees in that workplace and you feel the subordinate is receiving preferential treatment because they're "sleeping with the boss," you could potentially file your own sexual harassment suit arguing that you're being discriminated against because you're not. This stuff matters. Our professions are called livelihoods because they are inextricably tied to our survival and the survival of those who rely on us. Nobody should be more conscious of that than someone with power over the livelihoods of others.

Louis C.K. was the first comedian in history to sell out three shows at Madison Square Garden; he knew he had power in the comedy world. Kennedy and Clinton were presidents of the United States; bands played "Hail to the Chief" whenever they walked into a room. It would take a willful level of callous ignorance for them *not* to know that they were taking advantage of vulnerable human beings when sexually propositioning interns at the White House.

"People with power know they're in power," says Dr. Veronique Valliere, a clinical and forensic psychologist and a member of the Pennsylvania Sexual Offenders Assessment Board. "They use it day-to-day. It's always the person in power's responsibility to ensure they're not abusing it. It's something they know they wield at all times, in every situation. If you know you can get a good table at a restaurant, you know people are not going to say no to you, so, come on."

IT TOOK A LONG, long time for me to fully take Valliere's point. I'd spent years working for powerful people, marveling at how they never seemed to realize that it was not a coincidence that everyone always wanted to eat at the exact same restaurant they did, or that everyone always wanted to stay for another round when they did and yet were *also* always ready to call it a night at exactly the same time that they were. It wasn't until I became someone else's boss for the first time—at thirty-seven years old, when we hired a part-time nanny—that I realized just how right Valliere is.

I was describing my plans for my daughter's first birthday party when I said offhandedly to her nanny, "You should come on Sunday!" As soon as the words came out of my mouth, I realized how awkward and difficult it would be for her to say no. Would she feel obligated to come? If she came, would she think she had to help rather than be our guest? Was I taking advantage of her affection for my daughter? Should I offer to pay her to come or would that be insulting? After only a few months of being one person's part-time employer, I was keenly aware that I had put her in an uncomfortable position—and I was horrified. That was just a toddler's birthday party on a Sunday afternoon.

Now imagine how it would feel to take advantage of subordinates who are professionally and financially beholden to you to gain *sexual access to their bodies.* Imagine doing that to countless subordinates over decades and then claiming you had absolutely no idea that it might be abusive.

*The New York Times* reported that NBC management—including NBC News chairman Andrew Lack and NBC News president Noah Oppenheim—began questioning Matt about past relationships with employees in the weeks leading up to his firing, and each time he denied all wrongdoing. A senior NBC source told *Esquire* that "Matt was confronted by several of us directly, on different occasions. . . . We sat down with him, looked him in the eye, and said, 'Is there anything you can think of that even you don't consider to be harassment that might fall into this category?' And every one of those times he said there's nothing. On a couple of those occasions, he said, 'I've been racking my brain.' Those were his words."

If Matt truly didn't know that making sexual advances on female subordinates was predatory, I would think he would have jumped at the opportunity to tell management his side of the story *before* damaging allegations began appearing in the press under the glaring light of MeToo. Getting ahead of the story might well have saved his job. Instead, he said nothing.

People with power know they are in power.

In the coverage of Alford's story that followed ours, few others in the press discussed the issue of consent. Instead, the larger concern seemed to be whether Alford had a right to tarnish the Kennedy name by telling her story at all. On *The View*, Barbara Walters— whose bestselling 2008 autobiography included the story of her own yearslong affair with a married senator—introduced Alford by saying, "She'll make a lot of money! You will, Mimi Alford!"

"I have to bring something up that bothered me," said Walters later in Alford's appearance, "because, as I said, you're going to sell a lot of books . . . Did you think at all of Caroline Kennedy, who is still alive today, and her children, when you wrote this book, which did not have to be written?"

Walters's insinuation was that Alford was somehow more responsible for protecting Kennedy's family or his legacy than Kennedy himself, who'd had far more control over his choices than the nineteen-year-old intern he'd pulled into his wife's bedroom in the White House. Victims of popular or powerful abusers—a cherished uncle, a coach, a priest, a teacher, the king of pop, or even the president of the United States—are constantly blamed for "ruining" or "tarnishing" otherwise beloved figures by speaking out. The message this sends is unmistakable and unforgivable: *We'd rather not know. Stay silent. Suffer alone.*

I remember sitting in Alford's living room during her interview, listening as she described how it had taken her a lifetime to understand that "when you keep a secret and when you keep silent about something, you do it because you think it's keeping you safe, but in fact, it's deadly." Secrets separate you from everyone you love. I felt incredible empathy for her, but I mostly felt relieved.

*Thank God I'm not an intern anymore*, I remember thinking, *I'll never be vulnerable again.*

———

A YEAR AND A HALF LATER, in 2013, I worked on an interview with Elizabeth Smart, who was abducted from her family's home at age fourteen, held captive for months by her abductors, and subjected to daily rapes. Hers was the kind of black-and-white sexual assault story that the media typically races to tell. A beautiful young girl is kidnapped from her home by a madman. The victim is entirely innocent and the perpetrators obviously evil, without any thorny he-said/she-said issues or questions about agency or consent.

But for plenty of people, even Elizabeth Smart had not been innocent enough to be a wholly sympathetic victim. During the nine months she'd been held captive, her kidnappers had taken her out in public in disguise. At one point Smart had even been confronted by a police officer but remained obedient to her captors. Why had she not tried harder to escape?

Those doubts were echoed in our story. At the time, I remember thinking we were giving Smart—a child sexual assault victim—a chance to respond to her critics. "Why didn't she scream out, and beg for help? It's a question many have asked, and one that never ceases to infuriate Elizabeth," we said in voiceover.

Her voice took on an uncharacteristic fury that had been absent during the rest of the interview, even as she'd patiently described one unspeakable thing after another.

"It is wrong for any person to ever judge someone in any situation saying, well, why didn't you run? Why didn't you scream? Why didn't you try to do something? That is so wrong, and frankly, offensive to even ask that question," said Smart.

"Why do you say that?"

"Because you don't know, you weren't there, you don't know what I was going through—"

"Well, tell me what it's like, because people will wonder."

People do wonder, but why? How could a child sexual assault victim have critics, and why on earth would we have offered them a platform? I didn't ask myself any of those questions when I was working on Smart's story. Mainly, I remember thinking that exchange was perfectly reasonable and then being put off by her defensiveness. The interview aired as a primetime special and that was that. I left for Sochi a few months later and didn't think about Elizabeth Smart again until 2018, when I saw another interview with her by CBS News' Gayle King.

"You've said something interesting," said King, "you said, had this not happened to me, I might have naively thought that on some level, it's the victim's fault."

*That's ridiculous*, I thought. *What kind of monster would ever think that?*

"That's true," answered Smart. "I might naively have thought, what was she wearing? What was she doing? . . . That was silly of her. I mean, this is a terrible thing that's happened, but why didn't she do more?"

That sounded oddly familiar.

"Well, I've been there," said Smart, the same anger and indignation echoing in her voice as five years earlier, "and I will never be that person to ask those stupid questions. Because what you're really saying is, you should have done more."

"Elizabeth, you were in your house, though," said King. "It should have been the safest place for you."

"But it shouldn't make a difference," said Smart, then a thirty-year-old mother of two and much more assertive than she'd been during our interview. "It shouldn't happen if I was an innocent fourteen-year-old girl or a girl working the corner."

King later said that she'd had a "lightbulb moment" during the interview, "because I actually thought, you know, why didn't you run? Why didn't you? And she said, you know, that's not even a fair question to ask."

Oh, God. It was only then that I realized Smart could very well have been talking about our 2013 interview, and that *I* had been one of the people asking those stupid questions, blaming her for not doing more.

But how could that be? I was a feminist. I had one of those oversized, millennial-pink "The Future Is Female" mugs. We'd just asked her what everyone else was thinking. In all honesty, it was also what I had been thinking—that if I'd been in her position and a police officer gave me a chance to escape, of course I would have taken it. It was just common sense.

But did I think to do any actual research on the behavior of sexual assault or kidnap victims while I worked on Smart's interview? The impact of physical and sexual trauma on children? Called one of the victim specialists at the FBI, or somebody at RAINN (the Rape, Abuse & Incest National Network*), or even gone to the

---

* The hotline is 800-656-4673; RAINN also staffs a 24/7 live chat hotline on their website, rainn.org. The DoD's Safe Helpline is specifically for military personnel, and

damn RAINN website? No, no, no, no, and no. I didn't think I needed to. I'd watched about a thousand episodes of *Law & Order: Special Victims Unit.* As Smart said in our interview: *You don't know, you don't understand, you don't know what it's like.* She was right. I just assumed I did. And even though I'd never been through anything remotely like what she had, I thought she *should* have done more. Subconsciously, I blamed her.

———

ON SOME LEVEL, I think we all do this, and it's not because we are terrible people. It's because the world is a frightening place, and we need to believe that if we make the right choices, we'll be okay. The stuffy term for this is the "just-world fallacy"—the comforting but false idea that in a just world, people always get what they deserve. What goes around comes around. We reap what we sow. These ideas are deeply ingrained in our everyday thinking, and for good reason. They give us a false sense of control that makes us feel safe. Our fundamental, "commonsense" understanding of the world insists on this universal truth that is actually a lie.

An example: I used to keep a few rolls of quarters in my car to use for parking meters. One morning all my quarters—about thirty dollars' worth—were gone. Had my husband taken them? *Nope,* he said, *you must have left the door unlocked.* I dutifully mentioned the missing quarters to my neighbors. Each time, I got the same response: *You must have left the door unlocked!*

I made a bad choice, so something bad happened. Makes sense.

its number is 877-995-5247; it also has a 24/7 live chat hotline at safehelpline.org. For those under eighteen, RAINN is a mandatory reporter, meaning that it is required to report suspected cases of child sexual abuse if enough identifying information is provided to do so.

Well, yes, but we were all missing the point. The quarters weren't gone *because* I left the door unlocked. They were gone because a criminal stole them. Leaving the door unlocked made my car an easier target, but the thief and only the thief was the reason my money was gone. Telling ourselves that it happened because I left the door unlocked just gave us back the illusion of control. Blaming a sexual assault victim for what they wore or how much they drank or getting in the car or going to the room—or not escaping when a police officer gave her the opportunity—does the same thing. It makes us feel back in control. In a just world, we are all masters of our own fates.

But the world is not just. Even if we made perfect choices all the time, criminals would still exist and bad things would still happen. The truth is that I really have no control over a criminal's choice to break into my car. Twice when I've locked it, one has just broken my window, and I've left my car door unlocked plenty of times without having anything stolen. Yet neither my husband nor my neighbors ever suggested that I was lying about the coins being stolen in the first place. With sexual assault, it's different.

Why? We all know what stealing is, what kidnapping is, what murder is. With those crimes, our colloquial understandings roughly match the reality of how they actually occur. When we hear the word "rape," we all think we know what rape is—violent, terrifying, a windowless van, a guy in a ski mask, the hysterical victim shaking and covered in blood and bruises—but that's rarely the reality, which is much more complicated than the stereotype.

The stereotypical rape is straightforward. Even if the rapist is not a stranger but someone the victim knows and trusts, they abruptly change into some brutish "rape" mode that matches our image of a stereotypical rapist. The victim is either unconscious or screams "no" or says it repeatedly but is ignored, then fights back until physically overpowered. Afterward, they're beaten up and obviously traumatized. Everyone immediately recognizes that something terrible has happened. The victim may not go immediately to the police, but they're *at least* going to avoid the perpetrator because they know he's a rapist. There is no confusion. Everything is black and white. We've internalized this script so deeply that whenever we hear about a sexual assault that diverges from the stereotypical story we expect, something feels off.

In 2013, Smart's story struck me as weird because she cooperated with her captors to survive rather than risked her life to escape or fight off her rapist, which I assumed any "real" rape victim would do. Even though it doesn't align with the stereotype, what Smart did wasn't weird at all but perfectly rational. Ask most people if they would rather be sexually assaulted or killed, and they'll tell you they'd rather stay alive. Survival instincts nearly always overpower all others. Smart had seen her kidnapper outsmart the police before, had no reason to think he could not do it again, and the safer bet was to avoid antagonizing him.

The odd thing, though, is that Smart's story otherwise conforms pretty well to the typical sexual assault stereotype—she was a virgin, kidnapped from her home in the night by a terrifying, violent man with a knife—and yet when it diverged from the stereotype even the slightest bit, my subconscious alarm bells went off. Rather than questioning my own assumptions about how a sexual assault victim "should" react in that situation, I questioned her story.

———

"WHEN YOU SAY THE WORD 'RAPE,'" there's a script that goes along with it," says Kimberly Lonsway, PhD, the director of research for

End Violence Against Women International and one of the foremost researchers on rape myths. "That drives our thinking in all kinds of ways, mainly that the less a rape looks like the stereotype, the more skeptical we tend to be about it."

This script extends to every aspect of a sexual assault narrative, from how these crimes supposedly occur to who and what we expect the perpetrator and victim to be. If an accused rapist doesn't align with the stereotype—terrifying, monstrous, wearing a ski mask—we are more likely to doubt the allegations against them. If the accuser is young, white, and virginal like the stereotypical rape victim, we're more inclined to believe their allegations. If they are anything else, we're more inclined to doubt.

The concept of the stereotypical "ideal victim" was first defined by sociologist and criminologist Nils Christie in 1986 and remains disappointingly prevalent today: Ideally, the victim will have been carrying out a respectable activity in a place she could not possibly be blamed for being and is relatively weak compared to a "big, bad" unknown perpetrator. Whenever someone claims to be a victim and checks all five of those "ideal victim" boxes, the more likely we are to see that person as an actual victim. When they don't—for instance, when the victim is a man* or a woman who is drinking or was somewhere we feel she shouldn't have been, such as the perpetrator's hotel room—we struggle to see them as victims.

These expectations extend to behavior, too. Regardless of the circumstances surrounding a sexual assault, we subconsciously look for offender behavior that aligns with how we think a stereotypical rapist would act, and victim behavior that aligns with how we think a stereotypical sexual assault victim would react. Even though most of us have no actual idea how either rapists or their victims

---

* At least one in six men have been sexually abused or assaulted—for more information and support, see 1in6.org.

act, we measure the story against the stereotype because we assume it is true. If the victim's behavior strikes us as "counterintuitive" by these standards—for example, a victim who doesn't forcibly resist, who fails to capitalize on every potential opportunity to escape, who acts "normal" following the assault or continues her relationship with the perpetrator—we assume they are not really victims.

"The really unique part, I think, about sexual assault is that, when you go down the list of characteristics that cause people to question whether or not this was really a sexual assault, in many cases those are the common, typical dynamics of actual sexual assault," Lonsway says. "The very hallmarks of what sexual assault typically looks like are exactly the same characteristics that cause people to doubt the credibility of a sexual assault disclosure. That keeps us all busy in this field."

We aren't born believing these stereotypes. We internalize them as "common sense" because they're continually reinforced by how we see sexual assaults portrayed in media and culture. My work was a part of that—and I would soon pay the price.

But if you'd asked me when I left for Sochi a few months after our Elizabeth Smart interview aired, I would have told you that I knew everything I needed to know to protect myself from a sexual assault. Whenever I walked home alone at night, I held my key between my knuckles as I'd learned in the women's self-defense course I took in college. I never left my drinks unattended at bars. I didn't go home with strangers. I did all the things I'd been taught to do so I'd never be vulnerable to the stereotypical rape scenario.

"Whenever there's a big rape story in the press, there's an opportunity for the press to educate the public," says Helen Benedict, a professor at the Columbia Journalism School and the author of *Victim or Vamp*, a groundbreaking 1992 book that explored the ways the media unconsciously perpetuates rape myths. "To write stories about the myths, write stories about the background, and how often this happens—who it happens to, who actually commits these crimes—and the reality versus the myths. Most of the time that opportunity is completely missed."

---

OFF TO SOCHI I WENT, believing I was worldly and tough and well equipped to handle the perils of a tough, male-dominated industry—though at the time, those were the least of my concerns. I'd been working on a primetime special for nearly a year and a half and I was so worried about it that I'd literally diagrammed all the ways I thought it could potentially destroy my career. They were endless. I couldn't sleep, and I felt I had nowhere to turn for help.

The story started as too many broadcast news pieces do, with an article in *The New York Times*. In September 2012, there on its front page was Dr. Paolo Macchiarini, an Italian surgeon with a striking resemblance to George Clooney—which made the story all the more appealing for television. Dubbed the "super surgeon," Macchiarini was hailed as a pioneer in regenerative medicine for bioengineering and transplanting plastic replacement tracheas seeded with his patients' stem cells. He led a research group at the elite Karolinska Institute in Sweden, which awarded the Nobel Prize in medicine. His research, which was peer reviewed and published by the world's most prestigious medical journal *The Lancet*, was being celebrated as a miracle of modern medicine with endless possible future applications. Replacement lungs, hearts, kidneys, livers—you name it—could all follow.

Meredith saw the *Times* article and sent it to one of her long-time producers, Benita Alexander, who'd then forwarded it to me. I emailed Macchiarini. I remember being surprised that he responded right away that he'd love to talk to us. One of his current patients, he said, was a little girl in a hospital in Seoul who had been born without a trachea. Perhaps we'd like to follow her story?

Hannah was a pigtailed toddler whose smile radiated limitless joy and hope, even though she had never left the pediatric intensive care unit. Only Macchiarini, with his cutting-edge methods, had offered any hope. We flew to Seoul and filmed her in her NICU unit, alongside Macchiarini and her parents. Months later, when the U.S. Food and Drug Administration granted permission for Macchiarini to transplant Hannah with one of his bioengineered tracheas at a children's hospital in Peoria, Alexander was there with our cameras. The surgery appeared to be a success and received glowing coverage worldwide.

But there was more to the story. While she was in Peoria covering the surgery, Alexander began a secret romantic relationship with Macchiarini.

"I was in love and because I had made a very personal decision to take a leap of faith for love, I never looked back," she eventually told *Vanity Fair*. "I knew I was crossing the line at work and I made a very conscious decision not to tell anybody else at work what I was doing."

But the story did not have the heartwarming ending we'd hoped. In July of 2013, about three months after her surgery, Hannah— the radiant, pigtailed toddler whose life had been in Macchiarini's hands—died.

"The trachea was never a problem," Macchiarini told the *Times* after her death, adding that he would be performing another transplant that week in Stockholm.

With the loss of our young heroine, our story's focus shifted to Macchiarini. At that point, there was little reason to do otherwise beyond an arrest in Italy in 2012 for attempted aggravated fraud, but the arrest was public knowledge at the time the FDA approved Hannah's procedure and we included it in our story. Macchiarini's most publicly vocal critic was a professor of respiratory surgery in Belgium who'd published a paper calling engineered tracheas a "blatant scientific deception." But which was more likely to be correct, the global medical establishment that resoundingly supported Macchiarini's work or the one guy who said it was categorically impossible?

Yet in the weeks before Sochi, I thought Alexander seemed unusually secretive and defensive about Macchiarini. I wondered if the two had gotten too close. To even suggest an inappropriate relationship with the subject of a story was no small accusation to make, especially about such a seasoned, celebrated news producer. But what did I know? I had nothing concrete to validate my concern. Months earlier, I *thought* she had mentioned that Macchiarini had offered her frequent-flier miles so that she and her daughter could take a vacation. It's an obvious conflict of interest for journalists to accept gifts from sources, but she didn't say that she had accepted them. If there is one thing producers have in abundance, it's frequent-flier miles, so it wouldn't have made much sense. And in a few months we were both leaving the news division to work on Meredith's new syndicated talk show, where Alexander would be my direct supervisor. I could hardly afford to compromise my relationship with her by accusing her of journalistic misconduct.

Still, between her odd behavior and my growing, unsettling feeling that there was something that didn't add up about Macchiarini, I was worried. I started staying at work late, drawing my weird charts of the potentially disastrous outcomes should even *one* of my suspicions prove correct. For any one part of Paolo Macchiarini to be suspect, then *all* of Paolo Macchiarini would have had to be suspect— and that seemed impossible. Again, it made no sense.

Nothing about Paolo Macchiarini ultimately made much sense.

Nearly all the patients who received his bioartificial tracheas have now died; those who survived had their transplants removed.

He was eventually fired from Karolinska, which had overruled alarms raised by whistleblowers that later proved correct. Most of Macchiarini's papers have been retracted after discoveries that he had falsified his research, performed experimental procedures without appropriate permissions or adequate animal studies, and recklessly endangered the lives of his patients, causing them unconscionable suffering before their deaths. In 2019, he was sentenced to sixteen months in prison by an Italian court for forging documents and abuse of office. In 2022, a Swedish court found him criminally responsible for causing bodily harm to a patient, a felony conviction; in 2023, an appeals court found him guilty of gross assault against three of his patients and he was sentenced to two and a half years in prison.

That's just his medical fraud. Macchiarini also claimed to be a member of a top-secret international league of doctors who treated the pope, Vladimir Putin, the Clintons, and the Obamas. His secret love affair with Alexander collapsed when the elaborately planned wedding that he claimed would be officiated by the pope at his summer palace in Italy turned out to be a ruse (I still have my invitation). A Vatican spokesman confirmed that Macchiarini was not the pope's doctor and that the pope did not know anyone named Macchiarini. Instead, the surgeon appeared to still be married to his wife of thirty years back in Italy and had been involved with at least two other women during his engagement to Alexander.*

But as I left for Sochi in early 2014, I had no way of knowing any of that. No whistleblowers would come forward about Macchiarini until after our story aired, and even when they did,

---

* Alexander played no small role in his downfall, even as Macchiarini continued to be protected by Karolinska. After exposing him in *Vanity Fair*, she produced her own documentary (*He Lied About Everything*). Extensive interviews with her became the basis for a season of the Wondery podcast *Dr. Death*, which was then made into a crime drama starring Mandy Moore as Alexander and Édgar Ramírez as Macchiarini.

Karolinska sided with its superstar surgeon. In the meantime, here was a two-hour news documentary that we'd been working on for nearly eighteen months—my first field producer credit and supposedly the crowning achievement of my career to that point—which Alexander, one of the best news producers at NBC, wholeheartedly believed in. Again, what the hell did I know? Alexander was a mentor and I trusted her. She was soon to be my boss, and I'd already raised so many tedious concerns about the story that I knew I was on thin ice. As excited as I was for Meredith to launch her own talk show, I didn't want to leave news. If I ever wanted to get back to the news division as a producer, I needed at least one major news-producing credit and the Macchiarini story was all I had. What were the odds that Alexander was lying to us? Or that the global medical establishment was wrong?

By the time we left for Sochi, I was thrilled to be going to the other side of the world for three weeks and as far away from the Macchiarini story as possible. I wasn't going to the Olympics as an associate producer. I was just going as an assistant. All I'd have to do was book cars, organize hair and makeup, and make call sheets, and in between I'd be watching figure skating and hockey and skiing. There were security concerns, sure—but I'd be with the talent the whole time. Nowhere in Sochi should have been safer.

# FOUR

# How It Happens

've always taken comfort in the idea of fate, that even the most improbable events happen for a reason. As long as they happen for a reason—if God, at least, has a plan—then even the most random events have meaning, even if I don't yet understand them.

Then something terrible happens, and suddenly the idea of fate is no longer comforting but cruel. When the odds of that terrible thing are so improbable that they really ought to have been impossible, then the belief that everything happens for a reason becomes all-important. Why else could something so unlikely actually happen? And how?

Then you realize that, unless God is cruel, the most likely reason it happened is *you*. If everything happens for a reason, then the reason must be that you deserved it. Such terrible things, you tell yourself, don't happen to nice, normal people. Terrible things happen to terrible people. If that terrible thing is so unlikely, then it can only have happened because there is something specifically, unspeakably wrong or weak or weird about you.

Suddenly you see that all the people who ever loved you were either wrong or lying, that all the good things that have ever happened to you were aberrations, that your regrets were never mistakes but irrefutable proof that you are uniquely, irredeemably bad. The fallacy of a just world—that what goes around comes around, that we have some control over what happens to us in life, that my money was stolen only because I left the door unlocked—now brings a sense of hopelessness. You no longer see yourself as a person but as a problem that can never be solved, and so the only way forward is to try never to be discovered. To be loved, you must hide.

This is shame.

For years, the sheer improbability of what happened in Sochi made shame feel like the only rational response. There was no reasoning with it. It just was. It didn't matter that I hadn't been out trawling Russian bars, looking for married men to sleep with. It didn't matter that I left my hotel room and went very specifically to meet my female boss and longtime mentor, who'd just made history by becoming the first woman to anchor primetime Olympic coverage.

And how had that happened? Through another impossible series of events.

First, Bob Costas got, of all the things, pinkeye. Costas, who had anchored NBC's Olympic coverage 157 consecutive times since 1992, woke up with "full-blown viral conjunctivitis, not just generic pinkeye," which would impact his eyesight for months. The man had somehow survived not only childhood but raising two children without *ever in his life getting pinkeye*—until Sochi. What were the odds? And what were the odds that my boss would then become the first woman in history to anchor primetime Olympic coverage? Not Mary Carillo or Bonnie Bernstein or even Phyllis George—but Meredith Vieira, in 2014.

And so, having made a bit of television history, we decided to pop downstairs for a glass of wine to celebrate, where Matt Lauer—who wasn't known for being a guy you just bumped into and then hung out with—happened upon us.

What were the odds?

———

THERE WAS ALWAYS SOMETHING ominous about the Sochi Olympics. Putin had not yet invaded Ukraine, but had already overseen a brutal war in Chechnya, developed a reputation for silencing his critics and political opponents, and invaded the northern territories of Georgia. The games were widely considered a prime target for terrorists, who had carried out four separate bombings in the months leading up to the opening ceremonies. Putin responded by turning Sochi into a "ring of steel," a security zone sixty miles long and twenty-five miles wide, supposedly subject to near-total surveillance, guarded by forty thousand troops and twenty-five thousand police officers. The Olympics were typically among the most coveted assignments at NBC, but between the terrorist threat and Putin's new anti-gay laws, Sochi was not one of them. At least in comparison to other Olympics, NBC sent a skeleton staff.

But for those of us who went, that skeleton staff translated to bigger opportunities. As one of a relatively few assistants to go, I had been put in the same executive-level hotel as the talent. That proximity, plus the thin staff, meant that I spent much more time around Matt and the other talent than I otherwise would have. For the first few weeks in Sochi, that felt like the most incredible luck.

"After I left *Today*," Couric wrote in her 2022 memoir, "a producer friend told me that when Matt was on location for a week, a pretty PA was sent home early. 'We had to bring her back—for Matt's sake,' a male producer explained, alluding to the trouble

Matt could get into if she stayed. The trickle-down effect of sexual harassment: young women paying for the sins of their bosses."

My first thought when I read that was, *If only I had been pretty enough to be sent home early*—and then I realized that the concern for "the trouble" in question was not for the pretty young production assistant but for Matt. As ever, the priority was to protect the talent. Couric left *Today* in 2006, eight years before Sochi, which meant that, at least according to its former coanchor, *Today* management had been worried enough about Matt's behavior to proactively take one of his potential targets off the board. The skeleton staff meant already that there were even fewer potential targets in Sochi—but even if I'd been smart enough to realize that, I would never have considered myself one of them. I wasn't a "pretty young production assistant." I was perpetually exhausted and growing out an awkward pixie cut. I was still the wallpaper.

The Olympics meant long hours on my feet, shuttling from location to location, juggling research binders and wardrobe and a computer. I didn't bring any of the dresses or heels I would have been wearing at 30 Rock; I wore wallpaper-esque jeans and NBC Sports swag. The only remotely attention-seeking piece of clothing I'd packed was a bright orange Denver Broncos T-shirt that I wore when I stayed up all night to watch them in the Super Bowl.* As far as I was concerned, there would have been absolutely no reason for management to send me home.

For the first few weeks in Sochi, Matt treated me as he always had—like Meredith's awkward, tagalong kid sister. But once, early in the trip, a small group of us met for dinner in the hotel, and I remember him gesturing in my direction. Did everyone know about our "family connection," he'd asked?

For a moment I was at a total loss. I had no idea what he was

---

* They lost, 43–8. Fitting.

talking about. Then I realized that our "family connection" was my then boyfriend's brother, who had worked for Matt and his family for a decade. But that certainly didn't make me feel like family. It made me feel like the help—which, of course, I was.

I saw Matt at other group dinners, meetings, and shoots, and the smaller-than-usual team—and the vodka—had fostered a good-natured camaraderie. By the time we went to the hotel bar that night to celebrate Meredith's history-making turn, we'd all been together for weeks, and when Matt walked in, I patted the seat next to me at our table without much thought. Why not?

The look of surprise and joy on his face when he saw us was disarming. Still, I had worked for the talent long enough to know that whenever someone rushed over to the two of us with a thrilled look on their face, it was never because of me. *Why are you suddenly so friendly*, I remember Matt saying when he got to the table. I said we were celebrating Meredith, who'd just made history.

What a surreal experience it was, sitting between the two of them, in Russia of all places. For this one night, in these impossible circumstances, I had a seat at the table alongside two of the biggest names in journalism, who I'd known and idolized since I was a kid—just the three of us. It all had the air of the ridiculous. Bob Costas had pinkeye! We were in Russia under the personal protection of Vladimir Putin! Meredith was the First Woman in History to Do Something!* Reality had been suspended altogether, and so I felt like I could laugh and joke alongside Matt Lauer and Meredith Vieira as though we were the oldest of friends. And weren't we? I'd been watching them both on television since elementary school. I felt like I'd known them both forever.

But it was inevitable that reality would return, and it came with

---

* Meredith was also the original moderator of *The View* and the youngest-ever correspondent to join *60 Minutes* in 1989.

the sudden realization that I'd had at least seven or eight drinks in the course of about three hours: A few martinis before Matt arrived, another couple afterward, and then shot after shot of the cool, refreshing, and presumably expensive vodka that Matt had ordered for the table (*na zdorovie!*). But that realization really hit home when Matt held up the hideous pictures he'd taken of me and Meredith from his spot beside me at the table. Meredith still looked her usual, stunningly high-cheekboned self, while I looked like a stained pile of shoveled snow, my unsquared jawline melting into my neck as I tried to squeeze out of the frame. Embarrassing, yes, but the bigger problem was that I looked quite obviously drunk.

*Please delete them,* I asked; *Not in a million years,* he said. To him, they were just funny pictures, but to me, they were a nightmare. Years as an assistant had taught me to imagine and plan for every worst possible scenario, and I immediately imagined Matt the next morning on *Today*, chatting with Savannah and Al about what he'd done the night before—and these horrifying pictures flashing on the screen. *No, no, that would never happen,* I tried to reassure myself—I wasn't important enough—but then I imagined a more likely scenario, which was Matt showing them to other staffers as they tried to mine his fun night out with Meredith for potential chat items they could use on the air. That would have been humiliating enough—no one likes embarrassing, drunken photos of yourself floating around your workplace—but these were on Matt Lauer's NBC-issued phone, where they could theoretically live forever. But he wouldn't delete them, and the night moved on. Eventually Matt paid the tab and we all headed upstairs.

Then I saw Meredith grinning as Matt got off the elevator. The two of them were always playing pranks on each other, and out from behind her back came Matt's Olympic credential, which doubled as a visa in and out of Russia. We laughed hysterically after the doors closed behind him, and when we got off the elevator at our floor, we called him to gloat.

He had clearly been expecting the call. The man missed nothing. *Where are* your *credentials?* he asked.

Meredith's was around her neck. Mine was gone.

That meant that while we'd been at the table, Matt had not just noticed Meredith stealing his credential but also managed to steal *my* credential, and in the meantime, I'd been oblivious to both things at once. Was I that much more drunk, or was Matt just that sharp? Either way, I may have had a seat at the table that night, but I was just as out of my league as ever.

Deflated, I went down to his room to trade credentials and found Matt swinging mine from his fingers good-naturedly. He gestured for me to come into his room, where I stood awkwardly by the desk as he called Meredith to reverse-gloat. On the desk was a box of his personalized stationery, and I remember thinking that if Meredith had been there, she would have stolen some of it or written *sucks!* underneath his name. But that was just not something an assistant could do. My vodka-infused mind was moving so slowly that I hadn't noticed Matt had been watching me the whole time, practically daring me to try something. I wasn't that crazy. The talent never stops being the talent.

I got back upstairs to find Meredith waiting for me in the hallway outside the elevator. It was late, but for some reason she'd still waited to make sure I got back. We were so tipsy that neither of us could get her door open. While we were standing in the hallway, I began my usual routine of dashing off a thank-you note to whoever we'd been with that day—in this case, Matt. Really, though, I was doing it because Matt had picked up our considerable tab, presumably on his corporate card, which was technically my job to do—and by paying, he'd spared me the unhappy task of having to find a way to legitimately expense all those vodka shots. For an assistant, that was a big deal, and I genuinely was grateful. As I typed, I read the email aloud; I remember writing a joke in it about how we were so drunk we couldn't get back into our rooms. We'd had fun. I thought—and this is embarrassing to admit, even now—that we'd all bonded. That we were almost friends.

———

IN 2019, WHEN ASKED by investigative reporter Ronan Farrow to account for his behavior that night, Matt would say that he'd "considered her [my] concern about the photos to be a thin pretext, and her [my] messages to be come-ons."* While Matt Lauer might be able to get away with sexually propositioning staffers via his corporate email, I certainly couldn't, and even with seven or eight drinks in me I would never have had the nerve to risk my job that way by using my corporate email account to "come on" to the anchor of *Today*. But let's give Matt the benefit of the doubt and assume he really did believe that his former coanchor's awkward assistant was sexually propositioning him. Is this supposed to justify his actions?

This is a man who was famously called "the hunk next door" by Jeff Zucker in *The New York Times* in 1997, when he first became anchor of *Today*. In 2013, Brian Stelter wrote that "men fantasized about being him; women fantasized about sleeping with him (surely some of those men did, too)." Are we really to believe Matt was powerless to refuse what he interpreted as a come-on delivered via email from an obviously drunk, twentysomething assistant? Wouldn't any other adult have just as easily thought, *How cute*, and ignored it altogether, or written back "My pleasure!" and

---

* Throughout *Catch and Kill*, Matt's version of events is indicated by "sources close to Lauer," but Farrow has since confirmed publicly that one of the sources was Matt himself.

told the said-assistant to drink some water and go to bed? Matt was old enough to be my father, and included in this supposed come-on was *also* a description of myself as so impaired that I couldn't get a hotel key card into a door. Yet instead of feeling empathy or concern or indifference or even just plain old camaraderie with the girl he'd first known as the *Today* greenroom page, Matt apparently saw a promising possibility for the rest of his night.

We were not Jim and Pam from *The Office*, with years of affection and humor and chemistry built up between us. I was not some random woman he'd picked up at a bar. I was someone he'd worked alongside for years, admittedly as wallpaper but who he'd claimed just days before to have thought of as a "family connection." Moreover, how many times over the years had I gone out drinking with coworkers, or even just split a case of beer with the all-male camera crew in the hotel room where we'd just shot an interview, without incident? How many times over the years had I put drunk interns and production assistants and even producers in cabs after happy hour, texting them to make sure they got home safely? How many times had coworkers done the same thing for me? The anchor of *Today* isn't just any coworker but a leader, the moral and professional ballast of the show. There should have been nowhere safer for an NBC staffer at any time, under any circumstance, than with the anchor of *Today*.

I am more than a decade and a half younger today than Matt was in Sochi in 2014, but when a guy who worked for my husband drank too much bourbon at our house one night, my first thought wasn't how I could take advantage of the situation but how I could help the poor kid. Could I get him a glass of water? An Advil? A cup of coffee? An Uber? And this was a guy in his thirties on our couch, not someone young enough to be my child in Russia.

There is simply no world in which any decent fiftysomething father of three could have spent hours buying vodka shots for an assistant who idolized him—and who was alone, far from home, and young enough to be his daughter—and recognized her as anything other than vulnerable, let alone as an opportunity to exploit.

———

"WHAT WE THINK IS VULNERABILITY is really only exposed when there's somebody there to hurt us," says forensic psychologist Veronique Valliere. "Without danger, there is no vulnerability. We don't walk through the world as vulnerable. It's safe to ride your bike or go jogging, unless there's a drunk driver cruising by who hits you. It's safe to go to a frat party unless there's a rapist at that frat party. We don't walk through the world as vulnerable unless there's a dangerous person around us. It's the danger that's the problem."

I teach my toddlers never to go in the street without holding a grown-up's hand, because streets are dangerous. I should learn to be more precise with my words. Streets are safe to cross as long as no cars are coming. Cars are safe as long as the people driving them are not reckless. If there were no criminals, I could leave my car door unlocked. To Valliere's point, it's the danger that's the problem—and without it, there is no vulnerability.

After interviewing, evaluating, and treating thousands of offenders, Valliere is adept at describing—often using their own words—the many ways that they identify and exploit the vulnerabilities of their victims. Most of these "vulnerabilities," she points out, are not problems but simply normal human characteristics, like being kind or trusting or lonely.

"Being with someone dangerous who will rape or harm the victim is the problem," Valliere wrote in her book *Understanding Victims of Interpersonal Violence*. ". . . At each point, a person can offer care, comfort or resources to a vulnerable person rather than harming him or her, as an offender chooses to do."

A FEW MINUTES LATER, I was brushing my teeth when my phone buzzed with Matt's response to the thank-you email, which was something to the effect of *Hey, you should come back down here!*

I remember staring at my phone on the counter, as though it were some dead bug that had just jerked back to life. Drunk as I was, I was still well aware that people have sex in hotel rooms on work trips, and that Matt was rumored to do just that. But this was an email to *me*. I was the wallpaper. Had any other coworker sent it, I would have just assumed they were wasted and ignored it, but I couldn't ignore an email from Matt Lauer. There is no "ghosting" the talent. Still, enough of a subconscious alarm bell had gone off that I knew I should make it clear that everything was aboveboard, and giving him an easy out if he had meant otherwise. I wrote back that the only reason I would go back down to his room would be to delete the terrible pictures from earlier. I remember pressing send and thinking that it was a perfect response, crafted by a longtime assistant who knew never to create an awkward situation for the talent, to always leave a way to let them save face. *Consider it done!* he could write, and then we'd *all* save face. I started getting ready for bed and wondered how long I'd need to wait for him to respond before I could be sure that he'd gone to sleep.

Instead, the phone buzzed again: *The offer is all-inclusive but expires in ten minutes!**

I remember being, of all things, relieved that I hadn't made him mad. "All-inclusive" gave me pause, but then again, he wasn't

---

* Some journalistic housekeeping: these emails are in italics rather than quotation marks because I no longer have copies. That said, I was confident enough in my memory to report them this way to NBC in 2017, who presumably could have accessed and verified them.

sending it to some pretty young production assistant but to *me*. I had just been in his room, and he had treated me with all the sexual interest of a floor lamp. Matt Lauer? Making a pass at *me*? The thought went through my mind, and as soon as it did, I was embarrassed even to have thought it. Who the hell did I think I was? Marilyn Monroe? Yeah, right. When you're drunk, anything feels possible, but it still did not feel possible to me that Matt could think of me that way. But drunk people are not known for erring on the side of caution. We were friends! Drinking buddies! And now I was going to have *such* a great story to tell Meredith and the hair and makeup team—the drinking story to end all drinking stories. I pushed the alarm bells out of my head and thought, what the hell. In our business, Matt was a great friend to have. I was excited.

And I would get to delete those horrible pictures. That was reason enough to go.

But the offer expired in ten minutes. It was a ticking clock, like the one he'd given the hesitant production assistant fourteen years earlier in 2000, when he wrote—again, via the NBC messaging system—"I can't stay that long, I have a car coming at 3:00" when it was 2:42 p.m. I'd worked for the talent for so long that rushing to do whatever they asked before the clock ran out was practically a reflex. Anyway, when Matt Lauer asks you to do something or makes you an offer, you don't say no. Matt would have known that after seventeen years as *Today* anchor. What was the worst that could happen? That I'd get there and Matt Lauer would hit on me? Please. He was trying to be nice, and I was keeping him waiting. I rushed out the door. I didn't even stop to put on shoes.

———

*ALL-INCLUSIVE:* IN THE DAYS AFTERWARD when I read and reread that email exchange, this would be the word I used to convince myself that I must have known exactly what I was doing. It was better to be a bad person than a victim, I told myself. At least a bad person has agency.

In the aftermath of a terrible loss of control, even the illusion of agency can mean the difference between functioning and irreparably falling apart. I *must* have known what I was doing. Matt was the hunk next door, I told myself. Everyone wanted to sleep with him, right? On some subconscious, Freudian level entirely devoid of physical and personal reality, I probably did—and that was enough to blame myself, and only myself, for years.

So I can forgive that giddy young assistant for rushing back down to see the anchor of *Today*. She was hardly the first person in the world to do something stupid and impulsive while drunk out of her mind, and doing something stupid or even outright wrong doesn't mean I deserved what would happen to me in that room.

I remember bursting off the elevator, walking toward his door from the elevator in my socks. When the door opened, I remember that it seemed to pull back invisibly, and as I walked in, I realized he was standing behind it, now stripped down to his T-shirt and boxers. The lights were off. Matt Lauer was kissing me with his hands on both sides of my face.

For a long time when I described what happened, I would begin by saying, "It started like a normal sexual encounter," and by that I meant that it wasn't violent. I'm struck now by how many years it took me to acknowledge that absolutely nothing about how it began was like a normal sexual encounter. I can't think of a single time when I went to the door of any other man I was not dating and found him hiding behind it silently in the dark, undressed, having apparently already decided what he wanted to do.

Imagine that I had walked into that room and the lights had been on and Matt had been dressed, and without saying a word, *I* grabbed *his face* and began kissing *him*. My career would have been over, and it would not have mattered in the least whether I was drunk or sober or had read the word "all-inclusive" and gotten the wrong idea. Matt could have calmly explained to NBC management, who would in turn explain to Meredith, that he had just innocently offered to let me duck down to the room one more time to delete some pictures from his phone because he didn't want me to feel embarrassed, especially since we had "a family connection." It was unfortunate that I'd gotten the wrong idea, he might say, and that would have been the end of my career at NBC. There is no realistic scenario in which I could ever have instigated a sexual encounter with Matt Lauer without risking my job, and at the same time, neither is there any realistic scenario in which I could have *stopped* a sexual encounter with Matt Lauer without risking my job. Humiliate, offend, or anger the Most Powerful Face in News? That would have been career suicide, and he would have known that. People in power know they are in power.

But in the moment, I couldn't see the big picture; I couldn't think through my options and make a choice. Now his tongue was in my mouth, and I began to understand that walking into the room *was* the choice, and it had already been made. Had it been anyone else behind that door—except, possibly, Putin himself—an option would have been to laugh it off as a misunderstanding and then walk back out. But there was no laughing off Matt Lauer, and there was certainly no rejecting Matt Lauer in his underwear. There was only pleasing Matt Lauer. To do anything else would have been to become a problem, and Matt's problems at NBC tended to disappear.

I wish I could say that I thought about the life-changing moral and emotional consequences of what was happening, but I didn't. I couldn't. What I most remember thinking was that there was a very real possibility that his tongue could go too far down my throat and I might vomit all over the germophobic anchor of *To-*

*day*. Shots take a while to catch up with you, and between the unfamiliar tongue in my mouth—which belonged to *Matt Lauer*—and his weight pushing against me in a spinning room, I knew I was no longer buzzed but drunk, the sort of sloppy drunk where you just want to cradle a toilet bowl and then pass out on the bathroom floor. But in a way, that made the whole thing easier, because it gave me a singular focus: As long as I didn't throw up or fall over, I could figure the rest out later. It wasn't like I hadn't had drunk sex before. Matt was aggressive, sure, but not rough. As long as I held it together, it would be fine. It had to be. It was already happening anyway.

This is not to say, either, that my initial shock was followed by horror. It wasn't. Matt Lauer was kissing *me?* When you think of yourself perennially as an awkward tomboy, there is always a part of you that is overjoyed to discover that a man—any man—thinks of you as an attractive woman. Even sober, I would have been flattered. I was human, and this was a powerful, attractive, famous man. But I also was far from sober and Matt Lauer was kissing me in his underwear in a spinning hotel room. It didn't matter that the oldest man I'd ever been with until then was only a couple of years older than me, or that I'd never been with a married man, or anybody's dad, or a famous person, or someone who, in every other circumstance, usually intimidated me so much that I barely spoke. Drinking lowers your inhibitions, and I was very, very drunk. Compared to the alternative—jeopardizing everything I'd ever worked for—it never occurred to me to make a scene or run out of the room. Just as I was hardly the first person in history to do something stupid and impulsive while drunk, nor was I the first woman in the world to decide—as much as it was a decision at that point—to do the practical thing and not make an enemy out of a powerful man.

Would I have been willing had I *not* been afraid to say no to the

Most Powerful Face in News? I never would have been in the room if he had been anyone else. It's hard to conjure any other circumstance in which I would have cheated on my boyfriend with a married father in his fifties who made me feel like the help. The power, and the alcohol, can never be factored out of the equation. I can't possibly know.

And if I can't possibly know, neither can Matt—which means he certainly couldn't have known then. I don't think it really mattered. I can't imagine that a man who would summon a young, drunk subordinate to his corporate hotel room on a work trip is worried about consent. When I got to Matt's hotel room, he didn't act as though he had any doubts as to whether I would do what he wanted. But I never could have untangled any of this in those few moments, when the expectations in that room were not so much unfolding but already on top of me.

Nor would submitting be enough. The talent expected to be pleased, to be shown gratitude, for participation to be enthusiastic because I'd been trusted with the opportunity to be pleasing in this most personal of ways. The problem was that Matt knew next to nothing about me personally. It wasn't personal at all. Whatever the circumstances, he would always be Matt Lauer and I would always be the talent assistant whose professional function was to keep the talent happy.

Even in the most impersonal of my sexual encounters to that point—the hookups in college or the one-night stands in my twenties—it had always been personal in the sense that I could say whatever I wanted, make whatever jokes I wanted, or say "yes" or "no" whenever I saw fit. This was different. Imagine being expected to have sex, not as yourself in your private life but at work as the professional version of yourself who knows her place and can't speak out of turn or overrule the boss. In that room, I wasn't myself anymore so much as a body suddenly at someone else's disposal, but I didn't know how to extract my personality from that body, how to do something so personal yet impersonal at the same time.

At first, it seems easy enough; he is leading me to the bed, not violently, just perfunctorily, and my surprise shifts to basic human embarrassment. I haven't shaved my legs in a month. I'd been watching this man on television since I was ten years old and now he is going to take off my clothes and see me naked? I don't know what is allowed, but it seems like a no-brainer that I am not allowed to look at the talent's erect penis. I know I can't order Matt Lauer to do anything, but can I order him to put on a condom? If he doesn't have one, will he send me to go get one? I'm the assistant, but I have no idea where to get a condom in Sochi. Now he's pulling off my jeans, and since my legs are long and the pants are stretchy, it feels as though I am a child being undressed by a parent. I realize that my underwear has polka dots and so do my socks. I say, *I'm sorry about my socks.* Or maybe I said, *Do you like my socks?* I do not say *no* or *stop.* He's still pulling off the stretchy jeans, and I feel awkward, and to fill the awkward pause of the stretchy jeans, I say, *I didn't know I was your type.* He nods and says, *You're tall.* That, at least, was sort of personal. I smile.

*It's just sex,* I keep telling myself, *don't make it weird.* Still, in all the drunken hookups I've had in my life, there was always some discussion about actually having sex, some acknowledgment that a line was about to be crossed that cannot be uncrossed. Is this okay? Is this too fast? There was not always affirmative consent or some deep emotional connection, but there was always a basic acknowledgment that I had a say in what was happening. That night, though, I feel as though I'm just an observer, waiting for Matt to decide what he is going to do with my body. I think he's going to climb on top of me and I hope he's putting on a condom, but then I feel his mouth between my legs, and the possibility of throwing up no longer seems so embarrassing in comparison.

Then came the *oh shit* realization that I would have to react with enthusiasm if I didn't want to insult him, and I couldn't insult him. What was wrong with me? He was trying to be *nice*. This was supposedly for my pleasure, though at some point I realize that what he was doing did not seem to be in any way tied to my reaction to it. I'd taken for granted how much every other man I'd been with until then had cared—how earnestly they'd tried, how they'd looked for my comfort and approval and enjoyment—until I was naked and alone with a man who did not seem like he could have possibly cared less. Then again, why should he have cared? This was off camera. The hotel room was a safe space where the talent did not have to perform or be likable. After years of working with powerful, important people, a professional assistant learns to ignore so many basic personal boundaries. You laugh at jokes that you do not find funny and accept the blame for problems you did not cause. You lie at your own expense so that the talent can save face. You do things you don't personally want to do and you pretend to enjoy things you do not personally enjoy. What was the difference between all that and this?

In the immediate aftermath of that night, I probably would have said it was just awkward, uncomfortable, embarrassing. But it took years to process the sheer emotional carnage that took place during those few moments that I was staring at the ceiling. Feigning pleasure during sex can feel like an act of kindness to avoid humiliating a well-meaning partner, but this was not like that. It did not feel like a kindness but a betrayal of everything I thought I knew about myself, a horrific realization that I had allowed myself to become so beholden to this man and the system of power that created him that I was expected to show not only gratitude but enthusiasm as I was being used. How could that little girl who watched this man on television before school have possibly ended up here?

He maneuvers me onto my hands and knees, and for a moment

I'm relieved that I will be able to stare at the headboard because I can't imagine him looking at my face while he does what I think he is about to do. It's just sex, I tell myself again, and I stare at the headboard, not realizing that the image of the headboard is one that I will see again and again and again for years to come.

He's talking in my left ear: *Do you like anal sex?*

I freeze.

*No, that's not my thing,* I finally say.

*Are you sure? I think you'll like it.*

*I've never done that before.*

*You'll like it.*

*No,* I say again, *I still don't think that's my thing.*

*I think you'll like it.*

And with that—a few brief disagreements over what I wanted for my own body—I just gave up. For so many years afterward, I hated myself so much for this, was so ashamed of myself because of it, that I wanted to die. All the love and care that my parents had given me in the years since they brought me into this world—all the years that they had protected me, cherished me, done everything in their power so that their daughter would enjoy a happy, healthy life on this earth—and *that* was the best I could do? I threw myself away as though I was nothing, as though they and their love and care for me were nothing, as though everyone who had ever loved me were all nothing. It was unforgivable.

But giving up, I understand now, was really the only available option. It was to lose the battle in hopes of winning the war for myself and the possibility for the future I thought I'd earned. But I lost more than the battle. I lost the person I had been before I patted the seat, took the shots, sent the email, and walked so carelessly into that Sochi hotel room. But I have forgiven her for all that. Now I struggle to imagine the courage it would have taken, drunk and naked and on my hands and knees alone with Matt Lauer in a Russian hotel room, to say no *even once* after it began to sink in that this was why I was there.

And this, I knew, would not be okay. This was not just sex. This was my worst nightmare. It was everyone's worst nightmare, man or woman. Anal sex was not something a decent man springs on any woman he cares about, let alone a drunk young woman over whom he holds every conceivable advantage. This was not something a decent man pressures a terrified, decades-younger woman to do. And yet somehow, I still found the courage to say no that night—to argue with a man with whom there was no arguing. I'd said it deferentially, which was the only way you can ever say no to someone so powerful, but I still said it. Would a reasonable man have known I was afraid, was uncomfortable, and that, above all, I did not want this to happen? Yes, a reasonable man would. Any decent human being would, which meant that—in that moment—I realized that Matt Lauer was neither a reasonable man nor a decent human being.

Of course he wasn't. He was so powerful, he didn't have to be either. Fiftysomething-year-old married men who make tens of millions of dollars a year don't summon drunk young women who work for them to have carefully considered consensual sex. They do it to spare themselves any discussion, because they know that with a drunk young woman who works for them, there will *be* no discussion. I realized this, and I stopped arguing. What would have been the point?

───────

THERE'S NOTHING CONFUSING ABOUT the rape stereotype. It's black-and-white. It's overtly violent. You clearly recognize the threat and you know from the beginning that the situation is dangerously beyond your control.

But even then, what they don't teach you in self-defense classes is that the most common response to fear is not fight or flight but freeze—the deer-in-the-headlights response. The scientific term for this is tonic immobility. But because we expect our fight-or-flight response to automatically kick in and give us physical super-powers, we don't recognize that freezing is a survival response in itself.

"At that point, the logical part of the brain is not involved in the decision-making," says Jo-Ann Rojas, LCSW, a sexual violence counselor of more than twenty-five years and a licensed training supervisor at RAINN, the Rape, Abuse & Incest National Network. "The prefrontal cortex is not functioning anymore. The amygdala is in full effect and making all the decisions. You're not even conscious of how quickly these defense mechanisms make the decisions for you."

Blaming yourself for your defensive survival mechanisms makes as much sense as beating yourself up for blinking when something flashes before your eyes or throwing your hands in front of your face to shield yourself from a blast. Later, you can look back and tell yourself that it would have been smarter to grab something nearby that might have made more of a difference, but in the moment there's no opportunity to make the smarter choice. You're not making choices. You're just reacting.*

"Afterward, victims question what happened because they didn't necessarily say no or fight or scream," says Rojas. "There's self-blame. I've had people say, I took a self-defense class, I'm a martial artist, I still couldn't do anything. But sexual assaults may not

---

* It's also important to note here that both genital arousal and orgasm are involuntary physiological responses, do not constitute consent, and should never be considered an indication of consent. "The body responds to stimulus," says Rojas. "A physiological response does not mean that you liked it, wanted it, or enjoyed it."

always be seen as overtly violent or brutal. Coercion can be felt in a variety of ways."*

When the threat isn't overt, neither is the response. To the extent you're able to think at all, you're trying to get your bearings on what exactly is happening and whether it is really a threat. With the stranger in a ski mask holding a knife to your throat, that threat is unambiguous. There's no need to worry about making it awkward or finding a way to gracefully extract yourself from the situation. But when you're with someone you know and trust and have any sort of relationship with—who isn't forcibly holding you down or dragging you into a windowless van—accurately assessing how much or little control you have over the situation is impossible. There are too many unknown variables.

Some of those variables might even be your own: You might be into it at first, or willing to consent up to a certain point. When the other person suddenly begins to act in an unexpected way—they don't immediately stop when you say stop or listen when you say no—you might reasonably assume it was a misunderstanding, at least initially, and give them the benefit of the doubt. If this person matters to you at all, you're going to be mindful of their feelings and preserving the relationship you have with them, so you're not going to immediately scream and run out of the room or violently resist. If they aren't behaving violently, you won't, either. Most people don't react to nonviolent behavior with violence, especially when they aren't yet fully aware of the threat. Rather than fighting, victims try to evade the situation as tactfully as possible, trying

---

* A few of the CDC (Centers for Disease Control, which considers sexual violence a public health issue)'s examples of coercion include exploitation of vulnerability (e.g., immigration status, disability, undisclosed sexual orientation, age); intimidation; misuse of authority (e.g., using one's position of power to coerce or force a person to engage in sexual activity); economic coercion, such as the bartering of sex for basic goods like housing, employment/wages, immigration papers, or childcare;

to graciously deter the person without embarrassing or humiliating them.

"Even in cases of stranger rape, only about 30 percent of women respond with physical aggression," says forensic psychiatrist Dr. Barbara Ziv, a member of the Pennsylvania Sexual Offender Assessment Board since 2000 who has assessed more than a thousand convicted sex offenders and victims and testified in more than two hundred state and federal trials. "Women most often try to negotiate, and this is true in every kind of situation. They'll say, no, I'm tired. I have my period. You have a wife. And that's true even with stranger rape."

"Some victims made a strategic choice to remain frozen so as not to antagonize the attacker or prolong the assault," wrote forensic psychologist Valliere in *Understanding Victims of Interpersonal Violence*. "This strategy is adaptive, considering that the victim is facing someone acting in a confusing, chaotic, unpredictable way. Victims do not expect to be attacked, so have no plan."

"Often what victims say is that they're so confused, and that the whole thing happened so fast, they didn't even know what was going on," says Dr. Ziv. "Then they just sort of try not to make a bad situation worse, and they just go along with it until it's over."

There shouldn't be anything surprising about this. Women, in particular, are socialized to behave this way, practically from birth. We are conditioned to be compliant, whether as little girls told to hug our weird uncles when we don't want to or as grown women dancing around unwanted sexual advances at work. The "boys will

---

degradation, such as insulting or humiliating a victim; fraud, such as lies or misrepresentation of the perpetrator's identity; continual verbal pressure, such as when the victim is being worn down by someone who repeatedly asks for sex; nonphysical threats, such as threats to end a relationship or spread rumors; grooming and other tactics to gain a child's trust; and control of a person's sexual behavior/ sexuality through threats and reprisals.

be boys" mentality teaches us that an inherent, unavoidable reality of being female is not only that we must learn to tolerate what we don't want, but that we must do it without hurting male feelings in the process. Is that disempowering and anti-feminist? Obviously, but it's a lesson that has been passed down from one generation of women to the next for good reason. It's about survival: If you humiliate a man when he's vulnerable, or make him feel too small or too stupid, he might just kill you. Learn to tolerate bad things, because you can never really know whether you actually have a choice.

This means that the most practical choice—the smartest, most rational one—is often to go along, wait it out, and get it over with. When you know you can't win, you learn to compromise—*I'll let you do this if you just don't do that*—as a means of retaining some semblance of control over the situation. You do what you need to do to get through it, and that can very well include feigning pleasure to shorten a sexual encounter and avoid antagonizing a man by making him feel inadequate, especially when his behavior has already become unpredictable. It shouldn't be this way, but it is reckless and irresponsible to pretend that it isn't. Whenever we refuse to acknowledge reality, we leave ourselves dangerously unprepared for it. Then we blame victims for being unprepared—for being caught off guard, leaving their proverbial car doors unlocked.

In 2022, California's First Lady, Jennifer Siebel Newsom, testified against Harvey Weinstein in his second rape trial, in which he faced multiple sex crimes charges in California following his first conviction for sex crimes in New York.* Her testimony described

---

* In May 2024, Weinstein's New York conviction was overturned on appeal. He was reindicted by a New York grand jury four months later. That trial, in 2025, resulted in a conviction for one felony sex abuse charge, an acquittal on another, and a mistrial on the third charge of third-degree rape that, as of publication, New York prosecutors planned to retry.

oral sexual assault and rape, but also that she'd placated Weinstein by using her hand on his penis until he ejaculated so that he wouldn't ejaculate inside her.

"He was so determined, just so scary, just all about him and his pleasure, his need for satisfaction, so I just did it to make it stop," she testified. "I just made some noises to get him to ejaculate faster, just like pleasure noises."

Siebel Newsom made the practical choice, and horrible as it was, it worked: She made it out of the room, and did it without alienating a man she could not afford to alienate. During cross-examination, Weinstein's defense attorney Mark Werksman asked Siebel Newsom to specify how she "indicated her pleasure" during the assault—essentially, asking her to replicate a faked orgasm for the jury—and when Siebel Newsom refused, sobbing, he implied that she was being uncooperative. "She's made herself a prominent victim in the MeToo movement," Werksman told the jury. "Otherwise she'd be just another bimbo who slept with Harvey Weinstein to get ahead in Hollywood." His efforts to undermine her credibility seem to have worked. While Weinstein was convicted of three counts of forcible oral copulation, sexual penetration with a foreign object, and rape, the jury failed to reach a verdict on any of the charges involving Siebel Newsom, and a mistrial was declared on those counts.

"When we ignore a woman's cries of pain, when we tell her that she is to blame, that she asked for it, that this was just business as usual," said Siebel Newsom after the verdict, ". . . We don't just deny her experience. We deny her natural trauma response."

———

I REMEMBER WHAT HAPPENED as a headboard moving toward me and then receding, rhythmically coming closer to my face and then receding back again. When the headboard comes close, I feel physical pain, and when it recedes, so does the pain but my body seizes, preparing for it to return. Rationally, I know that the pain is caused by what I *don't* see in this memory, that I am choosing to look at the headboard for precisely that reason. Yet, in the memory, though I understand now what was really happening, it is only the headboard that hurts, not the man pushing my body toward it with his. I can feel my body tearing, but instead of screaming and yelling, I choose to stare at the headboard, still pulsing painfully toward me. The memory is perfectly silent, but I know that there must have been sound, that I continued feigning pleasure because to acknowledge the pain would have been to indicate that Matt Lauer had been wrong, that I did not like anal sex, and at NBC in 2014 Matt Lauer could never be wrong. The headboard comes toward me, it recedes. I don't remember it ever stopping. I just remember being grateful that he couldn't see my face, which I pushed into the pillow so that he wouldn't see the tears.

---

DISSOCIATION IS A PSYCHOLOGICAL defense mechanism common in sexual trauma. To cognitively separate from the physical reality of a traumatic event by fixating specifically on something else— such as a headboard—is a form of flight, in which the victim flees mentally rather than physically, minimizing the impact of the trauma. Another one is depersonalization, in which the victim mentally detaches from their body, almost as though they are watching someone else.

"I didn't fight, I just froze," said Brooke Shields in 2023 as she described a sexual assault thirty years earlier. ". . . Fight was not an option, so you just leave your body. 'You're not there. It didn't happen.'"

MATT ASKS ME IF I LIKED IT. I say yes, as though there is any other acceptable answer. He continues talking but I'm ashamed to turn over. I'm afraid of what's happened. When I flip over and lay on my back, I hold my hands tightly beneath me, trying to keep them between my body and the sheets. Something is wrong, and the pressure dulls the pain—but I keep up my end of the conversation as though everything is fine.

There were times when I was eight and nine months pregnant with my first child—the point in pregnancy when doctors tell you not to sleep on your back because the weight of your womb puts too much pressure on the blood supply to the uterus—when I would still have nightmares and would wake up having turned onto my back with my hands beneath me, still trying to hold myself together, terrified that my shame would kill my unborn daughter. I still can't stand anyone talking into my left ear. There was a night in 2017 after I left a wedding early because I'd had too much to drink and then fell asleep alone in our hotel room. Hours later, my now husband came back to our room, I didn't remember where I was and started screaming when he touched my arm. I got out of the bed and shoved him all the way to the door of the hotel room, kicking him. He sat down on the floor, his back against the hotel door, and it wasn't until my foot touched the side of his rib cage that I recognized where I was, and that I was safe. But I swore that there was nothing wrong with me, that I was fine, that I'd just had too much to drink, and it wasn't a big deal. I probably should have been hospitalized, but no, I was *fine*.

I AM A PRODUCT OF THE Great Midwestern School of Get Over It. It was only a few minutes of my life. I never thought I was going to die. I always knew I'd get out of the room. And maybe that is why it took me years to come to terms with what happened that night, when my understanding of the situation was so impaired by alcohol and ignorance that I could not even recognize how bad it truly was. It was easier, and safer, to fixate on how bad it *wasn't*, and then just to blame myself. If the fear I'd felt was not for my life itself but my life *as I knew it*, then it could only mean I was not weak but selfish. A stronger person, a less practical person, a more principled person, surely would have done better, or never gone to the room in the first place, or turned around the moment Matt emerged from behind the door in the dark.

At least that's what I told myself for years, and it worked. As long as it was my fault, then there was nothing else to be done but try to find a way to live with myself. Yet even I could not bury the harsher, uglier truth of what happened in that hotel room: that when I did finally say no, it meant nothing but a momentary delay of the inevitable. *What were the odds* was the wrong question to ask, because there is no escaping the inevitable.

There never was.

# FIVE

# "She Didn't Even Know
# She'd Been Raped"

*Why "Common Sense" Benefits Perpetrators*

ask if I can delete the pictures now.

The look of genuine surprise on his face was enough to convince me for years that the whole thing *had* been a misunderstanding. It was a comforting idea, too—one that I was glad to believe—because it was infinitely more flattering. In this pleasant fiction, I had been a knowing and confident enough woman to seduce Matt Lauer. Reality was much harder to accept: I'd been so excited to hang out with two of my childhood role models that I got sloppy drunk, threw caution to the wind and walked into an obvious trap.

What was disturbing, though, was what *followed* the look of surprise on Matt's face—or rather, what did not. There was no look of concern, or worry, or remorse, when it must have crossed his mind that I might have, actually, just come down to his room expecting to delete pictures. That look never came.

Still, he handed me his phone; I deleted the pictures and said thank you. There is friendly small talk between anchor and assistant as I get dressed, but none of the usual physical intimacies— kissing, holding, caressing, any hint of actual affection—that might have followed consensual sex. This was all business, until I reach the door. As he reaches for the knob, I misread the situation, thinking he is leaning toward me to give me a hug. He seems surprised but obliges, and it feels as though he's a parent humoring a child he's trying to hurry along. Then he asks if I'd told Meredith I was coming back down to his room. I hadn't. It seems a little late to ask.

*Don't*, he says, as though it isn't the one single thing I have plainly understood since I walked through the door. Discretion was part of the job. And anything else would have destroyed Meredith and put *her* in an impossible situation. If I told her, how could she ever sit next to Matt on television again, smiling and laughing at his jokes? I still don't know why, but in that moment, I wasn't thinking about my personal relationship with her, even though she was the closest thing I had to a mother on this side of the world. It was as if I went straight into pragmatic assistant mode—really, I'd been in it since I walked into that room—and every good assistant knows never to burden the boss with unnecessary information that will only make it harder for them to do their job. The only reason to tell Meredith what happened would be to unburden myself personally, but how could I do that to her? I'd be putting her in a position in which she would have to lie when her authenticity was what I'd always admired about her the most. I knew she wouldn't have blamed me. She would have blamed herself, and the thought of that was just as unbearable.

But for Matt to say specifically not to tell Meredith—as opposed to my boyfriend or his brother, who worked directly for him and his family—felt like another way of pulling rank, of reminding me that he was the more powerful between the two of them. I didn't need reminding. I was well aware that Matt was the network's $200 million man and Meredith was a former news anchor launching a new daytime talk show that would be very dependent on *Today* for on-air promotion. Every facet of my life, personal and professional and emotional, revolved around NBC and depended on the success of its on-air talent. More than that, I'd loved *Today* and its warm, caring on-air family since I was a little girl. Matt should have known he didn't need to bother.

He quickly pulls open the door, and the bright lights of the hotel hallway are momentarily blinding as he shuts the door behind me just as quickly. When I get back to my room, the image of myself in the mirror is similarly jarring, especially when I realize it was how I looked moments earlier in front of Matt. It is all there in the mirror, plain as day: I look drunk, not just wasted but wrecked. What remains of my makeup is streaked and smudged. There is no way that a man who misses nothing would not have noticed all this. Yet he'd acted so normal, as though everything was not only perfectly fine but fantastic. Maybe he was trying to be nice?

I start to wretch. I drop to my knees in front of the toilet but somehow manage to miss the bowl as I projectile vomit. I make it to the bed and pull off my pants. The next morning, the sheets are stained with a two- or three-foot swath of dried blood from where I'd rolled back and forth in my sleep, and my underwear is caked with it. It looked like exactly what it was—evidence that my body had been ripped open. But Matt couldn't have *meant* to hurt me, I told myself, so I began rationalizing. I bled when I lost my virginity, so maybe this was normal, too. It couldn't have been intentional. Of all the rumors I'd heard about Matt Lauer and women, none had ever involved him physically hurting them. It must have been a mistake, some weird thing that could only have happened with my weird, boyish body, and I was mortified to think that I must have bled in his bed, too. But then there was the pain, which was undeniable. It hurt to walk. It hurt to sit. It hurt to remember.

One strikingly clear thought crossed my mind, and then was instantly struck from my consciousness: If anyone else had done this to me, I would have gone to the police.

But it was an utterly useless thought to have, if only because I knew that I would never, ever have let anyone else do that to me, *and* because I was in freaking Russia. Who would I call? Putin? The KGB? The only authority was NBC, and if anything, I thought NBC would have blamed me for "the trouble" I'd allowed Matt to get into. Matt was Matt, but *I* should have known better. That he could ever be reprimanded never crossed my mind. In the news business back then, Matt's point of view was reality, and if you disagreed with it, you were wrong. The whole thing had to have been my fault. I had given him the wrong idea, failed to be clear, failed to convince him, failed to stop him, failed to find a graceful way out of the situation without embarrassing him. I certainly should not have bled. The only thing to do was to smooth it over, and smoothing things over for the talent was my job. That, at least, I knew how to do, and I would do it, whatever the cost.

But there was still the bleeding, and I did not know what to do about that. Had I been anywhere else, I could have gotten help, or talked to someone, or called my mother, or at minimum done a damn Google search. In Sochi, all surveillance was legal, and as a preventative measure, NBC had made copies of the hard drives of all our devices—even our personal ones—before we left New York. When we returned, they would take another copy and compare the two to check for evidence of malware. If I used my phone, my computer, or the internet, NBC would know about it. I couldn't go to a doctor because the only doctor available was employed by

NBC. The only people I knew in Russia were other NBC employees. I was inside Putin's ring of steel, surrounded by people dependent upon Matt's success. I was totally alone.

Maybe that was a good thing, for my ignorance was the only thing allowing me to function. Had any of those resources been available to me, I would have very quickly understood something even more terrifying, which was that what happened was neither normal nor likely to have been accidental. To have anal sex without lubrication is to virtually guarantee pain and injury, especially with someone both inexperienced and terrified. What happens to a panicked human body, aware that it has lost control over what is about to be done to it? Terror triggers a series of intense emotional and physiological reactions, including an adrenal survival response that can cause the body to tense up and freeze. Combine that rigid, freezing response with a lack of lubrication, and injury and pain are almost certain to follow. What happened in that room was an act of sexual violence.

But I didn't understand that back then. I had never had anal sex before, never planned to have anal sex, and never consented to anal sex in my life. Based on his behavior that night, though, one can reasonably conclude that Matt had considerably more experience with it and therefore would have known what he was doing. Most disturbing, it was obvious that I did not, and my ignorance and inexperience had served as one more vulnerability to exploit. Already, there had been no shortage of reasons for Matt to tread carefully that night. He was the anchor of *Today*, one of the most powerful and heavily scrutinized positions in all of journalism, and I was a subordinate. I was obviously drunk, and he had been an active participant in getting me drunk. I said I'd never had anal sex before and that I did not want to have anal sex at all. Had there been only *one* of those glaring red flags, ignoring it might charitably be called an error in judgment. But for the most powerful

man in news, who missed nothing—not even Meredith stealing
his credential—to ignore each and every single one of them? That
is no accident.

But in Sochi that morning, I was not looking for clarity but the
opposite. I was desperately clinging to every shred of ambiguity.
Ambiguity allowed me to avoid acknowledging the unthinkable,
which would have changed my life forever. Who would choose to
be a victim if there was any other option? I wouldn't.

I didn't.

I would handle it. I would take back control of the situation. I
would fix it. I *should* fix it, since it was my fault. I would put all of
it in a box and bury it.

I pulled the blood-streaked sheets off the bed and piled them in
the corner so that the maid would not see the blood. I wadded my
bloody underwear into a ball and threw it away. I cleaned the dried
vomit in the bathroom.

Good quarterbacks have short memories, I told myself.

Good soldiers fight another day.

Good girls don't make a fuss.

I got up and went on with my day as though absolutely nothing
had happened.

———

"VICTIMS ARE NOT IN A RUSH to use the word 'rape,'" says clinical
and forensic psychologist Dawn Hughes, PhD. "They are struggling to make sense of what happened, to figure it out, and especially when there were substances involved that cloud memory and
understanding, it's even more confusing. This is not a time when
you're going to rush to call the police and say 'rape.' We put this specifically in our epidemiological studies, our large-scale community-

based studies—we don't ask, 'Have you been raped,' because women will say no. But if I say, 'Have you been forced to have sex against your will,' then they will say yes."

"Rape" is not a word that can be said aloud without irreversible consequences. Rape is a felony offense, and to knowingly make a false allegation is itself, rightly, a crime. This is yet another reason why the confusion, false stereotypes, and tropes that surround sexual assault—what it is and is not, what constitutes consent and what does not—are so dangerous.

———

DESPITE THE BLOODY UNDERWEAR and the bloody sheets and the pain, I would never have used the word "rape" to describe what Matt had done. It's too freighted a word. Even now, I hear "rape" and think of monsters in dark alleys, then say "sexual assault" instead. But back then, I had no idea what to call what happened other than weird and humiliating.

Objectively, it was an aberration only in that most sexual assaults do not result in physical injuries—only about one in three female victims and about one in six male victims will sustain a physical injury. I did. Most sexual assaults are committed by people known and trusted by the victim, and most perpetrators do not use physical force or a weapon, but instead rely on confusion and coercion to make the victim comply. I used verbal rather than physical resistance, which is also common. Alcohol played a heavy role in what happened, and alcohol is the most-used date rape drug. There was nothing weird at all about what happened to me, or even the way I responded to it. It was textbook. The discrepancy was not between what happened and sexual assault, but between what happened and the stereotypical sexual assault.

AS PSYCHOLOGIST AND RESEARCHER Dr. Kimberly Lonsway said earlier, if we go down a list of characteristics that cause people to *doubt* a sexual assault, we find many of the common dynamics of *actual* sexual assault. That holds true for victims as well. Just as most victims are not in a rush to use the word "rape," neither are they seeking to interpret what happened to them in the worst possible light. If victims can rationalize what happened as a misunderstanding, then life can go on and nothing needs to be done. Ambiguity and confusion come as a relief.

But it is also isolating. Victims know that something wrong has happened, but they don't know how to process it or even what it is they are trying to process. Where, then, do they turn for help? They're not going to go to a rape crisis center or call a rape hotline if they don't know that what happened to them can be legitimately considered sexual assault. It's easy to wrongly assume, then—especially in comparison with the black-and-white stereotype—that if someone has to ask "Was I raped?" they probably weren't.

Yet according to Jo-Ann Rojas, LCSW, a sexual violence counselor of more than twenty-five years and a licensed training supervisor at RAINN (the Rape, Abuse & Incest National Network), it's an extremely common question asked on the RAINN hotline and its online chat. Because the circumstances surrounding sexual assault so rarely resemble the black-and-white, stereotypical scenarios they expect, callers are often confused by their own reactions. If what happened looks nothing like a "real" rape, then why are they so upset?

"They feel as if they're making a big deal out of it, or that it wasn't as 'bad' as someone else has experienced," says Rojas. "They minimize what they experienced and compare it to the horror stories or the stereotypes of 'brutal' rapes. If it doesn't involve all that, they feel like they shouldn't be so upset."

How deeply ingrained are these stereotypes? Look how often people appeal to them when trying to cast doubt on victims who come forward with sexual assault allegations that don't perfectly correspond to the stereotype.

"These are not allegations that [Weinstein] met someone in an alleyway and threw them down and committed a crime," Arthur Aidala, Weinstein's lead defense attorney in his 2025 retrial in New York, told the jury. "These are all based on relationships, friend-ships."

Aidala's appeal to the jury here is clear—if the story doesn't match the stereotype, it's not *really* rape—and it was apparently ef-fective. The jury's verdict on the three charges against Weinstein (two counts of criminal sex acts and one count of third-degree rape) came back split: guilty on one of the charges, not guilty on another, and no verdict at all on the third, in which the judge was forced to declare a mistrial.

Beyond the shock and emotional confusion victims experience in the aftermath of a sexual assault, trying to untangle whether what happened legally qualifies as sexual assault is objectively dif-ficult under any circumstance. Each and every state has its own le-gal definition and its own statute of limitations, which means the answer depends not only on what happened but also where it hap-pened and how long ago. In California, for example, rape is legally defined as using "physical force, intimidation, duress, or threats to persuade the victim to engage in sexual intercourse." Using that definition, Brock Turner, who was found sexually assaulting an unconscious woman on the campus of Stanford University in 2015, is technically not a rapist because he did not penetrate his victim with his penis but with his fingers and a foreign object. That also means that his victim, Chanel Miller, who, as "Emily Doe," delivered a victim impact statement so powerful that it was read online eleven million times in four days and aired on CNN in its entirety, is technically not a rape victim.\* But if we look to the FBI's definition of rape—"the penetration, no matter how slight, of the vagina or anus with any body part or object, or oral penetration by a sex organ of another person, without the consent of the victim"—we find that Turner is indeed a rapist and Miller is indeed a rape victim. Since both are technically correct, who gets to decide whether Miller can legitimately call herself a rape victim? How can this be so complicated for a felony offense that is supposedly black and white?

Even the FBI's definition—revised in 2012 from its original 1927 version, "the carnal knowledge of a female, forcibly and against her will"—requires victims to navigate another conceptual minefield because it hinges on the word "consent," as nearly every definition of a sex crime does. Because "the ability of the victim to consent must be determined in accordance with individual state statutes," victims next must untangle how their states legally define consent. Often, they will be looking for an answer that doesn't exist, because most states have no legal definition of consent at all.

To help victims find answers, RAINN maintains two online databases: "Laws in Your State," which breaks down each state's rape laws, and "Consent Laws," which provides state-by-state definitions of how, when, and if a person can consent to sexual acts. Helpful as these are, they serve more as a testament to the scope of the problem

---

\* After a jury convicted Turner of assault with intent to commit rape of an intoxicated woman, sexually penetrating an intoxicated person with a foreign object, and sexually penetrating an unconscious person with a foreign object, a judge sentenced him to six months in jail, three years of probation, and lifetime sex-offender registration. In 2019, Miller wrote a bestselling memoir, *Know My Name*.

than as a source of easy-to-understand answers. Most penal codes define only what consent is not. For example, under New York law, "lack of consent results from (a) Forcible compulsion; or (b) Incapacity to consent; or (c) Where the offense charged is sexual abuse or forcible touching, any circumstances, in addition to forcible compulsion or incapacity to consent, in which the victim does not expressly or impliedly acquiesce in the actor's conduct . . ." And while this continues for roughly another 1,200 words, the law never defines what consent actually is.

First imagine trying to navigate this as a victim in the aftermath of an assault, while also struggling with trauma, confusion, shame, fear, and self-blame.

Next try to imagine having to navigate it as a member of a jury.

In Bill Cosby's 2018 trial and Harvey Weinstein's 2020 trial, both juries asked their respective judges for legal definitions of consent during their deliberations. Pennsylvania judge Steven O'Neill's instructions to the Cosby jury were "You have the legal definition of the crime . . . If that definition does not contain the definition of consent, then the jury will decide what consent means to them." In his jury instructions, New York judge James Burke told Weinstein's New York jury that "the bottom line is that you should apply the same common sense in the jury room that you are called on to use in the rest of your lives," which was notable in that Weinstein's defense similarly instructed the jury in that trial to use its "New York common sense" to acquit him.

Common sense tells us that the Earth is flat, that heavier objects fall faster than lighter ones, and that flying is more dangerous than driving. Common sense is misguided or outright wrong all the time. When it comes to sexual assault, most of our common sense is based on rape myths and stereotypes that have little basis in reality. Because these tropes and stereotypes overwhelmingly benefit offenders, accused rapists and their attorneys will often appeal to "common sense" to try to dismiss or undermine the allegations against them. When CBS News' Gayle King questioned R. Kelly about decades of sex crime allegations against him, he screamed at her to "use your common sense!"* In her closing arguments to his 2020 New York jury, Weinstein's lead defense attorney Donna Rotunno said that the allegations against him "strips adult women of common sense."† In an open letter responding to my allegations, Matt wrote that my story "defies common sense."

"Common sense is that if you're raped, you're going to fight to the death," says Dr. Kimberly Lonsway, the director of research for End Violence Against Women International, and one of the foremost researchers on rape myths. "Or you're going to run immediately to the police department, or you're going to curl up in the fetal position and sob. Rape myths and common sense are the same thing."

When we tell jurors to rely on their common sense, we are trying to appeal to their reason. But in practice, we are telling them to rely on the assumptions they bring *to* court rather than the facts presented *in* court. We're asking them to patch holes in the law with their personal biases. It's dangerous.

"The word consent is used 162 times in the penal code of New York, but the definition does not appear even once," says author and activist Joyce Short, founder of the nonprofit Consent Awareness Network. "So without being able to tell a jury clearly what consent means, each time they have to reinvent the wheel, and we can't depend on the jury to reinvent the wheel identically in every

---

* R. Kelly was later sentenced to thirty-one years in prison after being convicted by two juries of multiple sex crimes and racketeering.

† Weinstein was later sentenced to thirty-nine years in prison after being convicted by two juries of multiple sex crimes in New York and California. His New York conviction was then overturned and retried, resulting in a split verdict: a conviction, an acquittal, and a mistrial.

case. If you're defining it differently in every case, then you're going to have disparate outcomes."

Short invited the jury forewoman in Bill Cosby's 2018 sexual assault trial into a conversation with lawmakers about passing a law to define consent in Pennsylvania. Since consent is the same regardless of context, the definition Short advocates leaves out the sex entirely: consent is freely given, knowledgeable, and informed agreement with a person with the capacity to reason. This allows juries to distinguish between different types of agreement, which is where common sense falls short. As discussed in chapter 3, consent rises above other forms of agreement because how it is obtained matters.

"If someone uses force, fear, or fraud, they're influencing you to say yes, and that 'yes' is not consent," says Short. "Bernie Madoff's victims ran after him with their money and said, 'Please, Bernie, take my money'—but that does not mean that they consented to the theft of their money, it means they were defrauded. If somebody is beating you over the head with a two-by-four and demanding sex and you ultimately say, 'Yes, get it over with, just stop beating me,' if a court does not have a definition of consent that allows the jury to distinguish between different kinds of agreement, then you have legally consented to sex."

The CDC (Centers for Disease Control), which considers sexual violence to be a public health issue, jumps through all kinds of hoops to try to address this. It defines both inability to consent ("a freely given agreement to have sexual intercourse or sexual contact could not occur because of the victim's age, illness, mental or physical disability, being asleep or unconscious, or being too intoxicated [e.g., incapacitation, lack of consciousness, or lack of awareness] through their voluntary or involuntary use of alcohol or drug") and inability to refuse ("disagreement to engage in a sexual act was precluded because of the use or possession of guns or other non-bodily weapons, or due to physical violence, threats of physical violence, intimidation or pressure, or misuse of authority"). Both of these circumstances, though, would be addressed by a simpler definition of consent that states what it actually is, rather than what it is not.

As it stands today, it's anyone's guess, and it leaves victims in a next-to-impossible position as they try to untangle what the hell happened to them. "Was I raped?" turns out to be a perfectly legitimate question—and yet when victims ask it, we use it against them.

"When I testified in the Weinstein trial, one of the lawyers said, *Ha ha ha, she didn't even know that she was raped*," says forensic psychiatrist Dr. Barbara Ziv. "Well, your archetypical sexual assault is actually very rare, and individuals who are sexually assaulted by somebody they know are often incredibly confused because women do buy into rape myths, just as much as men do."

Dr. Ziv was referring to Weinstein's defense teams' treatment of prosecution witness Annabella Sciorra in his first New York trial. Sciorra testified that Weinstein had sexually assaulted her in the early nineties. On cross-examination, Rotunno appealed to one rape stereotype after another to try to make Sciorra's story seem implausible to jurors—asking her what she was wearing, why she opened the door, whether she drank alcohol at dinner, why she didn't run, whether she tried to scratch Weinstein or "poke him in the eyes." She even asked whether Sciorra had complained to her condo board about the doorman who'd let Weinstein into the building on the night of the alleged rape.

"I felt confused," Sciorra testified. "He was someone I knew. I felt at the time that rape happened in a back alleyway in a dark place."

But this is far from uncommon. Another prosecution witness, Miriam Haley, also testified in that trial that she had not realized that one of Weinstein's alleged attacks qualified as a sexual assault because she "didn't physically resist."

"I felt like an idiot and I felt numb," she testified. "I didn't know how to deal with it. It's like I put it away in a box and pretended nothing happened and carried on as usual."

That, too, is a survival mechanism—dissociation.

"It can last hours and days and weeks," says Rojas. "Victims go on autopilot, and they feel numb. Maybe they're not crying or showing emotion the way people think they should. Instead they're very monotone. Their body is still in shock, and their brain is protecting them. Or maybe it's not safe to fall apart yet. If it's a perpetrator they see on a regular basis, then they have to figure out how to manage seeing that person all the time. Their brain protects and dissociates so they can function. Once you're in a trauma response, 'common sense' goes out the window."

Common sense—or rather, the rape stereotype they mistake for common sense—tells victims that if their reactions don't match what they think a "real" rape victim's would be, then they probably just aren't rape victims at all.

"Even if a woman comes to the realization that it was rape, that in fact it was an abuse of power and not consensual and they really didn't do anything to deserve what happened, the rest of the world doesn't, and they're going to face that," says Dr. Ziv. "People will blame them and say, *No, she was flirtatious. No, she led him on. No, it wasn't that bad, it was consensual, and now she's ruined a man's career.* That is a huge, powerful disincentive to come forward."

# SIX

# "The Mark of a Predator"

*How Victims Are Implicated in Their Own Abuse*

L ater that day, I was at a group meal when my phone buzzed with a message from Matt, from his NBC email to my NBC email. *You don't call, you don't write—my feelings are hurt! How are you?*

I remember looking at everyone else at the table and realizing that they were now in a totally different world. A couple of days earlier, we'd all been listening to the new Beyoncé album during a long car ride to a shoot and my life was an open book. We'd been working closely together for years, and if a problem was weighing on me, I could just talk about it. An argument with my mother? An email I'd missed or a dumb mistake I'd made? It wasn't so bad; everyone had been there. Yesterday I had been one of them and we were all in the same boat. Today I was not and we were not. Never again. Everyone had *not* been drunk and alone and in a room with Matt Lauer demanding anal sex, telling me that I wanted what I knew I did not want. None of *them* had been there with me in that spinning room, or in my drunk, unsteady body, or my blurred, frantic mind. No one could tell me I wasn't crazy or losing my mind or that it wasn't my fault or that it would be okay. The shame was so opaque and overpowering, there was no light or air left in the world. No one could help. No one could even know. And it would *not* be okay. I'd obviously done something wrong—*You don't call, you don't write* was talent-speak for *You should have called, you should have written, you've screwed up.* If that wasn't clear, *My feelings are hurt!* drove home the point. I had no idea how to respond, but I knew that to talk about it or ask anyone for help would only make the problem worse. Shameful secrets are like that. To trust anyone is to give them power over you. I was surrounded by friends and coworkers, but totally alone, drowning in plain sight.

And I was at a loss. I never thought I would hear from Matt. There had been nothing romantic about the night before, no talking about feelings or any pretense of affection or even attraction. I was just there, the only target on the board at the time. I thought I'd already done the right thing that day by acting as though nothing had happened, by not being difficult or making it awkward or causing a problem. The email said otherwise. The insinuation was that he had been forced to check in, because he was already worried that my silence was a problem. It is the job of assistants and producers to worry preemptively, to anticipate problems for the talent and solve them ahead of time. I should have anticipated his concern and assured him on my own that not only would I never be a problem but that I was grateful and happy. It's never enough just to refrain from making a powerful person feel bad about something they've done. You have to assure them that they have no reason to feel bad at all, lest they associate that nagging, uncomfortable feeling—personal accountability—with you. Why? Because we tend to avoid people who make us feel bad, and once the talent starts avoiding you for whatever reason, your days are numbered. Instead, you have to make them feel good.

Yet the email was also oddly comforting. It reaffirmed exactly what I wanted and needed to believe, which was that it had all been a misunderstanding, that everything was all right, that Matt couldn't have seen the blood or meant to cause pain.

Ignoring his email was not an option. Again, you couldn't just "ghost" the talent. If he needed reassurance, I would reassure him. I quickly wrote back, *All good*, or something similarly friendly, to show that there was nothing to worry about. What else could I say? This was still my NBC email account. As Meredith's assistant, I had access to her corporate email, so Matt's assistant probably had access to his, too. Even if not, NBC would scan our devices as soon as we returned to New York, but maybe Matt didn't know that. More likely in retrospect, he probably didn't care. He was untouchable. I was not.

There was no immediate response, though at some point there was another email exchange checking whether I thought anyone suspected something between us, though I don't remember the exact context. As far as I could tell, no one suspected anything and the trip continued as though nothing had happened. I saw Matt two more times before leaving Sochi, once on set at *Today* and again at another group dinner. Both times he not only ignored me completely but was specifically, markedly cold. I was used to indifference, which would have been a welcome relief. But to ignore me completely could only mean that I was a problem, and I knew I could not afford to be a problem for Matt Lauer.

I remember the end of my time in Sochi as interminable—a prolonged period of psychological torture that I would have said lasted at least a week—but when I look at a calendar, I see that it was barely four days. I just wanted to go home. Yet I knew that my home was not home anymore, but just another place where I would have to lie, where every moment in which I said nothing about what happened was a betrayal of someone I loved. Aside from my family, Meredith and my boyfriend were the two people in my life I was closest to, and now I could not look either in the eye without hating myself. If work was painful and frightening and home was painful and frightening, then there was nowhere safe for me anymore.

Before those emails from Matt, the way forward had been clear: I would bury what happened. But after those emails, there was no way forward. There was only panic, terror, confusion.

———

"IN AN INFORMAL SURVEY of the offenders in my treatment program, more than 60% of them said that they 'acted normal' after an assault, whether it was physical or sexual," wrote forensic psychologist Dr. Veronique Valliere. "They seem to intuitively know that acting as if nothing happened contributed to the victims' disbelief, confusion, and failure to identify the experience as an assault. They knew, too, that this shifted the burden of distress, acting out or confrontation onto the victim. The victim would have to make an active effort to create conflict. I've seen this technique used over and over again, with offenders who simply got up and invited the victim to breakfast, texted the victim after an assault to talk about what a great time he had . . ."

As New York City assistant district attorney Joan Illuzzi told the jury in the first of Harvey Weinstein's criminal trials, "He made sure he had contact with the people he was worried about. That's the mark of a predator."

This makes victims all the more confused, making them believe that anything weird or strange or upsetting about what happened must be in their heads. When victims then respond to normal behavior with normal behavior, rather than with the trembling hysterics of a stereotypical rape victim, they implicate themselves in their own abuse. Any cooperation whatsoever on the part of the victim—from choosing to drink, getting in the car, going to the room, engaging in consensual sex prior to the assault, returning text messages afterward—will later be used to discredit them. Even worse, victims see it as a reason to validate their own belief that they are to blame.

Defense attorneys for Bill Cosby and Harvey Weinstein showed jurors example after example of friendly communications between each man and his alleged victims. In 2021, lawyers for former *Good Morning America* executive producer Michael Corn responded to accusations of sexual assault by two of his subordinates at ABC News by releasing friendly emails from one of the women that had been sent hours after the alleged assault took place, with a statement saying that the emails proved her claims were "demonstrably false." In a statement released by his attorney, Corn argued that the emails were "not the words and actions of a woman who had been assaulted hours before." Corn claimed that his other accuser's allegations were "equally as fabricated," since she, too, had stayed in contact with him after leaving her job.*

"When there's a power differential, the women decide, I don't want to lose my job so I'll just placate, which is unfortunately a very female thing to do," says clinical and forensic psychiatrist Barbara Ziv, MD. "I apologize for not being gender-neutral, but it is a very female thing to do, because men don't respond that way, but

---

* Corn left ABC News in 2021. ABC investigated the allegations against him and found that Corn "more likely than not" violated company policies. After settling a subsequent lawsuit with one of Corn's accusers, ABC released a statement thanking her for "courageously speaking out about her experience at ABC News." As of publication, Corn is the president of programming and specials at NewsNation.

women almost universally do. They look inward and say, what did I do, and they look to calm things down, to try to smooth things over, even when they are the victim. It's really common, this bizarro dynamic where you're having to both placate and comfort the man who raped you. In that position, most women end up responding the same way."

"If the cost is losing your job, or even just making the person in the position of power mad at you, saying no does not bode well for an employee," says clinical and forensic psychologist Dawn Hughes, PhD. "People get fired. People lose their jobs. People get blacklisted in the industry. That's the consequence."

She pauses, then adds, "I say this all the time: People just want to go to work. No one should have to deal with this stuff, just to do their jobs."

———

IN A WORLD WHERE MATT HAD no power over me and what he thought of me didn't matter, that might have been the end of it. But this was NBC in the era of peak Matt Lauer, so it wasn't. My world as I knew it now depended entirely on staying in the good graces of one person, to whom my existence appeared to be either an afterthought or an annoyance. In either scenario, I was powerless. My only hope was to manage the situation, smooth things over, fix it. I couldn't have him mad at me, worried about me, even disliking me. I couldn't afford to be a problem.

The night before my flight home, I drank a third of a bottle of vodka, pacing and sweating as I packed. After enough alcohol, I'd worked up enough courage to do what I thought needed to be done, which was to "handle" the situation. I would clear the air, make sure Matt knew he had nothing to worry about, and then life could go on. After three days of a deliberately cold shoulder from him I was reasonably sure I had nothing to lose anyway. I thought I'd get back to New York and learn that I was no longer welcome on the *Today* set or that my boyfriend's brother was no longer employed or that Meredith's agent had gotten a call suggesting it was time for me to move on. I would say whatever I had to say to make everything okay again.

Now thoroughly intoxicated, I emailed and asked Matt if he had time for a quick chat. No response. An hour or so later, I emailed again, saying that we were leaving Sochi tomorrow and I'd be around for the rest of the night, if he just had time for a quick chat. No response. Even the emails were risky to send, because I knew NBC could read them and security would be imaging our devices, but with each passing moment—and more vodka—I became more and more convinced that I had nothing to lose, that my life and career would be over anyway as soon as I got back to New York. Another hour or so later, I emailed a final time, literally begging him to call me. I remember writing something like *I am just a normal person, I don't know what you want me to do.* No response. By this point, I felt like my lungs were collapsing, and the world around me with them. I was crying uncontrollably, working my way through the vodka, and then at ten thirty or eleven—who even knows what time it was—I used my NBC burner phone to call Matt's NBC burner phone.

He answered right away. He'd obviously been sound asleep. In tears, I said I really needed to talk before I left because I didn't know what to do.

He seemed to have no idea what I was talking about.

Then he said—as though he were trying not to wake all the way up, so that he could go quickly back to sleep—*Come see me when we're back in New York.* Then he hung up.

How easily he could have said, *Don't worry about it, kid. Pretend it never happened.* How easily he could have said, *It's all right, no need to worry.* How easily he could have said, *Are you okay? I'm so sorry, you said you were fine.* How easily he could have said absolutely anything to acknowledge how desperately scared I must have been to call him in tears the night before I left Russia.

Instead he said, *Come see me when we're back in New York.*

I saw it as a reprieve. I would throw myself at his feet. I would beg. I would fix it. The moments between now and then were just borrowed time. I would go back to New York and try to survive until I could talk to him and make everything okay.

It seemed as though to him, this was no big deal—but to me, it felt as though Matt had strapped a bomb to my chest and then sent me off to live with the people I loved, pretending it wasn't there. When you lie to the people you love, you rob them of their ability to make honest choices about their lives. You cheat them out of the integrity of their own choices, because you are choosing what they get to know about their own realities. I didn't see how I could do it. I didn't know if I was capable of it. If I were, I didn't know how I would live with myself.

But it was already done. With the emails, the phone call, the days that had already passed in which I'd said nothing to anyone, there was no going back and there was no way out. I had to do it. The only person who could help me now—who, with a word, could allow life to almost go back to the way it once had been—was Matt.

———

"THE ASSUMPTION IS THAT people will be so horrified by being sexually assaulted by somebody that they will never have any subsequent contact with them, and that's just not how it happens," says Dr. Ziv. ". . . Most women are confused by the sexual assault and it takes them some time to really understand it. Almost universally, they just want to go back to the way that it was before. They hope that it was just an aberrant day, hour, whatever—they just want to go on with their life. They hope that it's not going to impact them any more than it already has, and that they can just return to whatever normal relationship they had with the person. They just want it to go back to normal, so they will have subsequent contact with the individual. It's very common. In fact, it's more common. It's the exception of a woman who really understands that what happened to her was not consensual and that she didn't invite it, that it was rape."

This seemingly inexplicable compulsion to go back to the person who has betrayed and hurt you—is it insanity? Delusion? Denial? Weakness? It is none of these things. It is one of the most common human impulses we have. It's plain old loss aversion. The abuse is a known quantity that the victim has already survived, but the consequences of confronting or reporting the abuser—of losing their approval, the relationship, a job, a family, a support network—are unknowable, and therefore much more terrifying.

"It's only in the context of sexual abuse that we think this stuff is weird," says Valliere. "Victim behavior is not actually counterintuitive at all. It's actually quite logical if you understand the situation. The only people not surprised by the victim's behavior is the offender. They know. I have videotapes of these guys saying, 'I knew she wouldn't tell, I knew she'd come back.' The less we understand these things, the more we empower offenders. Silence is always empowering to the people who commit secret offenses."

Victims often think their silence keeps them safe, but it only makes them more vulnerable to their abusers. The abuser, after all, is the only other person who knows the secret, which makes them—in a perverse, backward way—the only person the victim believes they can trust.

# SEVEN.

# "Something Weird Happened"

*How Victims Disclose Sexual Abuse*

I couldn't breathe.

I needed help.

I needed to talk to someone.

But until I got back to New York, the only people I could talk to were other NBC employees—all of whom were as dependent on Matt's good graces as I was, which meant I couldn't risk saying anything to anyone that I would not want him to hear. The brow-beating insistence on anal sex, the pain, the blood, the terrifying torn-open sensation I still felt? Talking about that to anyone was out of the question. To say anything at all aloud about Matt and my body felt unthinkable, and so—in quiet desperation during the last hours before New York—I passed a tablet back and forth with a coworker, each of us typing a message and then deleting what the other had just written.

I remember writing that something had happened one night in Sochi with Matt, using a nickname for him. That was all the detail

I remember offering. Matt's affairs with women at the network back then were not considered abuses of power or sexual misconduct but gossip, and not even particularly shocking gossip at that. The tabloid rumors about his extramarital affairs were well-known, and anyway, ours was a hard-drinking business where everybody was always under pressure, on little sleep, and working out of hotels. People had affairs. They got drunk and hooked up with each other. It happened. I remember my coworker reacting the same lighthearted way I might have without the gory details: *Get it, girl!* or *Slay!* or *Yes!* or something not-at-all horrified. That nonchalant reaction was like being slipped a breathing line as the earth caved in all around me. It meant that it wasn't the end of the world. Life, or some version of it, could go on. It gave me permission to see what happened as a *good* thing—exciting, even—which was far easier to accept. Then the coworker asked how it had been.

*Wonderful,* I remember writing. What else could I have said? *Actually, Matt demanded anal sex and ignored me when I said I didn't want to, then he ripped my body open when he did it anyway but I've just been acting like nothing happened.* What would have happened then? I'd have either made my coworker complicit in covering it up or obligated them to report it. I let the conversation move on.

That was it.

---

IN THE STEREOTYPE, this is not how a rape disclosure goes. In the stereotype, the victim—even though she is hysterical and trembling and terrified—is never confused at all. Again, what idiot doesn't know she's been raped? She goes straight to the police or a trusted authority figure or to a hospital and gives a clear, concise, chronological, accurate account of exactly what happened. This account will never change. She'll tell it consistently and decisively every single time.

She is the perfect witness, an angel describing a monster committing a monstrosity.

But the reality is, as always, messier.

Most victims take time to process what's happened. As we've seen, even recognizing that a sexual assault has occurred is an extremely difficult task, compounded by emotional confusion, self-blame, shame, and fear. Yet there is no room for error. If the victim's reaction doesn't align with the stereotype, every word they say or write about their assault will likely be used against them later.

To return to the example of the first Weinstein criminal trial, prosecution witness Annabella Sciorra described Weinstein's assault—which she had not yet realized could be called a rape—to a close friend in the early nineties as "this crazy thing with Harvey." Weinstein's defense team called that friend, a former Weinstein employee, to testify against her.

"There was no component about what she said that I found shocking or alarming and I don't recall it being stressful," he testi-fied.* "My understanding was that she fooled around."

What victims do not say can be used against them, too. Weinstein's defense team attacked prosecution witness Jessica Mann as uncredible because she had "multiple chances" to tell her boyfriend about the assault but had not. Two of Mann's former friends testi-fied for the defense, one saying that she noticed nothing out of the ordinary about Mann's demeanor after the assault and the other saying she was "normal" with Weinstein after she claimed to have been raped. But none of this is unusual for a sexual assault victim.

Victims may not disclose a sexual assault for years and may not

---

* The witness, Paul Feldsher, earlier texted Weinstein, "I think the dog pile of actresses who are suddenly brave and recalling repressed memories is hideous." When asked about this text to Weinstein on the stand, Feldsher testified, "I stand by the description."

even realize they are disclosing one when they do. Researchers have described four general ways that rape victims tend to make disclosures: purposeful, accidental, behavioral, or piecemeal. Purposeful disclosures most closely adhere to the myth. The victim reveals what happened specifically for the purpose of stopping the abuse and exposing the offender, and does so immediately, definitively, and completely.

From there, it just gets messier and messier. In accidental disclosures, the victim intentionally withholds the complete narrative but then is accidentally triggered by something that compels them to tell the complete story—they see the offender, for example, or learn that they've done the same thing to someone else, and then the whole story comes out. Behavioral disclosures are similar in that the victim is also attempting to withhold what happened but reveals it behaviorally. They might isolate themselves, self-harm, or behave erratically. Their personality changes dramatically. Most directly, they might refuse to be around the offender again. Piecemeal disclosures are the most subtle. Victims reveal more information over time, and their narrative about the abuse or assault becomes more detailed and comprehensive as they gain a better understanding of what happened. At the same time, the disclosure is shaped by both the response of the person who hears it and the victim's own feelings of shame or self-blame and the fear of not being believed. Because piecemeal disclosures change over time, they are often disbelieved or discredited.

The listener may not even realize they are hearing a disclosure at all, especially if the victim does not explicitly say the word "rape." Disclosures are often intentionally vague because to share the information is to lose control of it. But withholding details is a form of self-protection, not dishonesty.

"Those first contacts usually are somebody close, and they'll say, 'Oh, this weird thing happened,'" says clinical and forensic psychologist Dawn Hughes, PhD. "And if the friend says, 'Oh, don't worry about it, that happens to all of us, just move on,' that will impact the disclosure. Or if they say, 'That sounds like rape, maybe you should go to the doctor, let's get checked out and figure out what we need to do,' that's a much more supportive response. It allows for the unfolding of the information, as opposed to somebody who's judging and dismissive, and then what happened will just get bottled up."

In 2013, researchers coined a term for this—a "test balloon." How the listener responds to the test balloon will directly impact how and whether the disclosure continues, as well as influence the way the victim views what happened.*

"How we tell a story is dictated by the audience, by the intent of the telling, by what's salient at the moment, and then we add on the elements of shame, blame and the listener's response," says forensic psychologist Veronique Valliere, PhD. "If you start telling your friend, 'Oh something weird happened last night, you won't believe what this guy did,' and she's like, 'I told you he was an asshole, why did you go out with him?' Then you're going to change the way you're telling the story. You're going to tell your mother something different . . . and with sexual assault or domestic violence, there's elements of protecting the offender, of what you're struggling with

---

* I recommend that you send your test balloon to RAINN. Use the hotline or their twenty-four-hour-staffed online chat; all services are confidential and anonymous, and not recorded in any way. RAINN is there for anyone grappling with anything that they think *might* have been sexual assault or abuse. This can be at any point in time, from fifteen minutes after what happened to fifteen years. That's why these services exist.
NOTE: RAINN is a mandatory reporter when/if personal identifying information (name, age, and location) is shared for vulnerable populations, i.e., minors, the elderly, or those who have a disability.

internally, of what you think the intended or unintended consequences of telling will be. All those things impact the disclosure."

For a sexual assault victim already struggling with a devastating loss of control, any disclosure is to risk yet another.

"I've heard family and friends say, 'You don't want this happening to anyone else, do you?'" says Jo-Ann Rojas, LCSW, a sexual
violence counselor of more than twenty-five years and a licensed
training supervisor at RAINN. "That's putting the fault on the
survivor. No matter what, the only person 100 percent at fault is
the perpetrator. When you say, 'Hey, if it's rape, you've got to report
it,' you're taking control away from the survivor, and that's the last
thing we want to do."

Regardless of how the victim defines—or does not define—"what
happened," to disclose any information about the incident is to lose
even more control. Texts, emails, and online chats can be shown to
others, or to investigators, without the victim's consent (RAINN's
services, for this reason, are never recorded in any way, and the online chat provides a safe option for those afraid of being overheard*).
The person hearing the disclosure may pressure the victim to disclose it, or threaten to disclose it themselves. Once a disclosure has
been made—even if the victim has not yet realized that they are
making one—it can change the lives of everyone involved.

Suggest that you might have been raped, and anyone who hears
you becomes a potential witness. Even if they're not legally obligated to report it, they may simply feel morally obligated to do so,

---

* The RAINN hotline *is* a mandatory reporter for vulnerable populations such as
minors, the elderly, or those who have a disability whenever personal identifying
information is given. RAINN will never ask for further information beyond what
has been shared, and those who share personal identifying information will be
notified of RAINN's status as a mandatory reporter. RAINN is not a reporting
agency in itself, so those attempting to make a report will be assisted in doing so
through the correct local authority.

and you have no power to stop them. Even a therapist can be forced to testify against their patient and their notes admitted into evidence. Later, if you decide to make a formal complaint, anyone you've confided in about the assault can be subject to questioning by investigators. Those people will likely need to obtain legal counsel, regardless of whether they can afford it. If your story is newsworthy, they will likely be harassed by reporters, too. Eventually they'll be asked for every detail of what you said and how you said it. Did you *seem* like a rape victim, whatever that means? Do they have any reason to suspect you are a liar or untrustworthy in any way? If you've ever exaggerated a story or told a lie—and we all have—then the answer will almost certainly be yes. But if they believe and support you, your rapist's legal team will set out to destroy their credibility.

But those are just some of the potential consequences for them. For you—the victim—they are infinitely worse.

Say "rape" and your body becomes a crime scene, subject to being spread open and probed and swabbed and photographed by strangers. Your naked body is no longer your own but evidence, and photos of it will be passed around by police and attorneys and eventually shown in court. That is, *if* your rape kit is ever processed, the police actually investigate your allegation, and a prosecutor chooses to pursue it. If a prosecutor does go forward with your case, it is no longer your case but the state's—the prosecution isn't the victim's lawyer but the government's. Regardless, there is no guarantee that any of these things will happen. Across thirty states and Washington, DC, as of 2022, at least twenty-five thousand rape kits remain sitting in law enforcement facilities, untested and uninvestigated. The actual number of untested kits is likely much, much higher. Yet, *not* submitting to a rape kit or going immediately to the police can be used to undermine your credibility.

Say "rape" and suddenly *you* go on trial, because your perceived credibility will determine everything that follows. In our justice system, suspects are presumed innocent until proven guilty, so a rape allegation must be presumed a lie unless it can be proven to be true. Unlike other crimes, in acquaintance rapes, physical evidence is largely irrelevant because the perpetrator can simply argue that the victim consented. The prosecution must then prove beyond a reasonable doubt that the victim did not. Because the only witnesses are likely to be the victim and the perpetrator, all evidence is circumstantial. Even the nature of the crime itself is broadly misunderstood. Reasonable doubt comes with the territory.

"There are a lot of unprovable allegations," says Valliere. "It doesn't make them false. It just means they're not going to show up in court. That's really important."

If you are seen as an "imperfect" victim—meaning your reaction to the assault didn't conform to the stereotypical, hysterical reaction we've all seen a thousand times in movies and on television—then your own uncertainty, confusion, and denial will be used to discredit and disbelieve you. While talking through what happened with anyone, did you ever admit you weren't sure, or might not remember correctly, or thought it might have been a misunderstanding? Write text messages or emails or journal entries expressing confusion over whether it was really a rape or defended the perpetrator's behavior? Even outright deny it was anything but consensual because the word "rape" was too horrifying to even think, or because you needed to believe it was consensual in order to function? Then you've created evidence that shows you've changed your story and made inconsistent statements. Now you're unreliable.

If these standards sound practically impossible for victims to satisfy, they often are. In Weinstein's 2025 retrial in New York, as prosecution witnesses Miriam Haley and Jessica Mann returned to the witness stand a second time to testify against Weinstein about their sexual assault allegations against him, defense attorneys sat with transcripts of their previous testimony from the first trial in hand, looking for any inconsistencies with what they said on the stand *five years* earlier that could be used to discredit their accounts. When accuser Kaja Sokola—who had not testified in Weinstein's first trial—was questioned by Weinstein defense attorney Michael Cibella, she was asked in detail about private notes she'd written ten years earlier in her Alcoholics Anonymous journal. Why had she written that two other men had sexually assaulted her, but not Weinstein, who she'd only described as having broken promises to her? Cibella then suggested that Sokola was perpetrating a lie by accusing Weinstein of sexual assault. She responded, "You should be ashamed of yourself." Still, when the retrial's split verdict was returned, it was only on the charge related to Sokola on which Weinstein was acquitted.

So if you've been sexually assaulted but you can't prove it happened, and you know you're going to be made to look like a liar either way, why go through all this? It's a heartbreaking but fair question. Legally, what tends to matter most is not whether a sexual assault actually occurred but whether the police and prosecutors believe they can prove that it did. The further the assault strays from the stereotype, the less likely the victim is to be believed. Police aren't going to waste valuable time investigating crimes that they know prosecutors aren't going to pursue. Prosecutors don't pursue cases unless they think they are likely to get convictions, and only an estimated twenty-five of every thousand sexual assaults result in incarceration. Combine all that with the other devastating realities of coming forward with a sexual assault allegation—being disbelieved and judged and alienated from everyone in your life, the loss of your dignity and privacy, and the overwhelming unlikelihood of ever receiving any kind of justice—and the easiest and quite possibly the most rational thing to do is nothing. If it was a stranger rape, you can try to bury it and pretend it never happened. If it was an acquaintance rape, you can decide it was a misunderstanding instead, or reframe it as something you wanted. Life will go on, and nothing changes for anyone but you.

Of course, that's true for the perpetrator as well.

# EIGHT

# Seeing What We Do Not Want to See

*Untangling Paradoxical Victim Behaviors*

Back in New York, a higher-up called while I was in the car home from the airport. While this wasn't altogether unusual, my first thought was that the Matt must have already complained about me and that this was the call telling me that my career at NBC was over. But as I remember it, they just asked how the trip had gone. I felt as though I had just dodged a bullet. I said it was wonderful.

When they asked specifically how working with Matt had gone—people in the business talk about the behavior and moods of the on-air talent the way normal people talk about the weather—I remember saying that he, too, specifically, had been wonderful. Once again, what else could I say? This was someone I'd long considered a mentor and friend, but ultimately they were still a television executive. But now I'd been back on the continent for less than two hours and I'd already built another wall of lies between myself and someone I'd known and trusted for years. I'd also created yet another potential witness for Matt's defense who could testify that I'd acted perfectly normal and said nothing about a sexual assault. How unwittingly I was building an open-and-shut case against myself.

I'd always thought of lies as acts of creation: to make something up, to embellish, to bridge a gap between events. It was to make a boring story more exciting by, as my Texan grandfather used to say with delight, *coming up with a real whopper.* But the lies that surround secrets and shame are different. They are acts of pure destruction, creating a void that grows and grows, separating you from the people in your life. What happened in Sochi was not just a secret between two people but a threat that could damage or destroy relationships, careers and families, and the all-important bond between American families and the sixty-two-year-old morning show that kept NBC's news division afloat. To keep the secret was to threaten and endanger. To tell was to implicate and burden. Every time I spoke to anyone I loved or who made their living at NBC, I was lying by omission, participating in Matt's deception, complicit in his behavior, enabling him to continue it. I was undermining my own credibility. I was hurting people, just by existing.

The honest thing to do would have been to go home, keep my suitcases packed, tell my boyfriend exactly what had happened, and then move out. At that point, it would almost have been a relief—in my head it had been a mistake, a drunken error in judgment, not a deliberate choice to cheat. But the truth felt as though it were not mine to tell. As soon as I said the words aloud, the consequences would ripple outward, well beyond my conscience and personal relationship. My boyfriend and I would break up and he would have every right to tell his family the reason, and that family included a brother who'd worked for Matt for years. How could I *ever* tell him? If what happened were to get out, Matt's facade of credibility would collapse. *Today,* and everyone who worked there, would be dragged into a humiliating, incestuous scandal. I would be blamed for all of it because I just hadn't kept my mouth shut. To ruin all that—and the *Today* family—for the sake of my own conscience felt selfish and unforgivable. Who cared about my conscience? These were people's livelihoods. And underneath all those perfectly legitimate and pragmatic reasons, I knew I would lose someone I loved.

Or I could just keep quiet, go see Matt at work the next week as he'd instructed, and hope that everything could just go back to the way it had been before. I'd put Sochi in a box and bury it, tell myself it never happened, be a good soldier. In the instant I made that choice, my home had become a place where I could never tell the truth, and the man that I'd loved for years, who *also* worked at NBC, now felt like a stranger.

From then on, every moment together felt like a betrayal, and loving him meant hating myself. Everything in life that was love and safety before Sochi had been perverted into pain and fear and secrets.

I look back at it now and only see how much worse it could have been. I was still only in my twenties. I wasn't married. I didn't have children. I had a boyfriend and a dog and a rented apartment; it didn't feel like it then, but I can see now that my life had barely begun. But had I returned to a husband and children—the people today for whom I would give my life without a moment's hesitation—would I have lied to *them*? Would I have been forced to choose between becoming a stranger to my children and providing for them?

When powerful people prey on those who depend on them to earn a living, they destroy families. They destroy marriages. They destroy homes. They destroy futures. And while single young women still establishing their careers may not immediately have as much to lose as those with children and mortgages, they still have *everything ahead of them* to lose. One predatory boss can alter their career trajectories forever. Yet again and again, their struggles are brushed aside—*You're young! You've got plenty of time to start over!*—which is both diminishing and fundamentally ignorant of another basic reality for women in the workforce. While no woman's time and opportunity should ever be considered expendable, young women who might want or already know they someday want to have children—as I did—risk the loss of the prime years in which they can focus solely on career advancement and growing their salary base and savings. As a mom of two young children, it's practically unimaginable for me to have the luxury of working an uninterrupted ten-hour day without guilt, or traveling for work without having to arrange additional childcare and dragging around a breast pump; my time will never be solely my own or my career's again. The opportunity cost of losing any of those career-focused years are incalculable, to say nothing of the unseen heights women *could* reach if we did not have to waste time dancing backward in heels around the inappropriate sexual advances of those who should be evaluating our work and not our bodies.

Matt's choices robbed me not only of my relationship with someone I loved and my career in television but the years I spent putting my life back together in the aftermath. Those years were not Matt's to throw away, and I will never get them back. Those years were the difference between the two children I was able to have in my late thirties and the three children I might have had if I'd been in a position to start a family earlier. But what were those years to Matt, or those of any other woman he targeted who had to rebuild her life and career? How many years of other people's lives is one man entitled to squander?

We can tell ourselves that a boss making a move on an employee is a tale as old as time, that it's not such a big deal, that women can just "get another job"—but these are people's lives and livelihoods. For most of us, making a living is not optional and our careers are not hobbies. Maybe you know a lot of astrophysicists willingly working as part-time janitors, but I don't. Most everybody I know is working the best job they believe they can get to survive. Every step back, every delay, every derailment has an unimaginable cost that can never be fully repaid.

---

EARLY THE NEXT WEEK, I found a work-related excuse to go to *Today* as Matt had asked. He grinned and waved me into his dressing room, shutting the door behind us. All smiles, he was so sorry he hadn't seen my emails, he explained—the pathetic, begging emails, the desperate pleadings of a terrified young woman afraid to go home, that had now been sitting in his NBC inbox for days unanswered—but if I wanted, I could come to his apartment that night. The look on his face was pleased, flattered, almost boyish. To him, apparently, those emails had been another proposition.

Another opportunity.

I was just relieved he wasn't mad.

And then I was flattered. This meant that it *had* been a misunderstanding. That he hadn't meant to hurt me and couldn't have seen the blood. It meant that he liked me, that I wasn't pathetic and weird but desirable. It meant that he was offering me a reprieve, a way to fix it, a do-over to not embarrass myself. This time I would not be drunk. This time I would never lose control. This time *I* would have control. I would make it okay. And anyway, it wasn't like I could say no to Matt Lauer, sitting in his dressing room at Studio 1A in Rockefeller Plaza. It was a given that I would go to his apartment, or do whatever else he asked. It was another trap, and I walked right into it. For me, there were no good options. Matt, though, had nothing but options.

For all the time I have spent since then questioning why and how I ever could have been so foolish, I have spent next to none questioning *his* choices. When he awoke in Sochi the next day and presumably saw those pleading, pathetic emails from Meredith's obviously distraught assistant—and remembered the panicked, secondslong phone call with her the night before—he could have written back, *Just seeing these! Nothing to worry about! Have a safe trip home.*

Or, considering Matt's description of interpreting my earlier emails as thinly veiled come-ons, let's be truly charitable and imagine that he saw those desperate, pleading messages as the beginnings of a romantic affair. Would he really have ignored them for days? A man *really* beginning a romantic affair might call or respond to a lover with concern and empathy: *I'm so sorry you were upset. I was half-awake when you called. Is everything okay?*

Instead, he told me to come see him in his office, where the power dynamics were the most explicit. Once there, he offered what felt like a reprieve to a desperate young woman, and I took it. After days of believing my life was over, I was in that dressing room for less than five minutes and somehow left feeling more in Matt's debt than ever, grateful that he was giving me a second chance, an opportunity to redeem myself and save my career. I left that dressing room feeling not trapped but triumphant. I thought I'd smoothed everything over. I thought I'd taken back control.

Then I got out of Studio 1A and back to my cubicle and spent the rest of the day panicked, wondering what the hell I had done. Sochi had been a mistake. *This* felt like a choice, despite the fact that there really was no other option. The damage to my relationship was already done and I could never undo it. The consequences of refusing Matt now would be even worse than in Sochi, and for what? But if I managed to salvage the situation, life could mostly go on as though none of it had ever happened. And wasn't it a compliment, that Matt Lauer wanted *me* to come to his apartment? *Get it, girl.* I would go there that night and instead of a drunk, oblivious assistant, I would be confident and in control. I would fix everything. I would go.

When I arrived, he ushered me quickly through a palatial apartment into a kitchen, where he offered me a drink. It was vodka, handed to me with a grin.

I was there to block out a memory, to erase it, to replace it with one less humiliating. Matt's objective, it seemed, was the opposite. His point, apparently, was to re-create that memory. To reinforce it.

To repeat it.

The shame flooded over me as I drank, realizing uncomfortably late that Matt was not drinking anything at all, but watching me intently, the way a parent administers medicine to a child.

He says he wants to show me something. He leads me into what I would have called a walk-in closet, though a more accurate description would have been a dressing room. I am surrounded by suits. I am at a loss. Why does he want to show me this? It is humiliating enough that I have spent years of my life carrying wardrobe bags and looking at racks of other people's clothes that are worth more than my annual salary. He cannot possibly think that I will feel anything but poor and small surrounded by suits worth six figures, as if his $8 million apartment hadn't already done the job. He unzips the back of my dress. Within moments I am sitting on the edge of a bed. He ducks out of the room and then returns, carrying an armful of towels.

*Just in case*, he says generously, *because of what happened last time.*

The implications of this radiate through me. "What happened last time" could only have been the blood. He saw it. He has known about it all along. It was not a mistake. And then afterward—*after* he'd seen the blood and known that it must have been excruciating— he'd asked me if I liked it, and I'd been so broken and humiliated and desperate to please him that I'd said yes. But that was then. Why would he have towels now?

Because he's going to do it again.

Because that has been the plan all along.

I should have thought, *He's a monster.*

Instead I thought, *You brought this on yourself.*

Yet I still find the courage to try to avoid the inevitable. I ask meekly, *Why this?*

*I like it because it's transgressive,* he says, plainly acknowledging the obvious, that what he likes is not intimacy but the degradation and humiliation of someone less powerful.

And then comes the trump card: *You said you liked it in Sochi.*

From that moment on, it is as though it is happening to someone else. He spreads the towels on the end of his bed and positions me on top. There is a rough woolen blanket that rubs my elbows as another headboard comes toward me painfully and then recedes, and I fixate on the scratching of the wool against my skin rather than the pain of what is happening. I tell myself to breathe. Then my memory just stops, and goes blank, until I am standing outside his door. I don't remember getting dressed or walking out through the endless rooms of that enormous apartment or saying goodbye. I remember standing in some sort of vestibule between the elevator and his door as he shuts it in my face, and I hear his footsteps striding briskly from the door. I remember that it seems to take an eternity for the elevator to arrive.

The memory seared in my mind, as terrifying today as it was then, is Matt Lauer walking toward me with towels to absorb the blood from what he is about to do to me. I will never forget that I was so broken and defeated that I actually got up from the bed to allow him to spread the towels and then position me back on top of them. I remember a feeling of weightlessness, of physical absence, of ceasing to exist as a human being, of extracting myself from the empty shell he was positioning on top of a towel on his bed.

I submitted. I submitted because I knew what was going to happen if I did—it would be painful and humiliating, but I would survive and life would go on—and I did not know what would happen if I didn't. I escaped in the only way I could manage. This is what it is to be a woman. Sometimes the only escape is a headboard, or the feeling of a rough wool blanket abrading your elbows. To be a woman is to play the long game; it is to be a big enough person to put aside your dignity to ensure your survival, and then to be made to feel small and ashamed for surviving. The humiliation, the shame, the degradation of that night—of both of those nights—was unforgivable.

But it is not me who requires forgiveness for it.

———

"RETURN TO THE MARRIAGE. Post-assault text messages. Consensual sex with the perpetrator after a reported rape. Going to breakfast together after the night of abuse. Going to work the next day after the superior sexually assaults the victim in the supply closet," forensic psychologist Veronique Valliere, PhD, wrote in *Understanding Victims of Interpersonal Violence*. "All of these are examples of continued contact with the offender, a victim behavior that frustrates prosecutors and baffles jurors. Why does she go back? Why doesn't she leave? How could she love him? Victims tend to display the most 'counterintuitive' behaviors in situations when there is a relationship with the offender."

"Continuing the relationship after a sexual assault is certainly one of the things that I get lots and lots of requests to do expert witness work about," says Kimberly Lonsway, PhD, a psychologist and research director of End Violence Against Women International. "Why did she stay in the relationship? Why did she text him?"

*If you had really been raped, why would you go back?*

This is the question I have been asked too many times to count—and it is an understandable question, one that people have struggled to answer and understand for years. A 1996 study—that is, a study from more than a quarter of a century ago, the same year that Matt is first known to have acted inappropriately with a subordinate at *Today*—found that about one in three victims will continue a relationship with the perpetrator after an assault, and that one in four will have sex with the perpetrator afterward. A 2022 review of existing studies put the number of victims who have consensual sex with their perpetrators following their sexual assaults at 19 to 32 percent. Given the confusion surrounding these kinds of sexual assaults and how little this issue has been studied overall, I'd guess that returning is even more common than these estimates suggest. But even at these numbers, we can certainly recognize that it is neither rare nor new.

Yet returning still feels incomprehensible to our "common sense."

In the standard, stereotypical rape narrative, it *is* incomprehensible: If I am walking home at night and a man in a ski mask jumps out of the dark and sexually assaults me in an alley, obviously I am not going to chase him down the street afterward and ask if he wants to go get a cup of coffee. But now assume that this hypothetical rape occurs in the way that most sexual assaults actually do, which is within the context of a preexisting relationship. The response will be entirely different, and when you think about it—and I know that no one wants to think about it—it is not counterintuitive at all.

Let's start with a straightforward example of interpersonal violence: an assault. I'm walking down the street and a strange man slaps me. I immediately recognize this as a crime and call the police. Once I've gotten away, there's nothing else to consider. Since my assailant is a stranger, neither his opinion of me nor his relationship to me matters at all. He can't cost me a job or harm my reputation. No one in my life will blame me for getting him in trouble. There is no reason not to report him, and so I do.

But take the same act of interpersonal violence and apply it within the context of a preexisting relationship, and everything changes. Let's say that it's my husband who slaps me. Just like the stranger, it's the first time he's ever done this to me, but unlike with the stranger, I'm not going to call the police immediately, nor am I going to promptly file for divorce. I have invested years of my life into my relationship with my husband. Our lives are intertwined physically, emotionally, and financially. He is the father of my children. It would be irrational to walk away from all of that, when what happened *could* have been an aberration, a mistake, a misunderstanding. Even though he committed the exact same crime as the stranger—a physical assault—I'm going to give him the benefit of the doubt and assume that it was a onetime thing, something that he didn't mean to do or that can be addressed. I'll feel ashamed that it happened at all, and I'll wonder what I did to make him do it, even though I know there is never any excuse for assaulting a partner. Maybe I recognize that the situation isn't my fault, but I will still blame myself for having married a man who would ever hit me. I'll be too embarrassed to tell my friends and family, because once I've told them, they'll never see my husband in the same way again, and I will lose even more control over the situation. They'll encourage me to leave, to go to the police, to get a divorce— and if I don't, they'll judge me. Or, instead, they'll ask what I did to make him so mad, as though I must have deserved it.

Even though the assault itself is the same—and still unconditionally wrong—the existence of a relationship between the perpetrator and the victim changes everything.

"It's complicated and confusing because there is a prior relationship that still has to exist after this happens," says forensic psychologist Dr. Dawn Hughes. "There are no rules for making that work. It doesn't work. And now the dynamic is forever changed."

Now imagine that it's not a physical assault but a sexual one. As we've seen, sexual assault by someone you know is confusing on every level. I'll be much less likely to immediately recognize the sexual assault for what it is. I'll blame myself. I'll try to reframe the incident as something I wanted, or smooth it over, or try to reassert control. If it's a relationship I can easily leave—if the perpetrator is relatively unconnected to my life—I probably will, because there's little reason not to. But if he's someone I've invested in emotionally, or someone I rely on professionally or financially—a person so entrenched in my life and community that I can't jeopardize the relationship—then I probably won't. Even if I immediately recognize what happened as a sexual assault, I will have to consider not only whether anyone will believe me but how losing the relationship will impact everyone else in my life. If it means losing a job, a church, a school, or a part of my family, then that's all the more reason to convince myself that it wasn't a sexual assault in the first place.

The context matters. It upends all our assumptions. The relationship between the perpetrator and the victim changes everything.

"Relationships are complicated," says Hughes. "So sometimes, we're back to our cost/benefit analysis: I don't want to lose my job, I still want to work here. I don't want this person to be mad at me. Especially if we're in the area where it's still in the unacknowledged rape category, when you haven't made heads or tails of what happened, so you're taking on the responsibility for what happened and you're not looking at it as victim/perpetrator in a binary way. There's always the hope that people can change, that maybe this was a one-off, that maybe he's really not like that. We tell ourselves these things so that we can maintain the relationship."

Imagine that you are in the military. To survive and do your job, you must categorically entrust your life to your fellow soldiers and your commanding officers. Then "something happens." To recognize what happened as a sexual assault would destroy the trust required for your unit to function. It would jeopardize the chain of command, the code of honor, and the bonds you share within it. To say you were raped is to ask your fellow soldiers to believe that one of their own is a rapist; it is asking them to choose sides against themselves. With that, all the institutional behaviors that allow a military unit to function come unraveled—and it's likely not your abuser but you who will be blamed.

Or it's the pastor at your church, the professor at the university whose body of work has inspired your career, the beloved athletic coach who has helped countless kids get full rides to college. Maybe it's someone even closer to home, like the family friend that invites your folks to his lake house every summer. Maybe it's your brother's best friend, someone you've been dating that your family adores, the family connection who got you your first internship. Victims trust and admire these people just as much as everyone else in their community. They don't want to believe that someone they admire and respect could be capable of wrongdoing, just as they don't want to feel they've "ruined" that person by speaking out about the abuse.

"Victims tell us that they can't disclose what happened because the perpetrator has a family, an important job, or maybe it's their family member and they don't want to 'ruin' the family," says Jo-Ann Rojas, LCSW, a sexual violence counselor of more than twenty-five years and a licensed training supervisor at RAINN, the Rape, Abuse & Incest National Network. "But they are not ruining anything. It's the consequences of the perpetrator's behavior that is doing that. But now the self-doubt and self-blame comes in: What if it wasn't a big deal, or it was unintentional? What if no one believes me and everyone blames me?"

"It is really hard for us to believe that nice guys can do this," says Hughes. "We want to believe that rapists all have horns and they're evil and they're bad all the time, but they don't and they're not. They can have other relationships that are normal, that are not abusive."

We never want to see the worst in people we love or need, and so we will go to remarkable lengths to avoid seeing what we do not want to see, or to remain ignorant of what we cannot afford to know. Ignorance, after all, is more than just bliss when it preserves a status quo that we need to survive—it is practically a *requirement* to continue functioning in that status quo. If acknowledging a truth destroys something we think we need to survive, our brain will subconsciously do everything in its power to keep us from seeing it. Simply put, if we cannot afford to see something—if the truth is quite literally too painful or its consequences will destroy our lives—then we won't.

The mental gymnastics we do for self-preservation are not the result of a lack of courage or insight, but an unconscious psychological defense strategy known as betrayal blindness, first identified in 1994 by Dr. Jennifer Freyd, a professor emeritus of psychology at the University of Oregon, as part of her groundbreaking work in betrayal trauma theory.*

"It's not willful ignorance because it happens without your being aware of it," says Freyd. "It's more effective that way, because you don't even know you're doing it. What's the alternative? If you're being mistreated by somebody that you are dependent upon and you fully perceive and are aware of the mistreatment, it's going to be pretty near impossible *not* to react. If you confront the person

---

* Betrayal trauma theory, also introduced by Freyd, suggests that "the degree to which a trauma involves betrayal by another person significantly influences the traumatized individual's cognitive encoding of the experience of trauma, the accessibility of the event to awareness, and the psychological as well as behavioral responses."

or withdraw from the relationship while you're dependent on them, you potentially put your life or your career or other people in your life in jeopardy. So sometimes it's just turning the facts around and saying, 'Oh, this is something I wanted,' or 'Oh, this is all my fault.' Those mental gymnastics allow you to preserve a relationship that you need. It's actually a very clever response."

Jennifer Siebel Newsom, who testified against Harvey Weinstein in his California sexual assault trial, described this perfectly as a victim's "basic instinct to protect herself by trying to turn her perpetrator into something positive in her mind so she can bury what happened in the recesses of her memory and move forward in her life."

"That is her survival mechanism, after all," said Siebel Newsom.

And though such mental gymnastics can allow us to navigate and survive terrible situations that no one should have to face, Freyd warns that they come with a price.

"People don't necessarily know what's happened to them, and so they don't know how to stop it from happening again," she says. "The thing that always breaks my heart is that they then blame themselves. They say, 'I let it go on, I should have seen it.' But it's not their fault."

Because abusers know their victims depend on them, they can leverage that dependence to further the abuse and protect themselves. Whenever the victim cooperates with the abuser or continues their preexisting relationship, they implicate themselves in their own abuse. But by the time they realize this, the abuse will have gone on so long that they assume they won't be believed, so they keep silent. They're trapped.

"Sometimes offenders, specifically, purposefully, push away their victims to make them come back, and they do that to affirm themselves, and they do that to assure that the victim can be held culpable," says Valliere. "They use that to say, 'If you didn't like it, why did you come back?' It's the same thing with domestic violence offenders who threaten to leave their victims, even though that's not at all what they plan to do. When you invoke fear in another person, it's just a way to control that person."

"Coercion in its simplest form is being forced to do something you don't want to do," says Hughes. "And when you have to make that cost/benefit analysis of something you don't really want to do, and the cost of saying no is too high, then do you really have equal power in that situation?"

"In the final analysis, people go for self-preservation over doing 'the right thing,' and I think you see that with almost every case of sexual assault," says forensic psychiatrist Dr. Barbara Ziv. "It's the same pattern. The victim's life is destroyed. It happens all the time."

---

I HAD BEEN HOME FROM SOCHI for less than a week. It had not been even a week and a half since Matt happened upon us at the hotel and I patted the seat next to me at our table.

How quickly my life had been derailed.

Even as I left his apartment, I knew that I had only made an already bad situation worse. There was no illusion of affection or a relationship. There were no texts checking to make sure I had gotten home safely. There was no *You don't call, you don't write* email the next day, and I didn't call, and I didn't write. I knew there was no reason. As in Sochi, we'd barely spoken. I knew what it was to have casual sex with a friend, and I knew what it was to have romantic sex with a lover, and this was neither. I might have called it transactional then, but it was not even that: Transactions are reciprocal, and for my part, there was only a continuation of the status quo. I got to continue pretending to be my old self so that my old life could go on. That isn't transactional. It is simply exploitative.

But if the objective was to demonstrate to Matt that I would never be a problem, I had certainly done that. I left his apartment on the Upper East Side, took a cab across the park, and got out on the other side. By the time I'd walked uptown from the Sixty-Sixth Street transverse to the Museum of Natural History, I'd already pushed the towels out of my mind and adopted a narrative that I could live with. I had just left *Matt Lauer's apartment*! I had even been greeted with a drink, as if I were a real person! I felt important. I felt special. Just because he was Matt Lauer, anchor of *Today* who I'd trusted and admired for most of my life, Matt had an incomprehensible power to make me feel good about myself by giving me nothing more than his attention—even if that attention entailed something degrading and humiliating to me.

I think back to those months in 2009 when I sat outside his office, to the countless times I overheard him ask his assistant to put through calls to people who weren't expecting them as though he were Ed McMahon delivering a $10 million check. People who are in power know they are in power. To use that power to take advantage of a woman's body, and to derail her life, can only be called predatory.

But only one person saw it that way at the time, and I had been dodging her calls: my mother. I could lie to everyone else in my life because I had little choice, but there was no world in which I could be a stranger to my mother. I usually called her during lunch at work, where I'd buy a cappuccino and watch the skaters on the ice rink and she'd make a coffee at home, and we'd sit and talk as though we were having coffee together. But I couldn't have this conversation with her at work. I couldn't have it with her in Central Park. I couldn't have it anywhere I might be overheard. It took weeks before I had the apartment to myself to call her, and by then, I'd almost convinced myself that she would be proud of me for handling the situation—and that this powerful man that even *she* admired had "chosen" me.

Even though I'd framed the situation as positively as I could manage, there was no pride on the other end of the line. Instead, it was a low, slow, labored breathing, as though she were struggling for air.

Then she said, in a voice I would not have recognized, *God damn him.*

No, I told her, it was fine. I was handling it.

*You think you're being a grown-up but you're being a stupid little girl*, she said.

It was, in all the years of my life, the meanest thing she had ever said to me. Of course, I could have no idea then of the sheer magnitude of the pain I had just caused her. Until I had a daughter of my own, I could never have imagined the primal rage she must have felt as she realized a powerful man nearly her age had preyed upon the body of the daughter who meant everything to her but nothing at all to him. I was oblivious to the powerlessness she would have felt to stop it, to the daily cruelty she endured as the man who'd done it was broadcast into her home every morning. The world she'd imagined for me at NBC was one of dreams coming true and hard work being realized. With that phone call, I shattered it. I shattered her.

She exhaled forcefully and her voice shifted again, the way you would punch the clutch of an old truck to pull a boulder up a mountain. She said that I couldn't see the truth because I was young, but that someday I would. She said that I thought of flight attendants as moms because she was my mom, but that it had not always been that way. When she became a flight attendant in the seventies, they were all young and glamorous. The acceptance rate for stewardesses at TWA was lower than at Harvard or Yale; this was the era of *Coffee, Tea or Me?* It felt like the male passengers and pilots were hunting them for sport, she said, and that she hadn't understood at first why so many of them were only interested in the married girls. Then she realized that the married girls kept quiet.

*You are nothing to that man but a convenience*, I remember her saying.

She was only my mother. What could *she* know of NBC, or media, or New York? She couldn't possibly understand. This was not *Coffee, Tea or Me?* but the era of *Lean In* and *#Girlboss*. It was the height of millennial hustle culture, and I hadn't spent years of my life earning $30,000 a year in Manhattan to walk away from my career just as my mentor was launching her own show. I was on the verge of finally getting promoted from assistant to producer. My mother was not wrong that staying at NBC was insanity, but so, too, would be leaving. If I left NBC as an assistant after six years with nothing to show for it, I would be an assistant for the rest of my career. All the dues I spent years paying would have been worth nothing.

The only thing to do was to find a way to put one foot in front of the other, to find a way to live with myself, to try to forget. I chose drinking. When life is too painful, alcohol is the most cost-effective escape. It also helped that drinking a little too much a little too often was socially acceptable in the news business. An occasional happy hour became a daily requirement. At least when I was drinking, I was only hurting myself. *Get it, girl.*

I started buying new clothes, wearing higher heels and more makeup. I got garish blond highlights, straightened my curly hair, and lost weight. Matt's point of view was reality, and in that reality, how I looked to men was all that mattered. Soon I was going to happy hours with coworkers and then staying out until four a.m., long after they'd gone home. Every bad decision became a way of proving to myself that what happened in Sochi had not been an aberration, but my choice and something I deserved. My mother saw me as a victim, but there was nothing I would not have done to feel any other way—even if it meant becoming a person that I barely recognized, and hated.

———

WE THINK OF SEXUAL ASSAULT victims trembling in corners, hiding from men, concealing their bodies in oversized clothes to avoid drawing attention, even deliberately sabotaging their appearances to make themselves less attractive targets. These are stereotypes. Every victim reacts differently, and this is not to say that no victim mirrors the stereotype—many do in one way or another—but plenty do not. Instead, many lean into their sexuality, seeking attention on their own terms to reclaim their bodies as their own.

Moreover, victims of sexual trauma often engage in high-risk, self-destructive, and compulsive behavior. They can even become hypersexualized, trying to reassert control over the area of vulnerability that was exploited. I would have called what I was doing "acting out." Freud would have called it a "repetition compulsion." Today, the term is "compulsive reenactment." Victims subconsciously reenact some aspect of the traumatic event, either in literal or disguised form, without realizing what they are doing. They chase a fantasy of changing the outcome of the initial event or believing in the comforting illusion that they can somehow "undo" or "fix" it by proving to themselves that they have regained control.

In her groundbreaking book *Trauma and Recovery*, Harvard professor of psychiatry Judith Herman, MD, interviewed a victim of gang rape who described a compulsive, almost incomprehensible need to return again and again to the place where she was assaulted: "I've always hated feeling like something's got the better of me. When this thing happened, I was at such a vulnerable age—I was seventeen—I had to prove they weren't going to get me down. The guys who raped me told me, 'If we ever find you out here alone again we're going to get you.' And I believed them. So it's always a bit of a terror walking up that lane, because I'm always afraid I'll see them. In fact, no one I know would walk up that lane at night alone, because it's just not safe. People have been mugged, and there's no question that it's dangerous. Yet part of me feels that if I don't walk there, then they'll have gotten me. And so, even more than other people, I *will walk up that lane.*" It makes no sense, but you can't stop yourself from doing it any more than you can explain to yourself why you are doing it.

Beyond the need to reassert power and control, reenactments also reveal a need to regain some of the sense of self-worth and value that was lost. Victims may offer sex to others casually or inappropriately, a type of sexualized transference in which the victim is reenacting their relationship with the perpetrator because they "may assume that the only value she can possibly have in the eyes of another, especially in the eyes of a powerful person, is as a sexual object," wrote Judith Herman in *Trauma and Recovery.*

"When you've been sexually assaulted, it's as if somebody has proven to you that your only value is sex," says Valliere. "And so, sometimes, pursuing sexual behavior feels affirming. As human beings, we all need affirmation."

———

EVERY DAY, I FELT MORE and more like I was being drawn into quicksand, disappearing. Everyone around me assumed I was the same fundamentally decent person I'd always been when I knew that I was not. No amount of alcohol could make that fraudulent, invisible feeling bearable, so sometimes some version of the story would come out after I'd had enough to drink. Even drunk, though, I would never have been reckless enough to say that Matt was anything other than the nice-ish guy he appeared to be on *Today.*

Somehow, I still wasn't sure that he wasn't. The weird, "transgressive" sex stuff—who was to say it *was* actually weird, that it wasn't something all rich, famous, older men did? The few times I'd been alone with Matt had a strange sort of unreality to them in my mind. I could replay fragments of them in my memory—the headboard, the scratchy wool blanket, the towels, the impossible number of suits in the closet—but they were just so divergent from normal life, from who I really was, that they felt totally disconnected from any reality that I understood. Maybe I had it wrong. Maybe I just wasn't sophisticated enough to understand how lucky I was. Maybe I wasn't seeing the big picture.

And, as Fran Sepler warned, these situations are complex. They don't exist as binaries. It's not an either/or between Matt as a monster and me as an angel. *Some* of Matt's behavior with women was innocuous. Some of mine—the lies I told to people I loved and the countless ways I betrayed their trust to stay in Matt's good graces—was monstrous, however valid my reasons for it. I would have thought that after all those years working with celebrities, I'd have been immune to the feeling of being starstruck when one flattered me. Now I think it was *because* I'd spent so many years working with celebrities—and being functionally invisible to them—that I was especially susceptible to it.

Even more confusing was that in the moments when I didn't hate myself so much that I wanted to die, I felt more alive than I'd ever felt, as though I'd become an adrenaline junkie from knowing that I could randomly walk down the hall at work and, in an instant, cross paths with someone who could ruin my life and career on a whim. The only thing more frightening than actually seeing Matt and worrying that I'd ruined my life by not being friendly or attractive enough was *not* seeing him, and worrying that I was already on the chopping block but didn't yet know it. I was waiting for the other shoe to drop. Should I should reach out in some flirtatious, affirming way so he'd know he had no reason to worry? Or maybe that was exactly the wrong thing to do, because I'd be bothering him and then becoming a problem? I had no idea, and I worried about it all the time. The only other time in my life I've felt that kind of obsessive, compulsive anxiety was when I was in the hospital after giving birth to my daughter, and I couldn't sleep because I kept peeking into her bassinet every few moments, checking to make sure she was still breathing. But with my newborn daughter, that obsessive worry was a function of endless maternal love. In 2014, it came from abject fear. I could think of nothing else but my current standing with a powerful man I barely knew. I knew, on some level, that I was losing my mind.

So I drank, and depending on the day, I'd think about Sochi as though it was either the best thing that had ever happened to me or the worst thing I'd ever done. Either way, though, Matt could only be blameless in it. When a lion bites a lion tamer, you don't blame the lion. Whenever I talked about it, I emphasized that I was the bad person, the cheater, the liar. Matt Lauer was Matt Lauer and that couldn't be helped, but *I* should have known better, been a better person, found a better way of handling it. Until I reported Matt in 2017, I probably told about ten or twelve people sanitized, idealized versions of what happened, never suggesting that it had been anything other than my choice. Most worked at NBC. Their lack of surprise or outrage, and the fact that they all kept quiet rather than rushing to the tabloids or to the company, only underlined Matt's power.

But for the few friends I told who worked in other industries— oddly enough, these were my male friends in supposedly misogynistic fields like finance, consulting, sales, and politics—the reaction was the opposite. Their faces went pale. Assistants and interns were off-limits, they'd say; everybody knew that. They said whatever I was doing, I had to get out of there. But if I wouldn't listen to my mother, I was never going to listen to them. What would have been the point? There was no escaping myself. I went to the Caribbean for a weekend with an old friend, but even that escape proved to be a trap when I returned to work the next week with a tan and Matt saw me waiting by an elevator. I hadn't seen or heard from him since the night he'd shut his apartment door in my face. Back at my desk, my phone buzzed with a message from him, complimenting my tan and suggesting I come by his dressing room the next morning.

I was floored. I was relieved. If he wanted to see me again, then the night at his apartment could not possibly have been as bad as I remembered. I wasn't some pathetic, powerless victim—a convenience, as my mother had put it—but attractive and irresistible. *Get it, girl.* It wasn't that I thought that any of this was okay or morally excusable. I knew that it wasn't. But it was done now and there was no fixing it. I couldn't salvage myself, but maybe I could still salvage what remained of the status quo. It felt like nothing mattered anymore. If I stopped now—said no and embarrassed him *now*, after all this—then it would have all been for nothing.

So I went to his dressing room the next morning, feeling gratified by his attention and determined to stay in control, to make this the time it wasn't humiliating but actually what I needed to believe it was. Before I could sit down, his hands were once again on both sides of my face, just as they had been in Sochi. This time he backed me against the edge of his desk. This felt almost comforting since he had not kissed me at all at his apartment. Then he pulled back and said, *I can't fuck you here*, as though it was even remotely normal to suggest having sex in the dressing room of one of the world's most famous television studios. Who had sex at work? Was he crazy? There were two hundred people outside and too many cameras and microphones to count. I'd have to come back to his apartment another time, he said, maybe the next afternoon. That was the bait, and then came the hook.

He pulled me toward an angled wall in his dressing room that partially concealed the view from the door, which, as far as I knew, was unlocked. That didn't seem to bother him as he pushed my shoulders down until I was on my knees, then began to undo his pants. *Oh God; not this. Not here.* I couldn't do this. I wouldn't do this. He was out of his mind. I said, *No, I hate doing this.* He said that it would only take a minute. It's shocking, how a simple phrase can fester in your mind, infecting every area of your life. *It will only take a minute,* said the miracle anesthetist who gave me the epidural when I was in labor the first time, but instead of feeling relief, I flashed back to the trapped, panicked feeling of being back on my knees in Matt's dressing room. *It will only take a minute,* said the sweet nurse giving my daughter her shots a year later; all at once, the blood flashed hot in my face and it was all I could do not to grab my child and run out of the room.

I tried to make an excuse. I said, *No, I'm terrible at this, there are people outside.* Soon he apparently grew tired of the discussion and pushed my mouth onto his now exposed, erect penis. Then there was only getting through it. He ejaculated. He watched me awkwardly stand up, and then gestured to my black tights and told me to dust off my knees.

Then he walked coolly over to his door, quickly pulled it open, and called his assistant's name. I left as though nothing had happened.

*You are nothing to that man but a convenience,* my mother had said.

At least he had invited me to his apartment, I told myself. I convinced myself that what happened had been "hot," that it was flattering and sexy to be desired that much. The next time, it would be better. He was just in a hurry. Then the next day my phone buzzed again, and Matt said he'd forgotten his cleaning lady would be at his apartment that afternoon, so he'd have to take a rain check.

Weeks passed. I knew my mother was right.

I wouldn't be a victim. I wouldn't be a convenience. I wasn't the same naive idiot I'd been in Sochi. I told myself I was Samantha in *Sex and the City*, sexually assertive and empowered. I was Bridget Jones, sending flirty emails to her boss. Whatever I was, I was not going to be some girl Matt could just summon to his office and push down on her knees. No. I would fix it. I would take control. This time it would go better. This time I would say the right things, and stay in control. I sat one night after work at a coffee shop that sold wine by the bottle and, after two-thirds of a bottle of Rioja, I texted Matt, asking about the rain check.

An hour and another bottle of wine later, he answered, all exclamation points, to come over one afternoon that week. It is heartbreaking, how vindicated I felt, when I had only fallen further into the trap.

When I got there later that week, Matt was warm and friendly. He asked how the new show was coming together and even offered me a glass of water. As he handed it to me, he said that he was surprised to hear from me. The last time I'd come over, it had seemed like I did not want to be there, which was why he hadn't texted until he saw me by the elevator, "showing off" my tan. Now he led me into a room with floor-to-ceiling mirrors and exercise equipment, where he began taking off my clothes. How sad and heartbreaking, that this—being stripped down in front of a mirror—could somehow feel like the least degrading sexual encounter I had with him. How sad and heartbreaking that there was ever a point in my life at which it felt normal to see sexual degradation as a matter of degree.

But that was also when I finally understood the apparent point. It was not attraction or attachment, obviously, but getting to do the sort of transgressive and uncomfortable things that most women wouldn't choose to do of their own volition. The point was the absence of discussion. The point was the assured discretion, the lack of risk in otherwise extremely risky behavior. It wasn't personal. It wasn't flattering or unflattering. It was just a means to an end, a fringe benefit of being powerful and famous.

A convenience.

Afterward, he looked at the time and said that his doorman would have noticed by now that I'd been there nearly forty minutes so I'd need to go, but to stay away from the windows as I got dressed. I left. Later, I met a coworker I'd been confiding in—though never once giving anything but positive accounts of my interactions with Matt—for a drink. As I remember it, their reaction was that I looked radiant. I have no doubt that was true. For once, I'd left an encounter with Matt Lauer still feeling like a human being. We'd even had some semblance of a real conversation. Maybe now we were actually friends.

And then—silence. Weeks passed. By then I knew better than to go silent—there would be no more *You don't call, you don't write* scoldings for me—so I sent some friendly, conversational texts. Unless they were about work, I don't remember him responding, and since these were on my NBC phone, I usually deleted them right away. I did not ask to see him again and he did not suggest otherwise. The more time that passed, the more relieved I felt, though I couldn't articulate why. Around that time, I confided in an old friend who had been through something similar with the anchor of her show. I thought she might know what to do. I told her that "something happened" with someone at *Today*.

"So the stories are true," she said quietly, before looking at me as though I'd just said I had been diagnosed with stage four cancer. She had no idea what to do. The anchor of her show was nowhere near as powerful, important, or famous as Matt Lauer. My problem, she said, was on another plane entirely.

Years later, I asked her what she remembered of the rest of that conversation.

"I remember you thought it was an affair because he brought you a glass of water," she said. "Before he took you into the room with the mirrors."

I was still describing it as an affair as late as early 2017, even as I described the blood and the pain and the towels he'd spread beneath me. I described it as an affair, even when I admitted that saying no had never been an option, that I had said no repeatedly and it hadn't mattered, and how trapped I'd felt. I described it as an affair because he was married and that was the only way I knew to describe it. I described it as an affair because that was the version of events that allowed me to continue functioning at NBC, where having an affair with a man known for having affairs was not so shocking. I described it as an affair because it was less humiliating to be seen as a mistress than a victim. We tell ourselves the version of events that we can live with, and then we tell that version to others.

Think of Annabella Sciorra, describing her sexual assault as "this crazy thing she'd done with Harvey." Prosecution witness Jessica Mann testified in Weinstein's first New York trial that she had faked an orgasm during an assault to pacify Weinstein, even telling him that it was "the best [she] ever had." She repeated that version of events to her roommate, who Weinstein's defense then called to testify against her. During Ghislaine Maxwell's child sex trafficking trial, one of Jeffrey Epstein's underage sex trafficking victims testified that another had bragged that she "got to sleep with [Prince Andrew]. She didn't seem upset about it. She thought it was pretty cool."

What would have been the fate of women who went around saying that Harvey Weinstein was a rapist in the years before MeToo? Are we really going to blame a sexually trafficked teenager for having a skewed perception of reality?

If you've ever claimed to have "let someone win" rather than admitting you've been beaten, or insisted you were in on the joke because it's less humiliating than acknowledging you were duped, then you've done the same thing.

# NINE

# Who We Believe We Are

*How Perpetrators Hide Behind the Shame of Their Victims*

had come to understand that I was just something around the office that Matt could either take or leave. As long as I was friendly and compliant, there was little need to keep obsessively worrying about what he thought of me because he likely never thought of me at all. I just didn't matter enough. The few times I saw him at *Today*, he would acknowledge me along with everyone else and then say with a sort of intentional loudness, *I'd give you a hug but I have all this makeup on!* Two or three times, he said the exact same phrase, verbatim. But now I knew better than to take it personally. None of it had been personal. All along, I'd thought I was handling him, when he was handling me. The only difference was that now I could see it.

One time, though, he saw me at *Today* and pulled me aside in the studio lobby, a look of genuine concern on his face. He'd heard from my now ex-boyfriend's brother—still his family's employee—that we'd broken up. *What happened?* I remember him asking

incredulously, seeming genuinely shocked. Standing in the lobby of
Studio 1A, surrounded by producers and stage managers and security guards, I wondered if the conversation was purely performa-
tive or if he truly possessed some sort of bifurcated consciousness.
He asked if I thought we'd get back together.

I did not, though I missed him—and our dog—terribly. I'd
told my ex that I'd cheated, though not with whom, and somehow—
probably because I was so plainly a disaster—he'd mostly remained
kind. But others soon confronted me directly about my increasingly out-of-control, incomprehensible behavior.

"I barely recognize you anymore," said one of my oldest friends
at NBC, demanding an explanation. We were at an Italian restaurant on Columbus Avenue, and I still remember looking out the
window over his shoulders, wishing I was in one of the taxis (he
remembers the conversation taking place after we left the restaurant, as we walked to the movie theater). I broke down and told
him that "something happened" in Sochi with Matt that had become "an affair." I waited for the NBC-requisite curiosity and excitement to wash over his face. Surely he would ask what Matt was
really like, or whether I knew how many of the other rumors were
true—but he didn't.

"Was this consensual?" he asked.

"Yes?" I said, giving myself away.

Soon I was avoiding him, like everyone else who told me uncomfortable truths that I could not afford to hear. I could not come
to terms with what had happened to my life, what had happened
to me, and who I'd become. At the beginning of June 2014, I wrote
an email to another old friend, ostensibly about my breakup but
inadvertently painting such an alarming picture of my mental health
that they offered me a place to stay so that I could get away.

"I just couldn't take the fraud feeling anymore," I wrote about
my breakup. "Yes, so I went through a 'bad girl' phase . . . but we

both know I am not really a bad girl. The thought of hurting a good man is literally unbearable to me, and [my ex-boyfriend] is a good man. Every time I looked at him, I felt lost and empty and confused and trapped and terrible, terrible things. . . . I feel like a total failure as a human being. . . . Trust me, you never want to find yourself questioning what kind of a person you are. . . . The words 'damaged goods' pop into my mind a lot."

I am struck now by how many of my friends back then—particularly those who did *not* work in media—have since told me how afraid they were for me, how obvious it was that I was in a terrible situation that was beyond my control, how they felt like they failed me, that they should have tried harder to help or to get through to me. I've told them all the same thing: Nothing would have gotten through to me. If I'd been able to see how precarious my situation was, I wouldn't have survived it.

By the time Meredith's new show launched, I'd gotten my own apartment, I was seeing someone new (who, of course, *also* worked at NBC), I had made new friends, and I was trying to put back together some semblance of a life as we built out the new show. Its set was decorated with Meredith's family furniture to make it feel like her home, and I was asked to reach out to members of the NBC "family" for informal snapshots to hang on the studio walls. I emailed the other talent assistants. Matt's assistant pointed me to a digital picture frame in his dressing room and said that I could swing by the next day to see if anything on it would work.

I had been getting the *I'd give you a hug but I have all this makeup on!* routine for months. I'd already told the new guy I was seeing about the "affair" with Matt, but only in the most self-aggrandizing and positive of terms. I wanted him to see me as desirable and in control, which conveniently was also the way I wanted and needed to see myself. I told him because I didn't want to be with another man I had to lie to, and because he worked at NBC, I could trust that he wasn't going to go running to the tabloids. He hadn't judged me for what happened—Who could say no to Matt Lauer?—but by the time I started seeing him, I'd thought the whole thing was over. Matt had clearly moved on, so the thought of going to his dressing room again didn't give me much pause. Anyway, getting the pictures was my job, so I would do it.

Matt was once again all smiles as he welcomed me inside his dressing room, pointed to the digital picture frame on a large windowsill behind his desk, and then pulled his chair back from the desk so I could reach the windowsill. The frame was plugged into the wall, so I had to bend over the desk, leaning on my elbows as I scanned through the pictures to one of Matt and Meredith on the *Today* set. To email it to myself, I had to manually input my email address using the fiddly digital keyboard, which probably took about two minutes. Soon I felt his hand on the inside of my thigh from behind, and he started touching me beneath my dress. My body by then felt so much more like a commodity than an extension of myself that I hardly cared. I kept answering his questions about the new show as his hand moved between my legs. I finished emailing the picture to myself, said thank you, pulled my dress back down, and left.

But as I walked away from the studio, the feeling of numbness began to fade. I knew it would be a matter of moments before I burst into tears, not because what happened was even remotely as devastating as all that had happened before—mainly, it had been awkward—but because I wasn't willing to lie or keep a secret from the new guy I was seeing and this would almost certainly mean the end of our relationship. I would just have to accept it. If I couldn't be with anyone without having to lie, then I would be alone.

I rushed away from Rockefeller Plaza, crossed Sixth Avenue to a public courtyard, and cried. I didn't cry quietly, either, but sat there for a long time and sobbed. One of my favorite quirks about living in New York is the way you can have a meltdown in the middle of a crowd of strangers and feel as though there could be nowhere more private. Even now, when I feel myself about to fall apart, I don't want to run upstairs to our bedroom but outside into the street. In the seven months since Sochi, I'd been crying all over the place. Now, for the first time, I started asking myself questions. Why had I just stood there, smiling and going along with it as though my body were not my own? Why hadn't I said no?

Because whatever Matt wanted was a foregone conclusion, and I finally began to understand what that meant.*

By that point, I was already carrying a bottle of bourbon with me to work in the same tote bag as the Keds I wore to commute. Sometimes when Meredith wasn't in her office, I would lock my-self inside, sit with my back against the door so that I could still hear the phone on my desk, and either drink or cry or both. Other times I would disappear altogether and go to one of the bars around Rockefeller Plaza, answering emails on my phone. I couldn't sleep and was taking all sorts of sleeping pills and benzodiazepines just to function. There was no escape from the shame.

I'd get to work at seven and there was Matt on *Today*. I'd go to lunch in the company cafeteria and there was twelve-foot-tall Matt Lauer on the wall. There was a cardboard cutout Matt Lauer in the doorway of the NBC store in the 30 Rock lobby. I'd get in a taxi to go home and there he was, on the taxi screen. My godparents came to New York that fall and I arranged for them to get a good spot on the plaza during the show. When I met them for coffee

---

* To corroborate this encounter in Matt's dressing room to NBC in 2017 and to Ronan Farrow in 2019, I described my disclosure of the incident to the man I was seeing at the time, as well as the bruising he'd seen on the inside of my legs. That man's job included working in the *Today* control room, which Farrow used in his description of him in *Catch and Kill*. To some readers—Matt included—Farrow's wording makes it sound as though I disclosed the incident *in* the control room

afterward, they showed me pictures they'd taken with Matt, saying he'd raved about me. I texted him to say thank you. He answered, "You owe me!"

I hated myself. Shame seeps into the very fibers of your being, populates your cells, flows through your veins, calcifies in your bones, becomes intrinsic to who you are. It becomes something to cling to, the last vestige of your decency, the last remnant of the person I'd been before Sochi who could afford to follow her conscience. I was resigned to it. As long as I worked in that building— and I still didn't see how I could leave—this would be my life.

I saw Matt a few times that fall, when he came on Meredith's show or she went on *Today*. He was perfectly nice. Once he texted "Nice outfit!" Another time, "Straight hair?" Some were just about work; at one point, he asked me to send him GIFs that he could forward to one of his children. My responses were always brimming with thanks, enthusiasm, exclamation marks, and xo's, as I'd tried to mirror his teasing banter with Meredith and awkwardly attempted to flirt. I can understand why it had been so easy for me to put what happened in Sochi and at his apartment in a box and bury it: Except for when I was alone with him, he was not monstrous at all but charming and charismatic, powerfully wielding the talent that all great interviewers have of making you feel as though you're the only person in the world. He could be friendly without being personal, a stranger who still feels familiar. At the time, I thought I sounded confident and in control. Reading some

---

immediately after leaving Matt's dressing room, which I did not. While Matt is correct that Farrow's wording here was imprecise, he does not appear to have denied that the encounter with me in his dressing room took place, either to Farrow or in his own writings (he maintains that all sexual activity with all women, including subordinates, was consensual). Because Matt has not denied the incident took place as far as I am aware, and to protect the privacy of the man to whom I made the disclosure, I have omitted that conversation altogether from this narrative.

of those texts now, I was exactly the stupid little girl my mother had warned me I was being.

Later that fall, my ex-boyfriend left the network for a better job, and since we were still on good enough terms and I was genuinely happy for him, I emailed our friends and colleagues at NBC to ask if they'd send short farewell messages that I could string together for a goodbye video. The talent often filmed these messages for departing employees, and one of the other *Today* anchors asked me to stop by her dressing room to film hers. That's what I was doing when Matt saw me on my way out of the studio and asked me to come to his dressing room the next morning to film his.

When I went the next morning, I thanked him profusely once again, and he joked that he was thrilled to help because he was such a nice guy. Then his whole demeanor changed, and it was back to the angled wall, back onto my knees, the pants unbuckling, the same pointless verbal objections, the same assurance that it will only take a minute.

Afterward, he does not rush over to pull open his dressing-room door but sits down in the chair at his desk. I remember asking, *Why do you do this?*

*Because it's fun*, he says.

I point out that I still need the video, and without a second thought, he does two perfect takes—the consummate professional. But memory is a strange thing. When I think of leaving his dressing room, I remember it as late at night. I know, rationally, that it was in the morning, right after he'd gotten off the air at *Today*. I know that it was the morning because of the time stamp on the videos—one at 9:44 a.m. for twenty-eight seconds, one at 9:46 a.m. for thirty-seven seconds. Then I left that dressing room and went on with my day as though it had never happened.

Later that day, though, I got a text from Matt: "Fun"

I responded, "Agreed!"

Four days later, an article appeared in *The New York Times*: LEADING SURGEON IS ACCUSED OF MISCONDUCT IN EXPERIMENTAL TRANSPLANT OPERATIONS. Four doctors at the Karolinska Institute alleged that Dr. Paolo Macchiarini—the subject of our two-hour documentary, which had aired months earlier—had misrepresented the success of his operations, and that none of the three surgeries he had done at Karolinska had been subject to ethical review.

I knew it, I thought to myself—and yet I had done nothing. It felt as though my life was collapsing around me. I was worthless. I didn't want to live anymore. A week and a half later, I met one of my oldest friends for drinks at the bar at the Carlyle. As was my usual habit by then, I drank too much and started crying as he told me repeatedly that I should look for another job. I said that there was no point. He wouldn't hear it, saying over and over, *Stay away from Matt, just stay away.* After he left, I stayed and kept drinking by myself.

Nothing mattered anymore. I knew the Macchiarini story would unravel. I knew that, with my drinking and random disappearances and ever-changing personality, I had no right to ask for a promotion at work; I would be an assistant forever. I was too ashamed to go home to my parents. I was drunk and alone, feeling ruined and worthless—and there was only one person I knew to whom none of that mattered. *Fun,* Matt had said, a week and a half earlier. Wasn't it? Wasn't it better to be used by somebody than wanted by nobody? I was drunk and alone and had nothing left to lose. I texted him. He answered right away, friendly as always, but in the Hamptons.

Then I felt the strangest thing. It was not rejection, or disappointment, or even embarrassment, but as though I'd dodged a bullet. The only thing more terrible than having to live with what had already happened was the possibility of having to live with more of it.

THAT WAS THE END OF IT.

I can say that now, in hindsight, where life's every chapter has a neat beginning, middle, and end. But looking forward from December 2014, there was only fear and uncertainty. I was living paycheck to paycheck in a month-to-month shoebox of a walk-up apartment I could barely afford, working as a thirtysomething assistant at a daytime talk show. Whatever my dream of making it as a journalist in New York, this was not it. *Fun*, Matt had said; as far as I knew, I could bump into Matt on an elevator at any point during the rest of my career and the "fun" could begin again, destroying any new life I'd somehow rebuilt or relationship I'd somehow begun. If I could not say no to Matt Lauer, then how could I honestly say yes to anyone else as long as I worked at NBC? Even if I left journalism altogether, I would still have to carry the secret of what had happened, and the shame. I knew I could not love anyone without telling the truth about what happened, but if I told the truth, I thought I could never be loved.

I was barely thirty years old, and the only thing I'd ever known absolutely about myself—that I wanted to have a family—now seemed impossible. What man would ever want to be with someone so disgusting? What children would ever want such a disgrace for a mother? I was worthless, useless, unlovable.

Where do you go from there?

You surround yourself with people who expect nothing so they will never be disappointed. You drink and lie and gossip and sleep around, so that anyone with expectations for your behavior is repulsed. You build walls, not to protect yourself from others but to protect others from you. When you feel lonely or heartbroken or hopeless, you tell yourself that you deserve no better. The more anyone values you, the faster you push them away. When you see yourself as worthless, the only way of existing that feels honest is to behave accordingly.

———

SECRET ABUSES DON'T JUST make their victims *feel* lost, erratic, dishonest, and alone; their victims often *become* lost, erratic, dishonest, and alone. Victims live through a nightmare, and then their lives become nightmares.

"When you tell somebody to keep a secret, you are making them a liar," says forensic psychologist Dr. Veronique Valliere. "They have to lie constantly, to cover up the abuse. And one thing that offenders understand perfectly is that, especially with ongoing abuse, they can create the symptoms that they use against the victim later. You rape someone and then they may start abusing substances, or they may start being promiscuous, or acting erratic or not showing up for work. And then the perpetrator can say, look, what an unreliable person."

In 2010, twenty-six-year-old actress Paz de la Huerta was at the peak of her career, starring in a recurring role on HBO's critically acclaimed series *Boardwalk Empire*. According to de la Huerta, that November she crossed paths with Harvey Weinstein at the Standard hotel in New York, where he offered her a ride home. She later alleged that Weinstein sexually assaulted her twice: first that night, and again the next month after he showed up in the lobby of her building.*

"I was very traumatized," de la Huerta told *Vanity Fair* in 2017. "I don't think I was taking very good care of myself. What hap-

---

* Two witnesses, one contemporaneous with the assaults and another from 2014, corroborated her accounts of the assaults to the New York district attorney's office in 2017, but no charges were filed.

pened with Harvey left me scarred for many years. I felt so disgusted by it, with myself . . . I became a little self-destructive."

She became depressed. She drank too much. Her *Boardwalk Empire* contract was soon dropped by HBO. Because she had already cultivated a reputation for sexy, provocative behavior—hardly unusual for an edgy young actress—few eyebrows were raised when she self-destructed in full public view. Weeks after the alleged sexual assaults, in January 2011, paparazzi captured her stumbling into a car, so drunk that she was refused entry to a Golden Globes afterparty. By March, she had been charged with assault after a drunken altercation with a reality TV star in a bar. De la Huerta's star abruptly stopped rising and began to free-fall.

In the meantime, Weinstein's star continued to soar. The Weinstein Company won back-to-back Best Picture Academy Awards in 2011 and 2012 and Weinstein burnished his reputation by hosting President Barack Obama at three fundraisers between 2011 and 2013.

Had de la Huerta come forward with her assault allegations back then, would anyone have taken them seriously? Who would have believed an erratic, out-of-work actress with a drinking problem over a celebrated Hollywood producer and friend of Obama? Years before MeToo, who would believe she'd been assaulted when she'd maintained a professional relationship with her alleged abuser? De la Huerta would never have stood a chance—and so Weinstein's power continued to grow, and along with it the number of his victims.

When abusers are well-known, well-respected members of their communities or high-performing workplace "superstars," people are already primed to see them as role models above reproach. Knowing that such a vaunted public image affords them another layer of protection against accusations, many abusers seem to play an active, intentional role in crafting them. Bill Cosby spent decades cultivating a public persona as America's Dad on *The Cosby Show* and starring in Jell-O commercials aimed at children. Jerry Sandusky started a nonprofit for vulnerable boys and wrote a book about it called *Touched.* Harvey Weinstein presented himself as a tireless champion of women, donating $100,000 from his H. Weinstein Family Foundation to endow a faculty chair at Rutgers named after Gloria Steinem. When the abuser has taken great pains to make sure they are seen as a good and trustworthy person, the onus then falls on the victim to convince the world otherwise. This is a built-in advantage for the abuser that most victims can never overcome, adding to their confusion and isolation in the aftermath of the abuse.

At the same time, abusers hold another advantage in that their credibility must only be superior to their accuser's for their denial to be believed—which abusers can ensure by selecting victims who are vulnerable, troubled, or just less well-known than they are. While the abuser only has to defend their specific behavior with that specific accuser, the victim, to make any accusation at all, will be expected to defend *all* their past behavior—from their sex life to their past relationships to their financial problems to their problems in general—in order to establish credibility. The abuser's credibility, in the meantime, is assumed.

Even though Monica Lewinsky, for example, never made any formal allegations of sexual harassment against President Bill Clinton, she still had her entire romantic and sexual history put under a public microscope. Her high school drama teacher—also her exboyfriend—called a press conference describing her as manipulative and obsessed with sex. Jake Tapper, now an anchor at CNN, wrote a 4,200-word essay in the *Washington City Paper* headlined I DATED MONICA LEWINSKY. ("I got with her because I figured that behind her initial aggressiveness lurked an easy, perhaps winning, bit of no-frills hookup.")

If you haven't spent your life auditioning to be the perfect victim—and you're not rich or famous enough to employ a team of lawyers and publicists to clean up your messes while getting maximal publicity for your good deeds—then there will always be someone or something in your past that can make you look crazy and dishonest. There will always be some ex-boyfriend, ex-roommate, grudge-holding coworker or neighbor or classmate. There will always be some story you exaggerated or embarrassing text messages you sent. For women in particular, the world is generally all too ready to see us as crazy anyway. But we all have meltdowns, have bad breakups, make bad financial decisions, and do stupid things while drunk (and sober) at some point in our lives. Traumatized people often do far worse. Usually, we're allowed to be human without having our lives reduced to our flaws, mistakes, and worst choices. Make a sexual harassment or assault allegation, though, and that changes. Now everything you have ever done wrong becomes a reason you cannot be believed, and every mistake you've made becomes an asset to your abuser's defense.

And even if the system were not stacked so heavily against victims, shame serves as a powerful silencing mechanism on its own, further empowering abusers who then benefit from the silence of their victims. Psychologist and bestselling author Dr. Harriet Lerner has been studying shame for decades, calling it "a steady call to silence, inaction and hiding."

Few forces in life, she has found, are more paralyzing than fear and shame working together.

"Fear and shame operate in different ways, but together they work to silence us, and to keep our lives narrow and small," says Lerner. "Part of the mystery of shame is that when a person is harmed or violated, it's not the wrongdoer who carries the shame. Rather, it is the innocent, harmed party who may feel to blame for what happened. Or, even short of remembering 'what happened' they may simply feel flawed, 'different,' unworthy of love, respect and belonging—alone, unprotected, and out of the flow of human connection."

In that sense, shame is different from embarrassment or guilt. As embarrassed as we might be when something humiliating happens, we know on some level that it could happen to anyone. Shame tells us not simply that something wrong has occurred, but that there must be something profoundly wrong with *us* for it to have happened at all. Even when we feel guilty about something we've done, our guilt is, in a way, reassuring because it tells us that we know right from wrong and can do better. Shame tells you that there is no point, for what is wrong is *you*—and can only be you.

"Guilt is about what you did or did not do, but shame is about who we believe we are deep down," says Lerner.

That sense that we are secretly, fundamentally, flawed and corrupt then becomes an imperative in its own right, telling us to keep hidden lest anyone else should find out just how flawed and unworthy we really are.

"Fear makes us afraid of the dark and shame makes us afraid of the light," says Lerner. "And the more we live a life of silence and hiding, the more shame grows, because only by speaking up and showing up can we shrink shame down to size."

———

YEARS AFTER REPORTING MATT, years after the front pages trumpeted a secret so painful that I kept it even from myself, and years after rebuilding a life from the wreckage, I wish I could tell you that the shame is gone. I can't. Instead I can say that it's in a sort of remission. I am strong enough now to confront it and beat it back when it resurfaces, but its building blocks are within me, integral to who I am, dormant but still there. Sometimes I am unexpectedly thrown back into the past—when I hear the Beyoncé album we all listened to in Sochi or smell the perfume I wore in 2014—and I find myself flooded all over again with the ugliness of what happened.

Far more devastating, though, is the ugliness that what happened revealed in me. That, I can never forget . . . my vanity, my arrogance, my blinding insecurity, my capacity for cruelty, the desperate need to believe that I was special and had power over men that I plainly did not have. The shame quite literally knocks me to the floor and suddenly I am consumed by a primal urge not to be alive anymore. A voice in my head reminds me that I don't deserve to exist, that I am disgusting—a fraud and a cancer on the world that must be cut out—that I never should have ruined my husband's life by marrying him or my children's by becoming their mother. I feel a desperate need to disappear, to never have existed at all, not because I *don't* love my children but because I love them more than life itself and the voice tells me, again and again, that the greatest act of love I could ever offer would be to vanish from their lives before they have any memory of me.

The difference now is that I answer that voice in my head, argue with it, remind myself of the first moments I held each of my children and *knew* that none of us can ever be worthless, that there was nothing I could ever have done or felt to deserve what was done to me. I tell it that there is no shame in survival because life is precious. Even when I manage to successfully quiet the voice, I still find myself sometimes recoiling from my husband, afraid to be near my children, terrified of hurting them simply by continuing to exist. What then? I listen to that Beyoncé album again and again. I wear my old perfume every day for weeks until the shame no longer has the power to level me. But I am beginning to accept that there may be no moving completely past shame, that it is as much a part of my being as my parents and grandparents and everything else that makes me who I am—and that I am still, nonetheless, worthy of love.

And always was.

# TEN

# A Turning Point

Some battle scars are worn on the inside, formed by things you've seen you can never forget. Experiences that move you, inspire you, change you. And for anyone who's been there, there's a secret: it doesn't harden you. It makes you more human.

So began a thirty-second *NBC Nightly News* promo, celebrating NBC News managing editor Brian Williams's tenth year as anchor in October 2014. *He's been there*, said the on-screen graphics, over tinkly, sentimental piano music. *He'll be there.*

While I began 2015 resigned to the belief that I was hopelessly flawed, with no meaningful future and a past too shameful to face, a series of bizarre and unimaginable twists at work somehow managed to make my situation even more precarious.

At the end of January, Williams went to a hockey game at

Madison Square Garden alongside a retired soldier he'd met in Iraq in 2003. As the crowd gave the serviceman a standing ovation, the overhead announcer explained that the soldier had been "responsible for the safety of Brian Williams and his NBC News team after their Chinook helicopter was hit and crippled by enemy fire." The next night on *NBC Nightly News*, Williams replayed the moment on the air, doubling down on the details of this harrowing story. It quickly emerged that very little was true, and more examples of Williams's exaggerations soon came to light (as Tavi Gevinson would later write, "When you're the star of the show, nobody can afford to correct your behavior"). NBC eventually suspended Williams without pay for six months and permanently removed him as anchor of *NBC Nightly News*. With this, the only real on-air rival to Matt's supremacy at the network had been taken off the board.

To manage the fallout, legendary executive Andrew Lack was hired as NBC News chairman. As NBC News president in the nineties, Lack had overseen the beginning of *Today*'s sixteen-year ratings winning streak and Matt's promotion to anchor. Because he was widely known to be one of Matt's close friends, Lack's new role atop the network's corporate hierarchy brought Matt's perceived power to its peak. When Williams returned from suspension to a diminished role in June 2015, he was reintroduced to viewers via a hard-hitting interview with NBC News' most trusted moral authority: Matt Lauer.

There Matt sat across from Williams, ironically tasked with confronting his colleague about honesty, integrity, and the responsibility of news anchors to be accountable for their behavior, even away from the news desk.

"Did you not deal with the reality that when you walked away from NBC . . . that the title and the responsibilities of anchor–slash–managing editor traveled with you?" Matt asked Williams earnestly. The interview made headlines, further underlining Matt's importance to the news division's credibility and bottom line.

I would have thought my life at the network—the only real life I still had—could not have grown more ridiculous and surreal. I was wrong. That spring, Benita Alexander handed me an invitation to her wedding to Paolo Macchiarini, to be held that summer at the pope's summer palace in Italy. Security would be tight, I remember her explaining, because the pope was performing the wedding. The Obamas, the Putins, the Clintons, and the Sarkozys would all be attending, along with Andrea Bocelli, Kofi Annan, Russell Crowe, and Elton John. She was also negotiating with one of our former bosses, NBC's senior executive producer for primetime news, to give NBC exclusive coverage of the wedding.* Did I ever say anything to Alexander—a longtime friend and mentor—about the fundamental implausibility of all this? Did I raise again my suspicions that something was off about Macchiarini, that I thought the whistleblowers' allegations against him were likely true? Of course not. I was too much of a coward, and I knew that when it came to maintaining self-justifying delusions, I was living in a glass house. Not only did I say nothing, I went to the bachelorette party.

Then, purely by chance, I received an emailed press release from the Vatican—I'd filmed an interview there in 2013 and stayed on its distribution list—detailing the pope's planned summer tour to South America, scheduled for the same time as the wedding. But how could the pope be marrying two divorcées at his summer palace if he was going to be in South America? I didn't even have the courage to talk to Alexander about that email myself. Instead I forwarded it to someone who then forwarded it to her, unraveling her life as she knew it. A week and a half after the supposed wedding date had passed, we learned that our documentary about Macchiarini

---

* Despite these conversations, no coverage of the wedding was ever planned by NBC.

had been nominated for a primetime news Emmy. Even *after* the wedding was canceled, Alexander assured me that the documentary itself remained journalistically sound—and a few months later, we all attended the awards together. Normally, an Emmy nomination would be a career-boosting achievement, the sort of recognition that secured promotions and opened doors at other networks—and to get one on my first piece as a producer was, at that point, the greatest professional accomplishment of my career. That fall, a full eighteen months after Sochi, I started producing my own pieces and my career was finally moving forward again.

Then came the bombshell *Vanity Fair* interview with Alexander, revealing publicly that she'd been romantically involved with Macchiarini in secret while we were filming the documentary—in clear violation of NBC's journalistic standards and practices. NBC rightly pulled the documentary from its website, the broadcast equivalent of a retraction. Those of us who'd spent nearly two years working on it in good faith were blindsided and humiliated. How could I ever get a producing job at another network now? NBC was all I had.

At the time, Alexander's choice to speak out felt like an unforgivable betrayal—but whatever the cost of exposing Macchiarini, I see now that she was still right to do it. Our embarrassment and anger were nothing in the face of what could have happened had Macchiarini never been exposed. Though she was not the first to try to tell the truth about him, Alexander was the one who finally made the difference. His downfall had begun.

———

MEREDITH'S DAYTIME TALK SHOW was canceled in January 2016. As unemployment loomed, an executive producer I knew at NBC News asked if I might be interested in helping her with a few projects. I was overjoyed. For the first time in my career—a career I'd thought was at a dead end—I was being offered a job for my own producing abilities rather than my connections to the talent. It would be a new beginning.

Then I thought about Sochi. If I took the job, I would be allowing this executive producer—a single mom—to vouch for me, when the secret of what happened with Matt could erupt into a scandal at any time. I thought of how blindsided I'd felt by Alexander when she'd risked all of our careers by hiding her relationship with Macchiarini, relegating years of our hard work to professional ridicule. I couldn't risk doing that to this woman. I would tell her about Matt and then let her decide for herself whether hiring me was worth the risk.

I asked her what she remembered of that conversation.

"I don't have exact words but I remember you saying something along the lines of 'You've heard the rumors, right?'" she says. "And, of course, I had heard the rumors. Then I remember you saying something along the lines of 'Well I can tell you they are true.' You didn't explicitly say you had had sex with Matt—or the details that you would later tell me—but you raised your eyebrows in such a way that I got what you were saying: You had been intimate with him. And frankly, it didn't change how I thought about you—or Matt, for that matter. I wasn't going to ask more."

I took the job. Years later—after Matt's firing and the decades of allegations by other female subordinates surfaced—others would question her choice not to report our initial conversation about Sochi to human resources.

"The idea of reporting it, or blowback, never occurred to me," she says. "I had heard enough stories about people at work hooking up or cheating on their spouse with a coworker that I never worried about it. Pre-Weinstein, this was just how it was. I had been the only female in production teams and smiled and played along when conversations went blue. It was just something that happened. You just ignored it. If you got pegged as a priss or problematic, no one would want to work with you. That, to me, was more of an issue. People having sex with people—it was just what happened. So it never occurred to me for a minute that I shouldn't work with you. I filed it away and ignored it. You were not in distress, as far as I could tell, at that moment. It had happened and ended years before I really knew you."

She talked about a time when she was an associate producer and an on-air correspondent had hit on her at a party.

"I remember telling the producer who I worked under the next day and she told me stories of him propositioning another producer in the past and we laughed about it and moved on to the work at hand that day," she says. "This is just how it was. So what was I supposed to do? Go to HR and tell them you indicated with your eyebrows—because you did not use the words at that time—that at some point you had sex with Matt Lauer but I didn't know any details or when or where it happened? If I had to do it all again, I would still not report it then. Not because I was part of some NBC conspiracy to suppress harassment stories, but because I was very much a product of the culture that enabled it. Your story at that point was not that shocking. I do think I asked if there would be an issue with you getting voiceovers from him and you assured me there wouldn't."

That was true. Two long years after Sochi, I'd become a much more assertive person. The few times I'd seen Matt at work since December 2014, he'd treated me with the same indifference as the pre-Sochi, wallpaper days. When the talk show was canceled, one of my longtime mentors suggested I ask Matt for advice about getting back into the news division, and I'd done it. I went to his dressing room one last time. He left the door open and we both behaved as though 2014 never happened.

So when my executive producer asked me to record Matt's voiceovers for one of the documentaries she needed post-produced, I said it would be no problem. Matt greeted me that day just as he would have any other producer, headed into the tracking booth, and recorded his voiceovers like the unparalleled professional he was. Then, as he left the tracking booth to return to his office, he paused and asked with the warmest of grins, *Weren't you in Sochi?*

In an instant, I was cut off at the knees. Gone was the capable, confident producer I thought I had become. A ghoulish grin lingered on his face. I realized after a moment that he was waiting for me to return the smile, and somehow I did. Then he turned and walked away.

With just a phrase, he could open a bottomless well of shame, humiliation, and self-loathing. I wondered, for a long while, whether he could have been so clueless as to genuinely believe I remembered Sochi fondly—but then I remember that he was once considered the best live interviewer in the business, that he was celebrated for his ability to instantly read his subjects and trigger the responses he wanted. As with so many things about Matt, the answer is unknowable. But that was the last time I ever saw him in person.

That summer, the EEOC released its report on sexual harassment specifically warning employers that "superstar" employees created a "breeding ground for harassment" (excerpted at the beginning of this book). Weeks later, Gretchen Carlson filed her sexual harassment suit against Roger Ailes that began the slow burn of MeToo. I continued trying to get jobs at other networks, interviewing at both *CBS This Morning* and *60 Minutes*—where I might have escaped Matt for Charlie Rose or Jeff Fager, both of whom would later be fired amid sexual harassment and bullying accusations. But, as always, my best connections—and chance of advancement—were at NBC, where Matt's dominance remained unchallenged.

My former executive producer remembers a conversation we had at the end of 2016, another one of my disclosure test balloons. "We met for cocktails, and that night you told me more details about what happened. Namely that you had been drinking a lot of vodka that night and that he had anal sex with you. I remember you telling me how you bled and how you were still bleeding the next morning. I asked if he used lubrication and was stunned when you said he didn't. . . . That really surprised me and struck me as very aggressive. You didn't use the word 'rape' then, but it was clear you didn't have fond memories of the incident. And you told me how you later went to his apartment and he put a towel down underneath you in case you bled."

I remember that the cocktail I was drinking as I told her had a sprig of fresh rosemary in it, and the look of shock and horror on her face as I nonchalantly recounted the blood and the pain as though it were in any way normal.

"Looking back, it is clear that there was something troublesome in what you were telling me but not quite totally articulating," she says. "I wish I had dug in a little more with you that night or had been able to offer you more than just a listening ear."

———

SIX MONTHS LATER, a childhood friend set me up on a blind date with one of his fraternity brothers from Kansas. I agreed to go only because I couldn't imagine that it would last very long: At the time, I was producing an episode of MSNBC's *Headliners* about George Clooney and the guy my friend wanted to set me up with was a Republican political consultant. These were the early months of the first Trump administration. I figured the date would last about as long as it took me to say either "MSNBC" or "Clooney." Expectations were low.

I suggested we go to one of the Irish pubs in Rockefeller Center since I'd just taken a red-eye back from LA for an interview and I thought I might need to go back to work afterward. By the end of the first round of drinks, the only things we appeared to have in common were our Midwestern roots and disdain for the other's profession. After about an hour, I found him so offensive that I reached across the table and put my hand on his arm to try to get him to stop talking. It felt as though I'd been struck by lightning, like in a Nora Ephron movie. This is the man I was supposed to marry, I thought. In that instant something strange happened: marriage and children and the possibility of loving and being loved once again all flashed before my eyes—the happy life I had long believed I had forfeited in Sochi. But an equally shocking thing happened in the same moment. After three years of test balloons and self-sabotage and holidays alone,* I decided I wasn't going to let the idea of that life go.

But shame is not put down so easily. The deeper you try to bury it, the tighter it takes hold.

Later that summer, we were walking down Forty-Second Street when my phone buzzed. It was my ex-boyfriend, sending me a video of a funny prank Matt had helped pull on one of his coworkers. The prank itself was hilarious. Matt was all charm and charisma. But I didn't laugh. Instead I stopped in the middle of the sidewalk and put my head between my knees, as though the air had been knocked out of me and I was about to vomit. If Matt had done a favor for my ex-boyfriend, I thought, I'm going to owe him again—and I would lose everything. The cycle was about to repeat.

No, no, no. Not now, not again. It shouldn't have been possible. My ex-boyfriend no longer worked for NBC. His brother no longer

---

* Christmas Day 2015—which I spent at the movies, seeing *The Revenant* by myself—was a real low point.

worked for Matt. The "family connection" was broken. It didn't matter. I could try to move on, try to start over, try to rebuild my life, but as long as I worked at NBC, Matt would be ever present on *Today*, imbued with the power to destroy my life on a whim.

It's easy to look back on this moment now from a place of sanity and security and calmly reason out that this was all in my head; back then, I had no such place of sanity and security. I hadn't known either for years. Since the talk show was canceled, my position at NBC was freelance and if I missed one paycheck, I wouldn't make rent. My heart started pounding and, to me, it was 2014 all over again. The sheer force of my panicked reaction physically doubled me over, functionally breaking me in two.

Fifteen feet ahead of me, utterly confused, was my new boyfriend, who had no idea why I appeared to be having some sort of breakdown on the sidewalk in front of Grand Central. He walked back to me and tried putting his hand on my shoulder. I swatted it away. I couldn't stand for him to touch me. He thought I was a good person, someone he could trust and love, when I'd known all along that I had no right to a normal, happy life. I would never be safe to love. I would always be alone. I deserved no better. I should have gotten up and walked out of the crappy Irish pub the moment I touched his forearm and fell in love. I should never have agreed to go out with him to begin with.

I started pacing and sweating on the sidewalk. Whatever this was—a sign, a coincidence, the beginning of the next phase of the nightmare—the world felt as though it was spinning out of control, the ground falling away beneath me. Almost compulsively, I frantically texted Matt, thanking him enthusiastically for doing the prank for my ex-boyfriend, letting him know that I was, as ever, grateful and compliant and in his debt. My boyfriend asked what I was doing and I couldn't explain, not only because he had no idea about Matt Lauer but also because I knew at once that it made no sense. I just needed—desperately, primally, as though my life depended on it—for Matt to know that I was still a good soldier, would never be a problem, posed no threat to him whatsoever. Then, seeing that it had been years since we'd exchanged texts, I added, "This is Brooke."

He answered, "Are you two back together?"

Matt meant my ex-boyfriend, of course—our "family connection." I answered that we were just friends, and even that felt like a damning admission of guilt. I knew that I should have stayed out of my ex's life altogether after we broke up in 2014, but our lives were so intertwined after years of working and living together that I hadn't known how. I still cared about him, missed him, loved him—those feelings don't just vanish overnight. I still loved our dog, and our walks through Central Park in the mornings with our coffee. I looked at my new boyfriend, next to me on the sidewalk—the man I already loved and knew I wanted to marry—looking at me as though I'd just turned into a feral animal, right before his eyes. I'd have to tell him something. I would not lie to another man I loved, but neither could I tell him the whole truth. I said I needed some space, that we could talk about it another time.

Later I called my mother, crying, and told her what had happened. I said I could not stand to make a wreck of the life of another good man, that I was damaged goods, that I had been unforgivably stupid to imagine I could have any sort of a future with someone I loved. I would always be alone. I should always be alone. I would end things before they went any further.

She exhaled loudly.

*If you can't let this go*, she said, *you might as well just jump off the George Washington Bridge, because you're throwing away your life.*

# ELEVEN

# The End

I t has been so long now that it is sometimes hard for me to remember the feeling of having a mother, of what it is to *be*
mothered—of what it was to be able to cry out for my mother,
taking for granted that she would always be there.

*Mom.*

I can tell you how thick the scar tissue has grown around the
name Matt Lauer, how I can say "rape" just as easily as any other
ugly word, but how paper-thin and fragile the scar tissue is over the
void where my mother used to be. Mom—to say her name, even
now, is to be broken into a million pieces. After Sochi, the concept
of unconditional love was lost to me—if I weren't her daughter, I'd
even told her, *she* wouldn't have loved me either—but then she died,
and for the first time in my life, I truly felt its absence.

I'd been in Washington doing interviews for an MSNBC series
and took the train back to New York on a Saturday morning. At
some point while I was on the train, my mother went to check

the mail and died before she reached the mailbox. It was August 19, 2017.

My father was out of town that weekend and texted that night, asking if either my brother or I had heard from her that day. Neither of us had. He sent a neighbor to check on her and the neighbor found her body in a flower bed, blue and swollen from where the blood had pooled under her skin against the ground.

What I remember is the right side of my face bouncing off the hard wood of my apartment floor. What I remember is deciding in that instant that I could choose to ignore my mother's death just as I had chosen to ignore the blood in Sochi, that I would bury it and it would be like it never happened. I would go to work on Monday. We would never speak again of the fact that my mother's body had lain undiscovered for hours in the front garden. You could do that and survive, I knew, because I had been doing some version of it since 2014. I had thought I could survive anything, but in that instant I knew I was wrong. I did not see how I could survive without my mother.

I can tell you what it is like to press your face into a wooden floor as though it will freeze time, because you know that life will never be the same again once you lift it. I can tell you what it is to see your father unable to make basic decisions, sobbing uncontrollably while telling his children that he has no reason to live. I can tell you how to talk through your mother's autopsy with the coroner, and the apparent indifference with which a heart just stops beating. I can tell you what it is to look at your children and know that one day you will likely die in exactly the same merciless way—my grandmother, my mother, and my uncle all died of sudden cardiac arrests—and the visceral urgency you will then feel to somehow impart to them the unfathomable depths of your love, so that it will still be there long after you are gone.

And so I can tell you that shame is nothing in the face of grief. Life is what it is, and in one oblivious moment on your way to the mailbox, it just ends. If my mother's death could be so arbitrary, so meaningless and devoid of reason, then I could see plainly that some random act by an indifferent man in a Russian hotel room three years earlier meant even *less* than nothing, was the very opposite of meaning. There were no more mental gymnastics to do, no more lies to tell myself. Sochi was just a horrible thing that a horrible man had done simply because he could. It was no more a reflection on me than my mother's death was on the bed of flowers where she fell. Life was what it was: mothers die, cruel and careless men exist, but none of it was personal. None of it meant anything. The end comes when it comes, and nothing matters but the choices we make before it does.

I could see all this now, but my mother was gone and would never hear it. I could understand, now, why she'd so desperately tried in the last years before her death to convey to her only daughter how much she mattered, how much she was loved, and how she could never, ever be worthless.

But she was still gone.

*Mom.*

The end came when it came, and she never met the man her daughter would marry. A month after her death, my brother's son— her first grandchild—was born, and she was not there. Three months after her death, the man who'd defiled and discarded her child like trash was finally discarded by the world like the trash she knew he was, but she did not live to see it. Three years after her death, I wore flowers in my hair and an eyelet dress to get married in Kansas, and she missed it. She was not there a month later, when my brother's daughter—her second grandchild—was born, or a year later, when her third grandchild—my daughter—came into the world, five days before the fourth anniversary of her death. Nearly two years later, my son was born, and she was still gone.

It wasn't personal; it's just what happened. My mother died three days before her sixty-eighth birthday.

The end comes when it comes.

When she died, I stopped throwing away my life. But what I can never undo is how carelessly I threw away the final years of *her* life, years consumed by her feelings of helplessness as she watched her daughter suffer. When my own daughter was born, a half second passed before she took her first breath, and I screamed out, *Why isn't she crying?* A half second of my daughter's struggle was too much for me to bear in silence, but my mother endured three years of it while the man who inflicted it was broadcast into her home every morning. I would eventually report Matt Lauer, but I can never undo what my mother endured. I can never ease her pain, never tell her that her voice was finally heard and that I am okay. That my life is beautiful, actually, but only because for three long years, she somehow held me back from the edge of the void. She was my mother. She gave me this life in every sense of that word.

And then, in an instant, she was gone.

But she wasn't. She'd done what she always did—the flight attendant constantly leaving, worrying that she would never come back—and left me a note. More precisely, she left me a folder labeled *for Brooke for Comfort in Event of My Death.*

It held a series of letters she'd written to me, copies of letters she'd written to friends through the years when their mothers died, a pulled-out article from a 1994 issue of *People* about a young writer named Hope Edelman who'd just published a book, *Motherless Daughters: The Legacy of Loss.** One passage feels as though it could have been written yesterday: "If everyone around you tells you not to talk about something that has affected you profoundly, you develop a

---

* Hope Edelman's book, *Motherless Daughters,* became a *New York Times* bestseller and is now in its twentieth-anniversary edition.

sense of shame . . . a daughter's longing for her mother never disappears, but you don't have to shut the door on the past."

The oldest letter was twenty-seven years old, dated September 4, 1990, on her familiar pink stationery.

My dearest darling daughter—these days this is how I often call you to my side for one of your sweet little hugs and kisses. Today was a very exciting, sad, important time for me, and equally thrilling, exciting and memorable for you. Today, my heart burst with pride and deep love for you as I watched you confidently begin your first day of kindergarten . . .

. . . Each time a door closes, another opens . . . I know that, and I am so happy and proud to observe you as you've so gracefully and joyfully celebrated beginning your school career, and I will do all I can to help you in this endeavor. At the same time, I will also be doing all I can to conceal from you, my sweet loving child, how very sad I am about the door that just closed. Ten years ago, before your brother was born, I was strictly a busy career woman. I worked as a flight attendant on weekends, and for a builder on weekdays, and I loved my life. Your brother's birth caused me to discover a part of myself that I'd previously not known—I discovered a sense of joy and simplicity in a mother's love for her children, and a whole new world opened for me. A reordering of values occurred. You may recall (and I hope with all my heart you do) that in between all the ruckuses and demands that you clean up your messes, that I called our moments together "gold." I'd snuggle you or your brother—or all three of us—and say, feel this? This is gold, it is so precious to me.

There has been much happiness in my life, and I am deeply grateful to God for my many blessings. Brooke, as I often tell you, if I'd been able to special order a child from heaven, I couldn't have asked for a daughter more delightful than you. I hope as the years go by, I will always be able to convey to you how much happiness being your mother has given me.

I look at my children now and worry endlessly that they will never understand how much they are loved, how precious and capable and wondrous they are—how much they matter—and in those moments I begin to comprehend my mother's torture. She spent her final years trying endlessly to bring her only daughter back to life, but I hadn't listened.

I broke her heart.

———

MUCH LIKE THIS WAS not the kind of book anyone ever dreams of writing, Edelman never dreamed of writing a seminal book about grief. Her mother died when she was seventeen, and when she could not find a book that spoke to her grief, she eventually wrote it herself. She has received letters from grieving daughters who find their own mothers' copies of the book, now decades old, and are comforted by passages their mothers left underlined and the notes left behind in the margins.

"I look at that book sometimes now, and I wonder, how did I know all that so young?" she says. "I had spent hours and hours speaking with women and listening to them, and I was living with all those stories when I was writing that book. I felt like I got to know those women's stories. And over time, our stories start to change because we start to change. We look back at the same set of facts and they have a different meaning over time. Meaning is not static."

I told her that, since my mother's death, I'd stopped looking for meaning in things.

"Meaning comes with time," says Edelman. "You just don't know yet, honey. I mean, is meaning something we find? Is meaning something that's ascribed to us? Or is meaning something that we make? I think it's all three things, at different times. Sometimes we force a meaning onto things, because it makes us feel better, like when we say, 'Everything happens for a reason.' Now, I don't really believe that's true necessarily. I think that we are active participants in that process. Your story of your mom dying leads to her death, and the story ends shortly after that . . . but we can only tell the story because the ending of every story is the beginning of another."

---

WHEN ONE DOOR CLOSES, ANOTHER OPENS.

When I opened that folder in 2017, another shift in values occurred. For three and a half years, I'd hated myself—for causing such pain to the people I loved, for making terrible choices to live with something that never should have happened, for the endless lies I'd told. But now I found that I could not hate my mother's daughter, the precious little girl that she had so loved, into whom she had instilled so much of herself. That little girl meant everything to her, and the time had come for her to mean something to me.

In the face of grief, shame lost its power.

My mother's last note was dated January 28, 2009, about the same time I began filling in for Meredith's assistant at *Today*.

> *Dear Brooke, Do you realize you have been in New York for a year now? And, instead of becoming more comfortable with that reality, I am realizing that I miss you more and more, as your being so far away becomes more and more permanent, and I really am discovering how sad that realization makes me. I love you very, very much, my baby girl.*

Alongside all this was a poem she had copied out on a scrap of paper.

I hope my achievements in life
shall be these—
that I will have fought for
what was right & fair,
that I will have risked for
that which mattered,
that I will have given
help to those who were
in need...
that I will have left the
earth a better place
for what I've done
and who I've been.

C. Hoppe.

# TWELVE.

# Me, Too

*The Media, the Myth, the Mirror*

A month after her death—September 19, 2017—I was back at my desk at 30 Rock when I saw that one of Matt's interviews was making headlines. It was with the ex–Fox News anchor Bill O'Reilly, who had been fired six months earlier over sexual harassment allegations.

"You were fired about ten months after Roger Ailes was let go by the network over allegations of sexual harassment," Matt began the interview. "So the network understood the subject matter. You were probably the last guy in the world that they wanted to fire because you were the guy that the ratings and the revenues were built on. You carried that network on your shoulders for a lot of years. So doesn't it seem safe to assume that the people at Fox News were given a piece of information, or given some evidence that simply made it impossible for you to stay on at Fox News?"

"That's a false assumption," said O'Reilly, who went on to say that it had been a business decision, a clause exercised in his contract, and that in forty-two years in the business, working for twelve companies, he never had any interaction with human resources. He was aware that Fox had paid settlements to five women who had accused him of sexual harassment but said that he hadn't been privy to the settlements, had no say in them, and that there were "many other people involved, not just me." Even though he felt he'd done absolutely nothing wrong, he hadn't countersued because "every allegation in this area is a conviction."

"Think of those five women and what they did," said Matt. "They came forward and filed complaints against the biggest star at the network they worked at. Think of how intimidating that must have been, how nerve-racking that must have been. Doesn't that tell you how strongly they felt about the way they were treated by you?"

You can almost admire the brazenness of it, were it not so disturbing.

". . . Let me put a period on it this way, Bill, by asking you over the last six months since your firing, have you done some soul-searching?" Matt asked. "Have you done some self-reflection and have you looked at the way you treated women that you think differently about now than you did at the time?"

Even now, I watch this interview and marvel that it could ever have taken place, though I know perfectly well why it did. On the left we have Matt at number five on *Forbes'* 2016 Highest Paid TV Hosts list making $25 million a year, and on the right we have O'Reilly at number seven, pulling in $18.5 million. What other talent at NBC was thought to have the moral and journalistic heft—or maybe just the chutzpah—to take on Bill O'Reilly? What sane producer would ever have dared to suggest aloud that, maybe, Matt shouldn't do this interview, and why? And so two weeks before the revelations about Harvey Weinstein would come to light, the pot squared off against the kettle: Matt Lauer and Bill O'Reilly, live on *Today*, dinosaurs battling beneath an incoming meteor.

O'Reilly's reason for doing the interview seemed both obvious and rational. He was there to promote his new book, the latest in his bestselling Killing series. He knew his audience and his audience knew him. He had only to show up on *Today* and be the same pompous, grandstanding ass he'd always been, and his book would sell itself.

Matt, on the other hand, appeared to be playing the opposite game. Unlike O'Reilly, Matt's success as anchor of *Today* was predicated on being someone and something he had never actually been. For years, he'd studiously presented himself to viewers as an honest, upstanding journalist and family man, all the while apparently leading something of a double life behind the scenes. About a month before his interview with O'Reilly, in August 2017, Matt even went so far as to establish his own nonprofit and name it the Lauer Family Foundation. O'Reilly was many things, but he can hardly be called inauthentic. He wasn't starting the Bill O'Reilly Foundation for Sensitivity. Because his brand was based on who he really was, it transcended his platform at Fox News. Unlike O'Reilly (or Tom Brokaw or Robin Roberts), Matt had written no bestselling books. His only audience was the *Today* audience, and not the other way around.* O'Reilly had little to fear from doing the interview because he was the real deal, so to speak. Matt was not. Even putting aside the years of rumors and tabloid stories, his behavior toward me *alone* made his choice to confront a fellow on-air

---

* Not for any lack of trying: Matt played himself in five movies (*Land of the Lost, The Beaver, Sharknado 2, Sharknado 3,* and *Zoolander 2*) and six television series (*Will & Grace, 30 Rock, The Michael J. Fox Show, The Blacklist, Unbreakable Kimmy Schmidt,* and *Entourage*).

news personality about sexual harassment—while presenting himself to viewers as the morally unimpeachable anchor of *Today*—shockingly hypocritical. To do it on live television ought to have been unimaginable—unless, of course, you were entirely confident you would never be found out.

But that was not what I thought in September 2017 as I watched Matt on *Today*, imploring Bill O'Reilly to do some soul-searching about his treatment of female subordinates. I watched the interview and wondered, at first, if the whole thing was a joke. Was it April Fools'? Apparently not. The interview was everywhere. By early that afternoon, *The Washington Post* had written about it, lauding Matt as the "hard-headed commentator" who'd confronted O'Reilly with "dead-on reality." Everyone seemed to think the whole thing was great, and that Matt was great.

I watched that interview at my desk in 30 Rock and thought, *Matt is absolutely out of his mind.*

<hr />

ON OCTOBER 5, 2017, *New York Times* reporters Jodi Kantor and Megan Twohey published their first article about Harvey Weinstein.

"Two decades ago," it began, "the Hollywood producer Harvey Weinstein invited Ashley Judd to the Peninsula Beverly Hills hotel for what the young actress expected to be a business breakfast meeting. Instead, he had sent her up to his room, where he appeared in a bathrobe and asked if he could give her a massage or she could watch him shower, she recalled in an interview. 'How do I get out of the room as fast as possible without alienating Harvey Weinstein?' Ms. Judd said she remembers thinking."

It was the perfect sexual harassment story. To start, its celebrity angle meant that people would be eager to read and understand it, and the allegations mostly conformed to the stereotypical sexual harassment story. Harvey Weinstein was the archetypical villain: Powerful and brash, he even looked like a monster. As far as victims went, Ashley Judd was a journalist's dream: She was blameless, widely respected for her talent, and already famous enough that no reasonable person could accuse her of making the allegation for attention. And the Peninsula Beverly Hills? It was the perfect setting. Even the name of the hotel made you feel surrounded, your way out easily blocked.

Kantor and Twohey's reporting was airtight and buttoned-up. Their story's allegations against Weinstein were straightforward and appalling: "In 2014, Mr. Weinstein invited Emily Nestor, who had worked just one day as a temporary employee, to the same hotel and made another offer: If she accepted his sexual advances, he would boost her career." It was a perfectly explicit quid pro quo, describable in one sentence. But if you didn't believe the victims or found them unsympathetic, Kantor and Twohey had those bases covered, too. They'd obtained copies of settlements, emails, and internal documents, as well as a (male) former Weinstein executive, all on the record, corroborating the hostile work environment at the company. Even though sexual assaults are rarely reported, they'd still managed to find a victim who'd filed a police report in 2015.

There was only one element of Judd's story that departed enough from the stereotype to leave room for subconscious victim blaming: Why had she, and all these other women, gone to Weinstein's hotel room in the first place? To most people, an invitation to a hotel room has obvious sexual undertones. But those of us who work in less office-centric industries like show business or journalism work out of hotel rooms all the time. Production, whether movies or television or news, is a fluid, improvisational business. Travel, tight budgets, and short timelines mean, quite literally, that you meet people wherever they are, whenever you can. A hotel suite can function as an impromptu interview location, a meeting space, a secure storage locker, a private dining room, and, as a bonus, you can even sleep there. Once I booked a suite at the Four Seasons in Washington, DC, to use as an interview location, slept in it the night before to save budget, then rolled out of bed half-awake to let the camera crew in for setup at five a.m., still wearing one of the hotel's bathrobes. Were the cameramen "asking for it" by showing up to my hotel room and still walking in when I opened the door in a bathrobe? Hardly. I'm pretty sure I even showered and got dressed in the bedroom while they set up their gear. Nobody batted an eye.

The *Times'* reporting earlier that year on the sexual harassment settlements paid out by Fox News on behalf of Bill O'Reilly had been just as neat and airtight. There were no messy women with messy stories and convoluted circumstances, only documents in plain black-and-white that detailed increasingly large payouts to female Fox News employees who'd made harassment allegations against O'Reilly. Even if you were inclined to believe O'Reilly's protestations that none of the allegations had merit since there was no admission of wrongdoing, the final settlement—which he paid personally to one accuser in January 2017—was for $32 million, one of the largest known sexual harassment settlements in history. That scale alone served as a pretty damning admission of wrongdoing, though the $25 million severance package paid out by Fox to O'Reilly probably robbed it of the intended punitive impact.

As a journalist, it was impossible *not* to be in awe of how flawlessly Kantor and Twohey had nailed the story, but I had no real reaction to it otherwise. I certainly wasn't surprised. Practically everyone in the business had heard something about Harvey Weinstein. And the stories sounded exactly like what I understood of sexual harassment and assault in that they conformed to the stereotypes.

Five days later, on October 10, *New Yorker* reporter Ronan Farrow published his investigation of Weinstein. Here was a wholly different type of story, one that immediately confronted readers with the messy and uncomfortable realities of sexual abuse. It said as much at the outset: "On October 5th, the New York *Times*, in a powerful report by Jodi Kantor and Megan Twohey, revealed multiple allegations of sexual harassment against Weinstein . . . The story, however, is complex, and there is more to know and to understand."*

Farrow's investigation described far graver, and also far messier, claims of sexual misconduct. It also included a recording of Weinstein attempting to coerce a terrified woman into his hotel room for "five minutes," warning "don't ruin your friendship with me for five minutes."

Unlike the allegations in the *Times* story, that sounded painfully, personally familiar.

*It will only take a minute.*

There was the story of a woman who'd been coerced into giving Weinstein oral sex in his office, saying "I don't want to do this, stop, don't," and then "I just sort of gave up. That's the most horrible part of it, and that's why he's able to do this for so long to so many women: people give up, and then they feel like it's their fault." Afterward, Weinstein "acted as if nothing had happened."

That sounded familiar, too.

---

* I don't want to suggest that one of these stories was superior to the other; fortuitously, the two very different reporting styles worked in concert to reveal widespread misconduct that might otherwise have been ignored. Kantor, Twohey, and Farrow shared the 2018 Pulitzer Prize in Public Service "for explosive, impactful journalism that exposed powerful and wealthy sexual predators, including allegations against one of Hollywood's most influential producers, bringing them to account for long-suppressed allegations of coercion, brutality and victim silencing, thus spurring a worldwide reckoning about sexual abuse of women."

Another victim described how she finally "stopped saying no and feigned enjoyment, because she thought it was the only way the assault would end," how Weinstein had then contacted her afterward as though nothing had happened, and that she'd had consensual sexual relations with him multiple times over the course of the next five years, which she knew would be used to discredit her.

"After the rape," she said, "he won."

I read this story and felt sick. I read this story and cried for my mother, who was no longer alive to read it. Had it been published only two months earlier, everything might have been different. She might have died knowing, rather than hoping, that I would not always feel so unconscionably alone with what happened, that I could see that I had not brought it on myself, and that I would not throw away my life because of it. She might have known peace.

What happened to these women was not being described by *The New Yorker* as "weird" things that happened, that they should have just gotten over. They were being described by *The New Yorker* as sexual assaults.

I read these women's stories and saw clearly for the first time that tearing my body open in Sochi had been one kind of violation, and then tearing my life apart afterward had been another. I saw how easily Matt had corrupted everything that I had once seen as good in myself: that I always looked for the good in people and believed they deserved the benefit of the doubt, that I never quit, that I put the team first. I blamed myself for what happened in Sochi because I thought that was what decent people did. Decent people take responsibility for their mistakes. Decent people are accountable for their actions. I patted the seat. I went to the room. I went back. I lied.

But by taking so much accountability, I allowed Matt to escape it—for years.

"When you are treated like an object, things about you that you cannot change are reframed," wrote *New Yorker* writer Jia Tolentino the day after Farrow's investigation was published. "If a man interprets your youth as sexual vulnerability, he can make it seem that you have no choice but to be sexually vulnerable—after all, you have no choice but to be young. And so you might conclude that you need to redeem the encounter within a narrative that you may not like but in which you can at least actively participate. This might mean engaging in consensual sex afterward, to make you feel like you wanted it the first time, though you know you didn't. Or staying friendly with the man in the hopes that you'll find out that he actually did value you, and he wasn't just hoping for access to your body. Or even trying to get something out of the transaction, whatever you can. This looks like weakness, but it's an attempt to gain control."

It was all there—everything I'd experienced and felt that I believed could only have happened to me—the imperfect, inconvenient, messy truth of sexual harassment and assault.

I thought of Matt's disturbing grin outside the audio booth in 2016—*Weren't you in Sochi?*—and the cold, calculated arrogance of his interview with O'Reilly. I thought about the posters for the Lauer Family Foundation flashing on the screens in the elevator banks of 30 Rock. On the surface, Matt was no Harvey Weinstein. Matt was charming, charismatic, handsome; Weinstein was objectively physically frightening, a notorious bully.

At the same time, I knew firsthand of the existence of another Matt Lauer, one who ripped your body open and made you bleed and then asked you if you liked it. That Matt Lauer had not bothered to be charming or charismatic as he laid out a towel on the bed of his apartment to keep a young woman's blood off his bedspread. That Matt Lauer existed, and I knew it, and had known it for years. A powerful person who preys on the less powerful is a predator. A powerful person who preys sexually on the less powerful is a sexual predator. It was a term so jarring, so seemingly incompatible with the breezy, charming Matt Lauer behind the *Today* desk who I'd watched as a child—and yet there it was.

And there he was, behind the *Today* anchor desk, appearing to be just as shocked and morally outraged by the Hollywood mogul's behavior as everyone else.

Maybe he was.

———

HAD WOMEN REALLY BEEN talking about this all along, and I just hadn't been included in the conversation?

Was I the only one who hadn't known that sexual harassment wasn't always a transparent quid pro quo? That it was *rarely* a quid pro quo? Was I the only one who thought you had to be all but unconscious, or physically fighting back, to even *think* the word "rape"?

Suddenly it seemed that rape was anything but straightforward, that sexual assault was profoundly confusing, muddled in context and power dynamics and all the social niceties of preexisting relationships that often continued afterward.

All of this was news to me.

How had I missed all this? Wasn't I supposed to be a journalist? After my mother's death, I had combed through our texts and call logs and emails, agonizing over every missed opportunity I'd had to speak with her. I was always traveling, or shooting, or editing, or prepping for an interview. While that was technically journalism, what had I really been doing? I wasn't telling hard truths or giving voice to the afflicted. Passion projects were for people who could afford them, and I had credit card debt and student loans. I pitched stories I knew my bosses would like or that I thought the talent would like. Their point of view became my point of view. Did I fail to question my assumptions? Yes, but it wasn't as though the network was looking to *my* editorial judgment in deciding what went on the air.

But they certainly looked to Matt's.

Still, the opportunities to learn more and do better had been there. There was the Mimi Alford story, and our interview with Elizabeth Smart. I'd been so focused on the questions I thought viewers would want to ask that I never stepped back to consider why they wanted to ask them, and what those questions said about our collective understanding of what happened to these women. Then again, nobody else apparently had, either.

"The media reflects what's going on in society much more than it leads it," says Helen Benedict, a professor at the Columbia Journalism School and the author of *Virgin or Vamp*. "Once in a while the media will lead a discussion by exposing something we didn't know before, but by and large it reflects the status quo more than it changes it. . . . You have to be a very clever reporter, and a knowledgeable one, to recognize the rape myths that are being used to trash the victim, and to be able to cover that without just being an echo chamber and further perpetuating the myth."

Clearly, I was not such a reporter. Even later, the opportunities to learn about and question typical rape myth narratives were there. I'd avidly followed the Bill Cosby case. All told, more than forty women eventually accused Cosby of sexual assault. Thirty-five had their stories compiled by *New York* magazine in an award-winning 2015 cover story, which detailed the assaults in graphic terms, portraying a shocking pattern of predatory behavior.

But the article did not describe the aftermath of those assaults— and so, when Cosby went to trial in the summer of 2017,* I was

---

* Cosby's first trial in June 2017 resulted in a mistrial. When the case was retried in April 2018, Cosby was found guilty of all three counts of felony indecent assault and

confused by the continued contact between Cosby and his alleged victim, Andrea Constand. When the defense argued that a rape victim wouldn't make dozens of phone calls to her alleged rapist, I began to doubt her credibility. When the defense illustrated how her stories about Cosby had evolved over the years, and argued that she and Cosby had been in a romantic relationship, her story struck me as too messy and weird to be believed. I could have dug in deeper, learned more about the prosecution's expert testimony on rape myths and victim behavior. I didn't. Four months later, I was blindsided by MeToo.

"This is part of the terrible frustration," Benedict says. "I keep reading about and hearing about and talking to women and men who are still discovering the power of these myths, who still grew up absorbing these myths as truth. The courts still use them, the police still use them, the press still uses them."

Dr. Barbara Ziv, the forensic psychiatrist, told me her office received more press inquiries after she was hit by a car than about her testimony on rape myths in Weinstein's 2020 trial. "How many of those people called to ask about rape myths?" she says. "Nobody! This is the stuff they should be covering. The average person on the street doesn't even know what a rape myth is, and who do you think sits on a jury?"

---

sentenced to three to ten years in prison. That verdict was overturned on a legal technicality in June 2021 and Cosby was released.

# THIRTEEN

# No Good Options

*The Uphill Climb of Reporting Sexual Harassment and Assault*

B y the end of October, MeToo was beginning to hit closer to
home. Mark Halperin, the political director at ABC News,
was fired after CNN published sexual harassment allegations
against him by five women.* I knew Halperin only tangentially.
One of my side gigs when I was an NBC page earning ten dollars
an hour had been transcribing interviews for his 2010 book *Game
Change*, but I'd only interacted with his coauthor, John Heilemann.
Still, someone who knew I'd worked on the book casually messaged
me about the Halperin news.

---

\* Halperin initially responded to these allegations with a brief apology issued through
a spokesman: "During this period, I did pursue relationships with women that I
worked with, including some junior to me. I now understand from these accounts
that my behavior was inappropriate and caused others pain. For that, I am deeply
sorry and I apologize." A few days later, facing mounting professional repercussions,
he issued a five-hundred-word apology: "I am profoundly sorry for the pain and
anguish I have caused by my past actions. I apologize sincerely to the women I

". . . I never really interacted with Halperin," I said, "but what a mess."

Then they mentioned that there was supposedly a reporter digging into Matt Lauer.

I stopped answering, my body overwhelmed by seismic waves of terror. I got up from my desk, walked to the elevator, and left the building. This could not be happening. Real reporters—meaning respectable, non-tabloid reporters from respectable, non-tabloid publications—*never* looked into the rumors surrounding Matt. Brian Stelter, while serving as media reporter for *The New York Times*, had written an entire book about the brutally competitive world of morning news shows and had barely mentioned them. For as long as I'd been in the business, the rumors surrounding Matt had been treated as mere gossip, well beneath the dignity of the mainstream press. Reporting on them would have been considered bad form.

Something had changed. But if real reporters were to start seriously looking into Matt, I knew there would be plenty to find.

Including me.

I remember exactly what went through my mind. It was not

---

mistreated . . . As I said earlier in the week, my behavior was wrong. It caused fear and anxiety for women who were only seeking to do their jobs. In recent days I have closely read the accounts of women with whom I worked at ABC News. I have not read these accounts looking for discrepancies or inconsistencies. Instead, in almost every case, I have recognized conduct for which I feel profound guilt and responsibility, some involving junior ABC News personnel and women just starting out in the news business. . . . Some of the allegations that have been made against me are not true. But I realize that is a small point in the scheme of these things. Again, I bear responsibility for my outrageous conduct at ABC News." Attempting to rebuild his career in 2019, he apologized again: "I am deeply sorry and hope to have a chance to apologize directly to those I treated badly. It is the right and necessary thing to do. I cannot imagine how difficult this experience has been for them," he wrote on Twitter. "If they decline to hear directly, that must be respected."

*please no*—I'd always figured that what happened with Matt would catch up with me, and on some level, it would be a relief—but *please not now*, not without my mother. Most of the time, it felt as though I could barely breathe. I could barely get through my day-to-day life. This, though—*this*, exposed to the world—I knew I would not survive without her.

It quickly became apparent that I would have no choice. It wasn't just one reporter "looking into" Matt, but at least two teams of reporters from two different publications, *Variety* and *The New York Times*, who were actively investigating. It would only be a matter of time.

In early November, two coworkers took me out for drinks, ostensibly to take my mind off my mother's death. The conversation turned quickly to MeToo, and then to me. "Brooke, what happened to you?" one asked, as though looking for confirmation of something she already knew. "Something happened when you broke up with your boyfriend. You were never the same after that."

She said it with such directness that evasion felt pointless. I said that something had happened with Matt in Sochi, and then I paused. The world truly had changed. To tell these women about Sochi now, in the glaring light of MeToo, would be to tell them a secret that multiple reporters were actively trying to uncover. It would make them complicit in keeping that secret. When the stories about Matt inevitably came out in *Variety* or the *Times* or both or some other publication, they could be blamed for knowing and doing nothing, for *not* reporting what they'd heard to human resources, for being seen to protect Matt. If I continued, I would be telling them more than they could afford to hear. If they wanted to look the other way, this was their chance to stop me from saying any more. Neither one took it.

What came out of my mouth stunned me.

"It ruined my life," I said.

Then I broke down, and sobbed, and told them what had happened—all of it, in an unguarded flood of detail. I explained that it had all been my fault, that I was an idiot, that I had believed what I needed to believe and I desperately needed to believe it had all been my choice.

One said, *That sounds like a rape,* looking at me as though I'd just been handed down a death sentence. It was not a misunderstanding. It was not my fault. None of it ever should have happened. Had I made bad choices? Undeniably; I had no business drinking that much at work, for starters. But then I had been put into a situation in which the only available choices were all bad choices. I couldn't run from it anymore. All of this was going to come out, and I needed to get a lawyer.

The next day, I asked Meredith if we could talk in private about a Harvey Weinstein–type situation, and we met soon afterward. I began the conversation the same way as I had with my two coworkers: I said it involved Matt and then paused, waiting for her to stop me if she didn't want to know more. As her former assistant, I knew that the consequences of what I was about to say would be far worse for Meredith than for anyone else at the company. People would question what she'd known and whether she'd covered it up. Her well-deserved good name would be tarnished, even though I'd done everything in my power to hide what had happened from her. It was unfair, and she didn't deserve it. But she did not stop me.

Ultimately, her advice was to report it to NBC.

But would it make any difference? I was no Ashley Judd or Gretchen Carlson. I was just one woman, and nobody's ideal victim. I'd done everything wrong, and I was a grieving mess who couldn't make it through the day without drinking. I gave my mother's eulogy with a glass of wine in my hand. If it had taken five women coming forward with allegations against Mark Halperin, at least six for Bill O'Reilly, at least seven for Roger Ailes, and dozens for Weinstein and Cosby, how many women would have to come forward about Matt Lauer before any would be believed?

In the end, I decided it didn't matter. I would never have asked anyone else to risk their career to come forward against Matt Lauer. It was a suicide mission—but when I looked back at my life since Sochi, it seemed plain enough that it'd been a suicide mission all along. I felt I deserved it.

Behind the scenes, Matt might have been doing similar probability calculations, tabulating how many women could potentially come forward. Katie Couric would later write in her memoir that she and Matt went to lunch around this time and discussed MeToo. According to her account, Matt looked concerned and said, "This MeToo stuff feels like it's getting out of control . . . it feels like a witch hunt." When she mentioned Andrew Lack—the chairman of NBC News—Matt said, "Andy is my best friend."

Then, on November 20, eight women made sexual harassment allegations against Charlie Rose in *The Washington Post*. Rose publicly apologized for his "inappropriate behavior" and acknowledged that "I have behaved insensitively at times, and I accept responsibility for that, though I do not believe that all of these allegations are accurate. I always felt I was pursuing shared feelings, even though I now realize I was mistaken." He was promptly suspended, and then fired, by CBS, PBS, and Bloomberg. Mark Halperin was no Matt Lauer, but Charlie Rose was close. If he could be held accountable, then maybe even Matt could.

Still, there was he was behind the anchor desk at *Today*, listening as investigative correspondent Stephanie Gosk reported on Rose's firing. Later that week he would swap his straight newsman role for his more affable, family-friendly persona as Dad-in-Chief of

America's First Family as he hosted the Macy's Thanksgiving Day Parade. The next week, it would be the Rockefeller Center tree lighting.

Meanwhile, alone in my month-to-month studio apartment, I tried to work up the nerve to talk to a lawyer. I'd never even had a speeding ticket fixed. The only lawyers I'd ever worked with were the ones at NBC. For the past nine years, NBC had been the closest thing I had to a family in New York. The company had sent flowers and catering to my mother's funeral, and two coworkers had flown from New York to be there. Since I'd moved to the city, I'd lived in six tiny apartments and walked to Rockefeller Plaza every morning from every single one of them. It felt like home. Since my mother's death, the routine of going to work every day had been the only respite from grief. To talk to a lawyer about NBC, to even think of myself as separate from NBC, felt like a betrayal.

There was, however, another way to look at it. No matter what I did, some version of the truth about Matt would inevitably come out. I didn't know any women who had actually reported their experiences with him to anyone in an official capacity. In that sense, reporting Matt to NBC was not a betrayal but an act of loyalty, a way of protecting the company that felt like my family. Would it make any difference? Almost certainly not. Matt was the show and the show was the news division. I, on the other hand, was a relatively junior producer whose career was already tainted by the Macchiarini scandal. The math here was not hard. Matt was going to win.

But I was tired of being a practical person. My mother's death meant I'd inherit enough money to pay off my student loans and credit cards, making me debt-free for the first time since I was nineteen. I didn't have a mortgage or children to support. My boyfriend and I were moving in together so I wouldn't be homeless, and I knew he would support me whatever I decided to do. Silence and complicity were no longer my only options.

For three years, I had been exactly the kind of worthless, weak person Matt must have estimated me to be.

Now I would be the kind of person my mother had always believed I was.

———

SO—YOU'VE DECIDED ENOUGH is enough, and you want to "come forward."

What the hell does that even mean?

It's not as simple as literally "coming forward," of raising your hand and saying you want to be heard. Instead you're about to leave the realm of ordinary life and step into a hideous, tedious legal process that, like every other aspect of sexual harassment and assault, is extremely complicated and not at all what you expect.

First, another hard truth: You have no "good" options. From the moral to the mundane, filing a formal complaint is an exercise in balancing harms. Here you are in a devastating, humiliating, painful situation that has become unbearable. To do nothing is no longer an option, yet the stakes of doing anything else are extremely high. You could lose your job or the chance to get a better one. Your reputation could be destroyed. Then there's the emotional and physical cost of the stress, the shame, the embarrassment, the feeling that you've lost control over your own life. You can't earn your living without confronting the situation, but you can't confront it without risking your ability to earn a living. You're trapped.

You really, really should talk to a lawyer—and lawyers cost hundreds of dollars an hour. Even if you can afford that, how do you find a good one? You can't just ask around, because sexual harassment and assault is not something that can be openly discussed. If you go around asking your coworkers if they know a good employment attorney to help you with a sexual harassment issue and confide in them about your problem, all those people become potential witnesses—and there's a good chance at least one of them will proactively report your situation to human resources as a matter of self-protection.* At minimum, they'll ask questions you can't or don't want to answer. If you do know anyone who has been through something similar at your workplace, they probably won't be able to tell you about it anyway because they'll likely have signed a nondisclosure agreement.

And then there is the shame, which is a powerful silencing mechanism on its own. You don't want the people you work with to know about this. You don't want *anyone* to know about it. You wish it had never happened.

"In these cases, people feel like they're alone," says attorney Tammy Marzigliano, a partner and cochair of the Whistleblower and Retaliation Practice Group at the leading employment law firm Outten & Golden, where she regularly handles sexual harassment cases. "They're really ashamed and embarrassed, and that is the theme I see throughout with my clients in sexual harassment cases specifically. It's almost like they blame themselves. They feel like they can't say anything, there's nowhere to go with it and they don't want to rock the boat. But they're not alone. There are so many people out there with similar experiences."

That "I don't want to rock the boat" mentality that Marzigliano describes is ubiquitous in the modern workplace. Women have fought so hard for a place at the corporate table that we're reluctant to complain about the service now that we've finally gotten a seat. We don't want to be seen as "difficult" or "crazy" or "overreacting."

---

* If you need an innocuous way to ask around without ringing alarm bells, say you need a good employment attorney because you're looking to have a contract reviewed or have questions about your benefits package.

Then there's still that generation of women in the workplace who don't want to hear it because they had to endure far worse to pave the way for you. Abusers, and the organizations that protect them, count on victims having this mindset. They depend on deference and a desire to avoid conflict and confrontation. That's why it doesn't work. What happens if you tiptoe into HR, shut the door behind you, and say quietly, *I don't want to cause a problem, but . . . ?* You learn the hard way that you've already showed your hand: Once you tell your employer you don't want to cause a problem because you want to keep your job, there's really not much of an incentive for them to do anything to help you. The squeaky wheel gets the grease. You have to squeak as loudly as you can. Be a problem. Rock the damn boat, or you're not going to get anywhere.

"You have to say, 'I am a threat to you,'" says attorney Lynn Hecht Schafran, a senior vice president, a senior staff attorney, and the former director of the national judicial education program at Legal Momentum, the longest-serving legal advocacy organization for women in the United States. "You have to say, 'I'm not going to go away.'" You may have to threaten a lawsuit, to demand monetary damages—which, to be clear, is usually the only form of justice available, and one that often reinforces the shame most victims already feel. No one feels good about money as compensation for sexual humiliation. But sexual humiliation without the money you need to help yourself and support your family feels even worse.

"You'd like to think you could go to your HR department and have it resolved in-house, and no money changes hands, and you just go on with your life," says Schafran. "That looks great on paper, since we passed all these great laws protecting employees, but then there's reality."

That reality is stark. If your employer sees you as a loyal and conciliatory employee, devoted to your job and wanting to get back to it with as little fuss as possible, then they know they can either ignore your complaint or offer you the smallest financial settlement possible and you're probably not going to ask for what you deserve. And, don't get me wrong, while many human resource officers genuinely do want to protect and help employees, they are also ultimately employees of the company that is liable for whatever problem you're reporting. Their overriding responsibility is to protect the company. HR people have bills to pay, too.

"HR is not your friend," attorney Nancy Erika Smith, who represented Gretchen Carlson in her sexual harassment suit against Roger Ailes, said in April 2017. "Going to human resources in a company like [Fox News] is like going to the KGB to complain about Putin."

"Most HR departments, like any employees, are very aware of who pays their salaries," says Schafran. "Their sense of responsibility is not to make things nice for the employees. I would say to anybody who's thinking about going to HR for anything serious, get a good lawyer first."

But again, finding a good attorney is no easy task—and once you've pulled together a few potential names, sexual harassment and assault is not something you're going to want to discuss in detail with fifty different attorneys as you shop around for someone to handle your case. These are painful, often humiliating situations. For most people, just making one call to an attorney is difficult enough, let alone discussing what happened again and again with relative strangers and answering their extremely detailed, shockingly personal but necessary questions. You need to do it anyway. This is par for the course, finding an attorney you trust is of paramount importance, and setting aside your shame or embarrassment is a crucial step toward addressing it.

Even if you do manage to find a good lawyer who will take

your case, Schafran warns, "it costs a lot of money, and that's very concerning from the get-go."*

But whatever the price, making any sort of complaint without consulting legal counsel will likely cost you more in the long run. A good employment lawyer can help you to explore other options beyond threatening or filing a lawsuit. They might be able to handle the issue on your behalf with a phone call, because just by hiring a lawyer, you're sending a message to your employer that you're serious about your complaint, you know your rights and you expect the problem to be addressed.

"We can find ways to be creative where people can still earn a living but keep their dignity," says Marzigliano. "A big part of what I do is advising people. When they have someone that understands the working of corporations and the law, they feel they're protected. And they're not in it by themselves and that there's a plan, and that changes the dynamic. They feel they have some control over the situation again."

Even if your case seems open-and-shut, you'll quickly find that there is no such thing as an open-and-shut sexual harassment case. Unless an employer is receiving public funding, employers have a fiduciary responsibility to limit their exposure to liability and resolve disputes as cheaply as possible. No employer will ever say, 'You're right, this was horribly wrong and we owe you.' It's their

---

* The National Women's Law Center offers resources for anyone facing sexual harassment or other sex discrimination issues. Its Legal Network for Gender Equity connects people facing sex harassment or other sex discrimination in the workplace, education, or when accessing health care with free, initial legal consultations with its in-network attorneys. For situations involving sex harassment and retaliation in the workplace, the TIME'S UP Legal Defense Fund offers funding to defray the costs of legal representation, as well as connections to media professionals and funding to defray the costs of working with a media professional (including working to keep your name out of the press). For more information, go to nwlc.org/legal-help.

job to fight you, every step of the way, until you give them no other choice—and then to pay you as little as possible in damages. This emotionally draining and isolating game of chicken isn't personal. It's just business.

"None of this is what anyone wants to be doing," adds Schaffran. "First you think, how do I make this go away? Do I really want to get involved with HR? And that just eats up time."

Another option: File a discrimination charge against your employer with the EEOC or one of its affiliated fair employment practice agencies (FEPAs) on the state level, though you could have as few as 180 days from the date of the alleged violation to do it. The EEOC will then investigate your complaint and either find in your favor or your employer's. If they don't find in your favor, you'll be given ninety days to file a lawsuit in federal court at your own expense. If they do find in your favor, they will give notice and invite your employer to join an informal, voluntary process known as conciliation to resolve the charge. If that fails, the EEOC has the option of filing a lawsuit in federal court to enforce its findings. If they don't, you will be given the option of filing your own lawsuit, again at your own expense. Long story short, the EEOC is not necessarily an alternative to hiring a lawyer. Even if it finds in your favor, you will probably need to hire one anyway—and as the EEOC receives tens of thousands of complaints each year (more than 81,000 in 2023), the process can be slow. On the bright side, filing an EEOC complaint does stop the statute of limitations on your claims, which could potentially buy you some time.*

At this point, you might think it'd be easier to just quit your

---

* The statute of limitations is the amount of time you have to take legal action. It varies from state to state and depends on the type of violation in question, which means you'll probably need to talk to a lawyer to figure out exactly how long you have in your specific case.

job, establish yourself with a new employer, and then deal with all of this later.

"People don't realize that just quitting a job has legal consequences," says Marzigliano. "They think, 'I'll just get out of the situation and then I'll deal with what happened,' then they'll call months later and explain they finally worked up the nerve to call a lawyer. That's understandable, but the statute of limitations has been running on their claims. If they never raised any complaints, there's no record of what happened. And who knows what they signed when they left because, at the time, they just needed to get out. That's how these problems continue, on and on."

If you're out of other options or you can't afford a lawyer, you might be tempted to take matters into your own hands by going public with your claims. Why not talk to a reporter, or just post what happened on social media? At a bare minimum, at least you'll know that you did something, and you'll know that you weren't complicit in the abuse by keeping it secret. Attorneys cost hundreds of dollars an hour (and for that, it should be emphasized, they are legally bound to put your interests first), while talking to a reporter is free.

But that does not mean it is without cost. It's one thing to speak about these issues anonymously or without naming your abuser—and that can be tremendously empowering—but it's another thing entirely to make a specific allegation against a specific abuser, who then has every right to respond with their own version of events. This, too, can have a devastating impact on your ability to earn a living, your mental and physical health, your relationships, even your personal safety. And as we've seen, even the best-intentioned journalists usually bring their own biases and motivations to their stories.

"I've had people tell me with much more grief and anger about what happened to them in the media than about the actual assault itself," says Louise Godbold, the executive director of Echo, a non-profit that offers trauma and resilience training. At the height of MeToo, Godbold spoke publicly about her own allegation against Harvey Weinstein, and knows firsthand the emotional and professional cost of speaking out about sexual assault in the press. "There's always a power differential at play. In the worst-case scenario, you become a 'subject,' not a person—and something we discovered as Weinstein survivors was that we were a commodity."

When it means getting a good story, journalists can be solicitous, understanding, and affirming, praising would-be subjects and sources for their courage and promising near-endless support and handholding. But once we have the story, it becomes exactly that—*our* story, to write, edit, publicize, and promote however we (or our higher-ups) see fit. For those grappling with the aftermath of sexual harassment or assault who have already been exploited by their abusers, that can be devastating and abusive in itself.

"Some survivors feel very empowered by having their story told by someone else, and by being heard on any level," says Godbold. "But it's important to remember that the story still belongs to the survivor, not the journalist. At the time of the trauma, power and control is taken from the victim, so the most important thing is to have power and control over your own narrative, your own sense of what happened. Even if you're talking to the nicest, most sensitive, most reputable journalist, it is essentially disempowering to have your ability to tell your story your way—to represent yourself accurately—taken from you."

While reporters can help you speak out, the one thing we can never give as journalists is that which victims most need: control over their own stories. Here, victims face another painful impasse. To try to take back control of their own narratives by telling their stories, they must first surrender that control to the journalist. That journalist's narrative—and motivation—may not align with yours.

"Talking to the press about a rape is a horrible thing to go through," says Benedict, the Columbia journalism professor. "Usually a victim gets nothing out of it but grief. It's not as if they're going to get money and it's not the kind of fame anybody really wants. Usually it just means harassment, hatred, threats, danger, humiliation, and defeat, when what the victim hopes for is justice."

# FOURTEEN.

# "He Is Beloved by Many, Many People Here"

## *Why We Want to Believe Denials*

n November 2017, I didn't know or understand any of this. I couldn't just google *smartest way to report NBC's biggest star to NBC*—actually, I probably did. I had no way of knowing that just by asking anyone at NBC for help or advice, I was making them a party to a massive news scandal and dramatically increasing the likelihood they'd be interviewed by NBC's legal team later. This is not a good way to win or keep friends. A small circle of well-meaning people were telling me what I should do, each with their own conscious or unconscious reasons for wanting me to do it: I should tell my story on the front page of *The New York Times.* I should threaten to sue both Matt and NBC for $75 million, roughly the amount Matt had earned since Sochi. I should report what happened to Interpol and try to have Matt sent to Siberia. I should go to Matt directly while wearing a wire and try to get him to admit what he'd done. I should go to Matt directly and offer to sign an NDA in exchange for $50 million—because if O'Reilly could pay $32 million, Matt could certainly swing fifty. There seemed to be an unspoken assumption that Matt had probably been paying off women for years. How else could he still be there?

I just wanted to talk to my mother, even if only for one more moment. I wanted MeToo to go away until I was strong enough to deal with it. I wanted to be anything other than the weak, ashamed, grieving train wreck of a person that I was.

I only knew two things with absolute certainty. One, that regardless of how I had responded to it, what Matt had done was unequivocally wrong—and, two, that my shame had allowed him to get away with it. It had to stop.

So I talked to a lawyer and began the painful process of digging through a past I'd been trying to bury and forget for years. I asked a friend I'd confided in back then what they remembered: "You said that it hurt and you bled." I asked my executive producer if she remembered either of the conversations about Matt in 2016, and she remembered both. I reviewed the few texts from Matt I hadn't deleted, fully expecting to be told there was no point in going forward since I'd been so friendly and enthusiastic and never once demanded he leave me alone. The texts told an obvious and embarrassing story, but not the one I remembered. I sounded exactly like what I was: a desperate-to-please assistant with no actual idea how to please a much older man she barely knew, over her head in a precarious situation she did not fully understand.

When I objectively outlined what happened in Sochi, it seemed increasingly impossible that Matt's actions that night—one after the next—could ever have been the result of an innocent misunderstanding. Could Matt have misunderstood that he was the anchor of *Today* and that I was a talent assistant? No. Was he aware that he was the direct employer of my boyfriend's brother? Yes.

He'd said as much earlier on the trip, in front of three other people. Was Matt aware that I was heavily intoxicated when he told me to come to his hotel room? Yes. He suggested the vodka shots, ordered them, watched me drink them, then signed for the entire bar tab. He responded to an email in which I said that I was so drunk I couldn't open a hotel room door. *Then* he told me I should come to his room. Had I expressed multiple times, including with the word "no," that I did not want to have anal sex? Yes. Had it made any difference? No. Any one of these alone might have been an innocent misunderstanding, but all of them? If I could employ a nanny part-time for six months and know instantly that the power imbalance made it wrong for me to impose on her by inviting her to a birthday party on her day off, then it's reasonable to expect the anchor of *Today* to know that demanding anal sex from an intoxicated subordinate is sexual exploitation. Innocent misunderstandings do not result in ripped bodies, bloody sheets, and an armful of towels. They just don't.

But did it qualify as sexual assault? What was blatantly predatory sexual behavior to some people was seen as "the way of the world" to others. To some, everything was rape. To others, nothing but a man in a ski mask with a knife to your throat—the rape myth—qualified as a "real" rape. Yet these clashing and contradictory social conventions were far less difficult to navigate than the statute books. I could look up every legal definition of rape in the United States—from New York's (which includes rape in the first, second, and third degrees; criminal sexual acts in the first, second, and third degrees; predatory sexual abuse; and aggravated sexual abuse in the first, second, third, and fourth degrees . . . and on and on) to the FBI's to the model penal code's—and none, technically, would apply, since the incident in question was in Russia.

I thought of Matt's twenty years as anchor of *Today* and found myself asking a new question: not Where in the World Is Matt

Lauer, but Who in the World Has Jurisdiction over Matt Lauer? The answer was plain enough: NBC, and only NBC. Of course, NBC had no authority to decide what was sexual assault and what was not, but the legal applicability of rape laws was already a moot point. I didn't have to convince NBC, or anyone, that what happened that night was sexual assault. I only had to prove that Matt was knowingly abusing his power to prey sexually on a subordinate NBC employee. There was at least some chance that I could do that.

And if I could stop him from doing what he did to me to someone else, then I would not have been able to live with myself if I didn't at least try.

On November 22, 2017—the day after Charlie Rose was fired— I emailed my human resources representative and asked to meet. I said I would be bringing a lawyer. The meeting was scheduled for Monday, November 27, in the news division's legal department. It was late enough that the office would be empty, an important consideration as NBC was legally bound to protect my identity. HR and the company also had to keep the contents of my complaint confidential. In my mind, to make the complaint would be to put its contents, once and for all, into a vault—the place where I could finally put down all the shame and humiliation that I felt and leave it behind.

But in the five days between sending that email and the meeting, I heard a rumor that a woman supposedly had gone into NBC HR the week before to make a harassment complaint against an anchor far less important than Matt. Supposedly—at least according to the rumor mill—she'd been laughed out of the room, MeToo or not.

What the hell was I doing? Reporting Matt Lauer to NBC was insanity. His best friend was the chairman of NBC News. Who the hell did I think I was? NBC wasn't going to fire Matt Lauer because of something he'd done to *me*, if they even believed he'd done it. Telling the company would accomplish nothing but make it so that I could never get another job again. I emailed HR and canceled my meeting. There had to be another option.

One of O'Reilly's accusers had sued him personally, and he'd settled with her for $32 million. But O'Reilly had been allowed to remain on the air, with no admission of wrongdoing as a result. I didn't want Matt's money. I wanted to clear my conscience, to know I'd done everything I could to stop him from abusing his power again. From behind the anchor desk, he would have the money and influence to assemble a legal dream team that could get him acquitted of male pattern baldness. For all I knew, he'd been quietly settling suits like this for years. Suing him would change nothing.

The press was the only other option, though this, too, would mean risking my job. No news employee was allowed to speak to reporters without explicit permission. But how much of a risk would it be? Surely *The New York Times* would never betray a source. And if NBC failed to act, I would at least have done something.

I met with two reporters, off the record, on the morning of November 27. But I very quickly realized I had nowhere near the courage to talk about what had happened publicly. I had barely begun to process it myself. My father and brother shared my last name, and neither knew anything about any of this. Nor did I want to humiliate my ex-boyfriend, the "family connection," who *also* knew nothing about any of this. And then there was Meredith, who would inevitably and undeservedly be dragged into Matt's disgrace, and I would never, ever have done that to her willingly. She was the closest thing to a mother that I had left.

But what if I let them use my story, without using my name? The problem with that, I knew, was that talent always got the benefit of the doubt—and the bigger the talent, the bigger that benefit. Brian Williams had told tall tales about being shot down in combat for years, humiliating not only himself but the entire news division. Not only was he still employed by NBC News, he'd been given a new show. If the *Times* and *Variety* used a single unnamed account of Matt's behavior, Matt could dismiss the accusations against him as rumors and gossip and that would be that. Even if I gave my entire story to the *Times*, I didn't think it would make any difference without my name on it. And as soon as Matt read the word "Sochi," he would know it was me and that would be the end of my career. This, too, would likely change nothing. You can't demand accountability without taking accountability, and I was still trying to hide. It wouldn't work.

Going to the press would also forfeit my only advantage: Because Matt and I were both still employees of NBC, we were—in theory—bound by the same rules, and both entitled to some degree of due process. Matt would at least have to answer my allegations if they could be substantiated, and unlike the *Times*, NBC could easily substantiate them by looking at their own internal communications. After all, Matt had only communicated with me using his NBC News phone and email. And while I couldn't force anyone to talk to a reporter to corroborate my account—asking that of another NBC employee would be asking them to risk their job—NBC could certainly compel their own employees to cooperate with an internal investigation.

If NBC didn't believe me, fine—but when the *Times* and *Variety* published their investigations, at least the network would never be able to say they had no idea what he was doing. They would have to explain to the world how they let him sit behind that anchor desk at *Today* after hearing about the blood and the towels and *It will only take a minute* and "fun." If they let him light the Rockefeller Center Christmas tree after that, then they deserved everything that was coming to them—but I felt the company deserved the opportunity to do the right thing.

I emailed HR again, and asked if we could still meet.

THERE WAS A BRIEF PAUSE in the conference room that night as my human resources representative and NBC's in-house counsel waited for me to begin. I looked up at the fluorescent lights, and for a moment considered running the hell out of the room.

I looked at the two women sitting before me, with their legal pads and poised pens. I thought of myself sitting at the table at the hotel bar in Sochi, the moment before I patted the seat next to me to invite Matt to join us, changing everything. This was that moment for them, and they had no idea. They were just here doing their jobs, as I had been then—but the moment I started talking, their careers would never be the same.

I knew that NBC was aware of the reporters' investigations into Matt, so I figured HR had to be expecting some version of this meeting. But there was no great sense of dread, no apparent anticipation or anxiety in the women sitting across the table from me. They waited graciously for me to begin.

Finally I said, "You know who this is about, right?"

They both shook their heads.

"It's about Matt Lauer," I said.

And then I told them everything, with as much detail as I could manage, pausing only to name people who could corroborate what I said. I emphasized, again and again, how flattered I'd been by the attention, how I'd described it as an affair for years to coworkers while omitting details too painful or humiliating to acknowledge. I made it clear that there had been no explicit threats or quid pro quos. I told them that they would find nothing but friendly, enthusiastic communications from me to Matt, and how deferential I had always been, even when trying to refuse anal sex in his corporate hotel room in Sochi or oral sex in his *Today* dressing room.

I did not use the words "rape" or "sexual assault." Instead, I just described exactly what had happened.

At one point, my lawyer interjected to clarify that what I was describing represented a lack of consent. Silence hung briefly in the air as, presumably, we all contemplated what that meant—but practically speaking, even I knew that it did not mean much. NBC could only decide whether Matt's behavior violated its policies, and beyond that it was just a matter of degree. By the time I finished and had answered their questions—had I reported this before, and when? Who had I told, and when? Was I aware of any other women who'd had similar experiences? How many? How long ago? Did any of them still work at NBC?—hours had passed, and my face was streaked with dried tears. In the end, it was as easy as jumping off a cliff.

The swiftness and determination and courage of those two women must have been a thing to behold. Late on a Monday night, I'd handed them a grenade with no pin. They said they would take care of it, and they did.

I thought that maybe, later that week, I'd get called back to the legal department, and they'd sit across from me and point out all the discrepancies they'd found. I'd be suspended and then fired. Matt would stay on *Today* as though none of it had ever happened. I got up the next morning—Tuesday, November 28—and went to the office, shocked to discover my badge still worked at security. I went to my desk and waited for that call to come. I heard nothing. I did my work. I went home.

Later I learned that some of the people I'd named were called that day, but I understand now that NBC would have had little need to corroborate every single detail of my story. They would only have needed to determine whether it was credible enough to confront Matt directly—which they did.

"On November 28, 2017, Lauer was interviewed by senior members of NBCUniversal corporate HR and Legal," reads the report of the NBC internal investigation. "During the interview, Lauer admitted to engaging in sexual activity with the complainant. The Company determined that his conduct violated Company policy and terminated Lauer's employment on November 28, effective immediately."

⸻

*FROM NBC NEWS, THIS IS TODAY . . . live from Studio 1A, in Rockefeller Plaza.*

The next morning, *Today*'s famous opening lines had been edited, making the show sound strangely anchorless. It was the first time in two full decades that the familiar sound of Matt Lauer's name was not among the first words heard by millions of viewers, along with the day's headlines. Even the name of *Today*'s other anchor, Savannah Guthrie, had been removed—and she'd survived longer as Matt's coanchor than anyone since Katie Couric. It was an early indicator of the uncanny degree to which Matt, in even the most literal sense of the word, had been the show's true anchor— its moral and emotional ballast, steadying its course even as his $25-million-a-year salary weighed heavily against the show's budget while its ratings steadily declined. Now that anchor had been cut loose, and *Today* was adrift.

I'd had no idea. It was November 29, 2017, and I had to vacate the tiny, month-to-month studio apartment where I'd lived since 2014 by the first of the month. I'd stayed up half the night packing, leaned my mattress against a wall to make room for boxes, and slept on a yoga mat. My phone rang around 6:40 that morning, waking me from a dead sleep. It was a friend on the *Today* staff, voice low, asking if I was okay. I was barely conscious as I said yes and fell immediately back to sleep, without even asking the reason for the question.

Then *Today* went on the air.

"This is a sad morning here at *Today* and at NBC News," said Guthrie. Seated next to her was Hoda Kotb, who would eventually succeed Matt as coanchor.

"Just moments ago, NBC News chairman Andy Lack sent the following note to our organization," she continued, reading from the teleprompter. "'Dear colleagues, on Monday night, we received a detailed complaint from a colleague about inappropriate sexual behavior in the workplace by Matt Lauer. It represented, after serious review, a clear violation of our company's standards. As a result, we've decided to terminate his employment.

"'While it is the first complaint about his behavior in the over twenty years he has been at NBC News, we were also presented with reason to believe this may not have been an isolated incident. Our highest priority is to create a workplace environment where everyone feels safe and protected, and to ensure that any actions that run counter to our core values are met with consequences, no matter who the offender. We are deeply saddened by this turn of events. But we will face it together as a news organization—and do it in as transparent a manner as we can.'

"We just learned this moments ago, just this morning," said Guthrie. "As I'm sure you can imagine, we are devastated. And we are still processing all of this. And I will tell you right now, we do not know more than what I just shared with you. But we will be covering this story, as reporters, as journalists. I'm sure we'll be learning more details in the hours and days to come. And we promise we will share that with you."

She then turned to Kotb.

"And, Hoda, I mean, you know, for the moment, all we can say is that we are heartbroken," Guthrie said. "I'm heartbroken for Matt. He is my dear, dear friend and my partner. And he is beloved by many, many people here.

". . . And I'm heartbroken for the brave colleague who came forward to tell her story, and any other women who have their own stories to tell. And we are grappling with a dilemma that so many people have faced these past few weeks. How do you reconcile your love for someone with the revelation that they have behaved badly? And I don't know the answer to that. But I do know that this reckoning that so many organizations have been going through is important. It's long overdue and it must result in workplaces where all women, all people, feel safe and respected. As painful as it is this moment in our culture, and this change, had to happen."

"Yeah, it did," said Kotb. "This is a very tough morning for both of us. I've known Matt for fifteen years and I've loved him as a friend and as a colleague. And again, just like you were saying, Savannah, it's hard to reconcile what we are hearing with the man who we know, who walks in this building every single day. We're both woken up with the news kind of predawn. And we're trying to process it and trying to make sense of it. And it will take some time for that."

*He is beloved by many, many people here.*

Of course he was. Matt was the hand that fed the news division, the morning tide that kept afloat a $200 million sinking ship. Whatever else he was, for twenty years, he'd shown up without fail to Studio 1A every morning at the crack of dawn and kept a lot of good people employed in an otherwise shrinking industry. There was no denying that. It is only human to want to avoid acknowledging what is painful—but it is also dehumanizing to have your pain barely acknowledged, relegated to an afterthought. It was not as though the loss that *Today* was feeling that morning was the unavoidable result of some senseless tragedy. Instead it was the direct result of Matt's deliberate choices. To use his words to Bill O'Reilly, he was "the last guy in the world" the network would want to fire, and they wouldn't have done it without irrefutable evidence. All the heartbreak and hurt felt by the *Today* family that morning was entirely avoidable. My mother's death was a loss; what *Today* had suffered was a betrayal.

But the talent, for all their poise and wit and unflinching charisma, are just people. Watching that morning's broadcast today, I don't feel so much hurt but empathy for two deer in the headlights, struggling just as anyone would to reconcile conflicting feelings about someone they'd trusted with their livelihoods and reputations. It had benefited all of us to believe Matt's years of denials of the tabloid rumors. Our minds will go to remarkable lengths not to see what we cannot afford to know. That's how betrayal blindness, or adaptive blindness, works: It's a cognitive survival mechanism that prevents us from acknowledging a truth that destroys something we think we need to survive.

"Whether the betrayal is in our closest relationships, in our workplaces, or in our society, we often have a powerful motivation to remain ignorant," wrote psychologist Jennifer Freyd, PhD, a professor emeritus of psychology at the University of Oregon, who first identified betrayal blindness. "We remain blind to betrayal in order to protect ourselves. We fear risking the status quo, and thus our security, by actually knowing too much."

And so we look the other way, decline to ask questions, go along to get along—just as I had done when I first started at *Today* in 2008 and 2009 and was told of Matt's "inappropriate sexual behavior in the workplace" separately by two different people. Both times, I didn't want to know.

There are other cognitive biases at play here, too. There's also plain old confirmation bias, where we ignore new information that conflicts with our assumptions while clinging to information that confirms them, and denial bias, which makes us reject unpleasant or unsettling information. When we're told something terrible about someone we love and we say *I refuse to believe that*, that's denial bias. It's much easier to believe a denial than an allegation because our minds find a way to believe what we want or need to believe, and to doubt or deny what we don't.

In Matt's case, all this plus twenty years as the star anchor on a news broadcast expertly crafted to make him appear trustworthy, likable, and decent meant that viewers were already primed to believe his denial. He was a known quantity that Americans had been groomed to trust by the best producers in the business. By contrast, his accuser was some random woman without a name or a face or a life or a family, who'd walked into one meeting, complained, and ruined Matt's career. But for anyone who worked at *Today*, there would have been a strong personal incentive to refuse to believe in the possibility of Matt's wrongdoing. In our business, working relationships with big-name talent are a professional currency, and with Matt's firing, many longtime *Today* employees lost a proverbial fortune. Employees who spent their careers producing Matt's segments suddenly found they had little to show for twenty years of work. On November 27, 2017, to be close to Matt Lauer meant being a powerful and important person. Two days later, it meant being either a fool or an enabler. That would have been difficult, and extremely painful, to accept—and, again, it is only human to avoid what is painful.

Soon, questions would have to be answered. Who knew what, and when? How could this have gone on so long? Had everyone been looking the other way, or helping to cover it up? Whatever the answers, there would be devastating consequences for everyone. A *Today* news archive of Matt Lauer material two decades deep had become practically unusable overnight, if not an outright embarrassment. Would viewers ever see the show the same way again?

Would ratings fall even faster? Would there be layoffs? Lawsuits? Would everything change?

Three hours of live television later, Kotb sat beside a visibly upset Kathie Lee Gifford.

"I'm grappling with whether I should even share something but I guess I really should," said Gifford. "The feeling when you've been—and I don't feel that Matt has betrayed us in any way at all—but when I found out that my husband had betrayed me, you question your own judgment. You question, you say, was everything a lie? And I think we have to fight against that. Very much fight against that. The man we know and adored was the man we loved and adored and continue to. I texted him this morning and said, 'I adore you.'"

The rawness of Gifford's honesty is what makes her unfiltered reaction so telling: Apparently, her mind immediately went to her own husband's infidelity because the automatic assumption in the media world was that Matt had been fired for his. If the longstanding rumors about Matt's "affairs" with female staffers had never been much of a secret, then neither could it be much of a betrayal.

*I don't feel that Matt has betrayed us in any way at all.*

---

"MOST OF US HAVE PEOPLE in our lives that we believe we know well," wrote forensic psychologist Dr. Veronique Valliere. "We judge him or her on how that person presents to us, without acknowledging that people live private lives where they show parts of themselves that are intimate, sexual and secret. This is sometimes called the 'double life' of the offender. Offenders rely on status, position and convincing others that they are incapable of offending. They put effort into their public persona so that when allegations arise, the victim is disbelieved." Moreover, successful abusers know how to appeal to the egos and empathy of those who admire them.

In her book *Unmasking the Sexual Offender*, Valliere describes a treatment session with a group of sex offenders—"they looked and acted 'normal,' chatting with each other before the group about work and sports"—in which a thirty-five-year-old offender broke down in tears describing a particularly demeaning sexual assault he had committed against a woman in a wheelchair. When Valliere asked him why he was crying, he said that he was ashamed. She asked him why.

He was ashamed, he told the group, because his victim had been "so ugly."

"I hope that answer made your blood run cold, as it did mine at that moment and still does," she wrote. Even the other offenders had been stunned into silence by the response. "I learned a profound lesson of the egocentricity of empathy, that what we call empathy is often filling the space with ourselves and not the other."

In a formal study of fifty offenders in her program, Valliere found that in 83 percent of cases, the people close to the offenders believed in their innocence, even when the offenders confessed or were caught in the act.

I'm going to repeat that: 83 percent of the time, the people close to the offenders believed in their innocence, *even when the offenders confessed or were caught in the act.*

"What makes us want to believe them?" asked Valliere. "What about us embraces their denial?"

Our decency, our humanity, our desire to see the best in everyone; our egos, our survival mechanisms, our instincts for self-preservation. We believe what we want and need to believe, and subconsciously find ways to doubt and deny what we don't or can't accept.

"It is very tempting to take the side of the perpetrator," wrote Harvard professor of psychiatry Judith Herman, MD, in her groundbreaking book, *Trauma and Recovery*. "All the perpetrator asks is that the bystander do nothing. He appeals to the universal desire to see, hear, and speak no evil. The victim, on the contrary, asks the bystander to share the burden of pain. The victim demands action, engagement, and remembering."

# FIFTEEN.

# The Attention

didn't see any of this until hours later, when I was already at my desk at work.

Around 7:40 that morning, the incessant buzzing of my phone against the floor beside my head woke me again, and in my NBC News inbox was the email that Guthrie had read aloud to *Today* viewers forty minutes earlier.

What had I done?

Then a comforting thought: If Matt had already been fired, then the nightmarish NBC tribunal I'd imagined in which I sat in a conference room as he hurled insults at me would never happen. The complaint was confidential. I would never have to talk about any of this again. I wouldn't have to relive it ever again or be haunted by it anymore. It was over.

Next, a chilling one: The email about Matt's firing had made clear that he had been fired directly in response to one complaint from one woman. Now every reporter covering his firing would be trying to find out who that woman was and what she'd alleged. I worked in a building filled with such reporters. Guthrie had just said as much: *We will be covering this story, as reporters, as journalists. I'm sure we'll be learning more details in the hours and days to come.*

Should I stay home? It would look suspicious to just no-show at work. But if I went, people would ask questions. Everybody knew that I'd been Meredith's assistant, which meant that everybody knew that I'd worked closely with Matt. Since the first Weinstein story, we'd been congregating in edit rooms and around coffee machines to talk about the latest MeToo'ed man, comparing who'd known what and who was shocked and what we believed. It would probably be all anyone would do that day. Everyone would speculate on who'd reported Matt and what was in the complaint, and *I knew.* Would I pretend I had no idea, or would I lie outright? I'd thought I was done with lies and secrets. Now I was drowning in them all over again.

I just did what I'd been doing for years and pretended none of it was happening. I put it all in a box and got dressed. Nobody had told me not to come to work—no one from either legal or human resources had emailed me at all since I'd given the complaint—so all I could do, really, was go. It was my job. But I stopped for a Bloody Mary on my way. It might have been two.

No amount of alcohol could have fortified me for what awaited at 30 Rockefeller Plaza that morning. Every photo of and reference to Matt Lauer had vanished overnight. The cardboard cutout of him that greeted tourists from the doorway of the NBC Store was gone. His ten-foot-tall *Today* promo poster in the lobby was gone. It appeared he'd even been removed from the giant digital mural in the commissary. He had been scrubbed from *Today*'s website and his social media accounts had been deleted. He was more than just gone. It was as if he had never been.

In that strange alternate reality—one in which my life and career would have been very, very different—I came to a terrifying realization.

As long as Matt had been behind the *Today* anchor desk, appearing in Super Bowl commercials and on the screens in the back of taxis—as long as he was being paid tens of millions of dollars to be watched by millions of people—then he had everything to lose. What did he have to lose now?

And if he had been fired directly because of my complaint, then he had already been confronted with it. If he'd been confronted with it, then he knew who'd gotten him fired. His only way out of all this—the disgrace, the accountability for his behavior, the tens of millions of dollars he was no longer making—would be through me. Where was I? Standing in 30 Rockefeller Plaza, surrounded by the highest concentration of Matt Lauer loyalists and beneficiaries in the world.* Nobody here was going to see me as a victim, or a whistleblower, or even a colleague. They were going to see me as a traitor. Part of me *felt* like a traitor. I'd broken the code.

That day, *The New York Times* reported that "Mr. Lauer's involvement with the woman who made the complaint began while they were in Sochi, Russia, to cover the Winter Olympics in 2014, and that their involvement continued after they returned to New York."

Sochi.

I still used one of the NBC Sports–branded Nike backpacks with the Sochi Olympic logo as a gym bag. I had a Sochi Olympics notepad somewhere on my desk. I had a Facebook album of Sochi pictures. Should I hide the backpack, get rid of the notepad, delete the album, or continue using them as though I had nothing to hide? Which would be more suspicious? Was this all in my head?

---

* According to Katie Couric's memoir, that very morning—deprived of his round-the-clock NBC car service—Matt was driven out of the city by a *Today* senior producer.

Reporting Matt was the first thing I'd done in years that I knew was the right decision. It was the only decision. Just about every choice I made in its immediate aftermath, though, would quickly prove otherwise.

The *Times* asked my lawyer for comment on Matt's firing, and because I felt guilty for not giving them my story, I thought it was the least I could do.

"My client and I met with representatives from NBC's human resources and legal departments at 6 p.m. on Monday for an interview that lasted several hours," read my lawyer's comment. "Our impression at this point is that NBC acted quickly, as all companies should, when confronted with credible allegations of sexual misconduct in the workplace."

But I didn't think about the fact that my lawyer would now immediately become one of the lawyers at the forefront of the MeToo movement, and that I'd have no control over what other interviews and press he did on his own behalf. I didn't know that the *Times* would report that "The woman met with reporters from *The Times* on Monday, but said she was not ready to discuss it publicly," which suggested that at some point I would be. I never, ever wanted to discuss it publicly. I wanted to bury it and move on with my life. The more pressing problem was that talking to reporters without permission violated NBC News policy, and I had not disclosed that I'd met with the *Times* when I reported Matt to NBC. I'd asked them to listen and do the right thing, and they'd done the right thing. Now they would think I was playing both sides against the middle, that I'd had so little faith in the company that I'd hedged my bets. I went straight to my human resources representative— the same woman who'd taken my complaint—and apologized, praying she wouldn't fire me on the spot.

She didn't. She said that she thought my mother would have

been proud of me. It was the kindest thing anyone in that building ever said to me in the eleven years that I worked there.

Then I went back to my desk. I went to the same staff meetings as everyone else, listening as network executives emphasized the amount of power Matt had wielded as anchor of *Today* and his culpability in abusing it as staffers pressed and pressed for more information about the complaint. I saw that NBC was in an impossible position: As a news organization, it was ethically required to be transparent about Matt's termination, but as a corporation, it was legally required to keep the underlying complaint confidential.

By that afternoon, media reporter Sarah Ellison had published a piece in *Vanity Fair* with more details.

"For weeks, amidst the deluge of revelations about sexual misconduct by powerful men in media, executives at NBC News had been hearing rumors of stories being reported at *Variety* and *The New York Times* about Lauer's alleged sexual relationships with NBC bookers and producers," Ellison wrote. "Those executives asked Lauer 'if there was anything that he thought we should know or could fit into this category, and he adamantly denied that there was.' According to one NBC insider, [NBC News chairman Andrew] Lack reported to other top executives that Lauer had denied any sexual impropriety.

"Then, on Monday, a woman who had already met with *The New York Times*, but who wished to remain anonymous, went with her lawyer to meet with representatives from NBC's human-resources department to lodge a formal complaint about Lauer. According to a person familiar with her complaint, neither 'rape' nor 'assault' was used in her complaint to NBC. Nevertheless, the complaint was serious and specific enough to result in the firing of NBC News's biggest star and most powerful figure. The allegation related to an inappropriate sexual relationship that started when the colleagues were covering the Olympics in Sochi."

I hadn't "wished to remain anonymous." I had *never* been anonymous: I sat face-to-face with NBC and put my name to every single allegation, risking my career and credibility in the process. What I wished was that my right to make a confidential complaint to my employer be respected by the press. And even though the *Times* and *Variety* had quickly published their investigations into Matt—which detailed many other allegations of sexual misconduct, including another sexual assault allegation—the *Vanity Fair* article supported the assumed narrative in the building, which was that Matt was no more than a lying adulterer. That made him a bad husband, sure, and an embarrassment to the show and the network, but if I hadn't said the words "rape" or "assault" in my complaint, then the assumption would be that he hadn't done anything seriously wrong; it all must have been consensual. Matt may have engaged in predatory sexual behavior, but he wasn't a predator like Harvey Weinstein—everyone would think he was just a regular guy busted for having an affair, a victim of MeToo hysteria.

Soon my lawyer would be inundated with not only interview requests, but also hate mail: *Shame on your client for throwing her c—t at a married man.* Even though trying to shame me was about as worthwhile an exercise as trying to set fire to the sun, it was as if those messages had been written by the voice in my head. Now that voice was everywhere. It was in the comments of news articles and on Twitter. I overheard it in elevators and at the commissary and in line at Starbucks.

So I left early that day, stopping on the way home to have a drink with two coworkers who knew I had made the complaint— I remember toasting my mother's memory, but little else—then I went back home to keep packing my studio apartment for my move that weekend.

The next day, Matt's public relations team released a statement. "There are no words to express my sorrow and regret for the pain I have caused others by words and actions," it read. "To the people I have hurt, I am truly sorry. As I am writing this I realize the depth of the damage and disappointment I have left behind at home and at NBC. Some of what is being said about me is untrue or mischaracterized, but there is enough truth in these stories to make me feel embarrassed and ashamed. I regret that my shame is now shared by the people I cherish dearly. Repairing the damage will take a lot of time and soul searching and I'm committed to beginning that effort. It is now my full time job. The last two days have forced me to take a very hard look at my own troubling flaws. It's been humbling. I am blessed to be surrounded by the people I love. I thank them for their patience and grace."

Oddly, I had no personal reaction to this, but a purely professional one: *Wow, his PR people did a great job.* After two months of reading the public apologies of once-powerful men, I thought that—as a piece of crisis communications—Matt's was pretty good.

Think of how difficult it is to apologize without actually taking any responsibility for your behavior—which could then be construed as an admission of liability, inviting any number of lawsuits. When he was fired, Matt's net worth was reported to be around $80 million. Multiple women were accusing him of sexual harassment and misconduct. Should any one of them file a civil suit against him, the burden of proof for a jury to find him guilty would not be "beyond a reasonable doubt" but only "a preponderance of evidence." Bill O'Reilly had personally paid one woman $32 million to settle one sexual harassment claim. Gretchen Carlson received a $20 million settlement in her sexual harassment suit against Roger Ailes. Matt faced the very real possibility of a cascade of expensive lawsuits just as he lost his $25-million-a-year revenue stream. His estimated $60–80 million net worth suddenly looked like an uncomfortably thin financial cushion.

This meant that Matt and his team would have to craft an apology with enough emotional heft to win over viewers at home—the target audience he'd need to cultivate for a potential comeback—but *without accepting any actual responsibility.* It was an incredibly fine needle to thread, but they'd done it: Matt was sorry to the "people I have hurt" and for "the pain I have caused others by words and actions," but that could mean anybody and anything, nobody and nothing, especially since "some of what is being said about me is untrue or mischaracterized." There was no promise to make amends to any of his victims, only to his family—who, conveniently, was already legally entitled to them.

I just went back to work. I had my lawyer refuse every interview request on my behalf. I deflected the awkward questions from coworkers. I told myself I would bury it and move on, just like before.

But moving on was not nearly so easy this time. The day after Matt's firing was announced, my personal cell phone buzzed with a message from Stephanie Gosk, a correspondent with NBC News' investigative unit, assuring me of her complete discretion if I wanted to speak to her off the record.

Gosk, for her part, never revealed my identity to anyone, though eventually it became an open secret among the media reporters covering MeToo. There is a well-worn trope that victims of prominent abusers come forward for "the attention," as though accusing someone famous and powerful is a quick and easy shortcut to wielding fame and power ourselves. If anything, it may be the quickest route to feeling utterly alone and powerless that I can imagine. The platform victims are given by the media is neither a pedestal for admiration nor a podium to reclaim their voice. Instead it is to be thrown under a microscope and redefined by strangers, the subject of overwhelming scrutiny, criticism, judgment, and suspicion. Intensely private pain becomes public fodder, and, at an extremely vulnerable time when they are most in need of support and understanding, victims find they are suddenly treated as socially and professionally untouchable.

I'd already spent my career in proximity to every variety of fame and had seen firsthand its impact on people. I wanted no part of it. From my comfortable place off camera or blurred in the background of red-carpet photos, I'd learned that there is no shield more precious or powerful than simple anonymity. Because of Matt's fame, the confidential complaint I'd made as a private citizen to my employer was deemed newsworthy overnight and now that shield was gone.

"The attention" meant, in my case, being hounded by reporters sliding notes under my apartment door, flooding my personal cell with texts and voicemails every time Matt appeared in public or there was another MeToo story involving NBC. That was frightening enough, but more frightening was the knowledge that at any moment, any one of those reporters could publish my name and picture and there was absolutely nothing I could do about it. Even refusing interview requests added to the shame and guilt I felt: *If you would only speak out*, the reporters would say, *you could help so many other women!* The implication was not subtle. By staying silent, I was letting Matt win, and all those women down. Did I really want to live with that for the rest of my life? On the other hand, simply by reporting Matt at all, I was cast as a shameless fame seeker, doing it for "the attention." Matt won either way.

Winning, to me, was just getting to live my life knowing that Matt would never again have the power to make me a stranger to the people I loved. Winning, to me, was getting to walk into 30 Rock every day without being afraid of losing control of my life just because a powerful man might see me waiting for an elevator. With Matt's departure, the culture at NBC was beginning to change. By January 2018, *Today* announced that Hoda Kotb would permanently replace Matt as co-anchor, creating the show's first all-female anchor team, and Libby Leist was named as the show's first female executive producer. I was thrilled. But at the same time, it seemed the Matt Lauer era at *Today* would never end. A headline soon appeared on *People*'s website: MATT LAUER SENT HODA KOTB A CONGRATULATORY TEXT AFTER 'TODAY' CO-ANCHOR ANNOUNCEMENT. Within hours, *US Weekly*, *Vulture*, and *Time* all ran their own versions.

"He texted me and he said congratulations and some really nice words, and it meant the world when I saw the text pop up," Kotb told *Entertainment Tonight*, appearing truly elated. "My heart just went like, you know, it meant the world to see that."

". . . You know, Matt is our good friend and continues to be, and I think for both of us, we've just been trying to navigate this time and honor our love and friendship with Matt, but also understand and try to learn more about these circumstances," added Guthrie.

I imagined that, somewhere, Matt was breathing a sigh of relief. No victim in her right mind would talk about him now, when *Today*'s anchors were publicly professing their love for Matt. Somehow, I felt responsible. Why hadn't I reached out to either Guthrie or Kotb myself, so they would at least hear both sides of the story? Why hadn't I had the courage to talk about what had happened publicly, so they wouldn't have been put in this position? My silence had made them vulnerable and allowed Matt to muddy the waters. Once again, I'd failed to protect the talent. It was all my fault.

---

"HI BROOKE, THIS IS Ralph Ortega from the *National Enquirer*. I'm investigating a story about Matt Lauer and your role in his termination. Please call me at this number. I'm on deadline. Thank you."

It was April 2018, and I was in Los Angeles doing field interviews, sleeping on my brother's couch so that I could spend time with my nearly seven-month-old nephew. I was still on Eastern time, and though it was barely eight a.m. on the West Coast, I was already sitting at a coffee shop near my brother's apartment, revising my questions for an interview later that day with Suzanne Somers at her house in Palm Springs. Then my phone buzzed against the metal café table, and I stared at the screen in denial for a good, long time. I am a normal person, I told myself. This must be a mistake. What could the *Enquirer* possibly want with me?

I flipped the phone over as though the text had been a figment of my imagination and finished my work. I reviewed the route to Palm Springs, studied the traffic, tried to decide what time I would leave, and told myself I would deal with the text message in the car. How would I deal with it? I had no idea. I would call my lawyer. I would call NBC. Then I would go on with my day, as though none of it was happening.

That was the plan, anyway. I ran into the first problem as soon as I got back to my brother's apartment and found it eerily silent. Everyone was still asleep. No one was watching. There was nothing between me and the overwhelming, all-consuming rage.

I walked into the kitchen, set the coffee on the counter, and my knees crumbled beneath me. I curled into a ball on the floor, my eyes fixed on the line where the linoleum met the bottom of the dishwasher. As soon as I tried to inhale, my torso was racked by giant, rolling sobs as I gasped for breath. I didn't want to wake the baby, so I bit into the top of my right knee. This was how my brother found me.

I remember the rest of that day in disparate images of the random objects I'd locked my eyes onto while trying to keep myself under control: the front of an Albertsons as I sat in a parking lot and cried; a row of Tesla charging stations as I sat in the car and cried; the takeaway coffee cup from the shop near my brother's apartment that I clutched all day as though it were a child's teddy bear, reminding myself of what it would do to my brother to lose both his sister and mother within months. My brother, though, remembers that day well.

"I remember until everything fell apart, it was actually a nice visit," he says. It was only the second time I'd seen his son, born barely a month after my mother's death. "It had been long enough since Mom died that it wasn't so fresh, and at some level, life was going on. Then, the *Enquirer* thing happened and you got the calls, didn't know what to do, were on the phone with your boss and someone from human resources, and they were trying to convince you to fly back to New York. They told you that under no circumstances were you to drive yourself to Palm Springs while you were upset. You lied and said that I would drive you, but I had the baby and there was no way I could take a baby to Suzanne Somers's house. Your boss tried to get you to cancel the interview but you wouldn't, because you'd done all the work and it was important for your story. You put on makeup in our bathroom and you cried at the same time, so you kept having to stop and start over. Then you just left, drove to Palm Springs, did your interview, and came home twelve hours later like none of it had ever happened."

I can remember him standing in the doorway of his spare bathroom, watching me try to put makeup on my contorted, soaking-wet face and looking as though he was earnestly trying to decide whether I was having a mental breakdown. Then I just got into my rental car and left. My most immediate concern was that I wouldn't be able to drink all day because I had to drive to Palm Springs and back. Then my phone started ringing.

First it was the main NBC number in New York, and then it was my editor's cell number. Then it was somebody I'd worked with years ago. Then it was my executive producer. My phone rang and rang—production assistants, associate producers, editors, former coworkers, seemingly anyone who was connected to me online or credited alongside me on IMDb. They were all being called by the *Enquirer*, which was describing me as Matt Lauer's mistress who'd gotten him fired. The questions themselves, as they were relayed to me, were just as degrading. Had I deserved to be promoted to producer, or was that a payoff to keep me quiet about my affair with Matt Lauer? Why had I reported him when the affair had helped my career? Did I actually do any work at NBC, or was my job a vanity role?

"One associate producer came to me directly and I immediately took her to human resources," says my executive producer. "I was so frightened for you. I wanted to go out there so you wouldn't be alone, but I couldn't leave my son. Human resources wanted you to fly home that day, but you said no. You had shoots to do. You told us your brother would come with you to your shoot in Palm Springs, but I am pretty sure you went to that shoot without him."

Of course I did. I drove to Palm Springs, I did the shoot, I drove back, then we all watched a David Attenborough documentary while I knitted a baby blanket for a pregnant coworker.

"Eventually the *Enquirer* ran an article about the woman who brought Matt Lauer down," my executive producer continues. "It didn't use your name but it said it was Meredith's assistant, so it could only be you. A friend of mine at *Today* had been sent a press release about the piece and she sent me a screenshot of it. . . . The next morning everyone knew that it was Meredith's assistant who made the complaint, and that it was you. But it was clear it was getting more and more difficult for you to work at 30 Rock. Going to the commissary or the edit rooms made you anxious. You were living all the time in that awful Sochi space. You were drinking. You were making yourself vomit. You were self-destructive. It was time for you to leave, and I know that broke your heart."

From within the bubble of 30 Rock, reporting Matt—who

seemed to be dearly missed, his absence and the heydays of his success openly lamented by many—felt as though it had been pointless. Then *The Washington Post* published a poignant reminder of
why I had done it.

"Thirty-five current and former NBC staffers said that while
some of [Lauer's] relationships were consensual, some were not,"
wrote media reporter Sarah Ellison. "Twelve women interviewed
said they were sexually harassed but did not report it. Three of the
twelve told The Post about sexual advances from Lauer. One woman
said that the anchor exposed himself in his office and asked her to
touch him, and a second said he had sex with her in the middle of
the day in his office—alleged incidents that have not been previously
reported."

Though I had declined to be interviewed for the *Washington Post*
article, Matt—evidently done with his soul-searching—provided a
fulsome quote.

"I have made no public comments on the many false stories
from anonymous or biased sources that have been reported about
me over these past several months," he said. "I remained silent in
an attempt to protect my family from further embarrassment and
to restore a small degree of the privacy they have lost. But defending my family now requires me to speak up. I fully acknowledge
that I acted inappropriately as a husband, father and principal at
NBC. However I want to make it perfectly clear that any allegations or reports of coercive, aggressive or abusive actions on my
part, at any time, are absolutely false."

Matt no longer appeared to be "humbled" by his own "troubling flaws," or "truly sorry" to the people he hurt. Here was a
man who, almost as an aside, acknowledged that he had been fired
as a direct result of his own actions, but in the same breath declared
himself a victim of "anonymous or biased sources." These accounts
of Matt's behavior—dozens between three different stories in three

different outlets—were not blind items in the *Enquirer* but fully reported investigative pieces in the *Times*, the *Post*, and *Variety*. These weren't tabloids but reputable publications in which unnamed sources are vetted and verified just like any others; they were "anonymous" only to the reader. As a journalist, Matt would have known that. And was anyone who didn't accept his narrative at face value a "biased" source?

Two weeks later, NBC released its internal investigation into Matt's sexual misconduct. The company found his accusers credible. Once again, I refused all interview requests and declined to comment. Once again, Matt released a statement, his third in six months.

"There are aspects of the NBC report with which I clearly disagree. However, I spent 25 wonderful years at the network, 20 of those at 'Today,' and I'm extremely proud of what we accomplished as a team. On November 29, 2017, I was terminated by NBC after admitting to past relationships with co-workers. A day later I took responsibility for those relationships, apologized to the people I hurt and promised to begin the process of repairing the damage I had caused my family," he said. "I have worked every day since then to honor that promise."

Next, Matt appeared on Radio New Zealand to argue against a proposal to allow New Zealanders expanded access through his $13 million, 16,000-acre ranch to reach a public park. Once again, he presented himself as the victim of his own actions.

"I believe the groups that are behind this are in some ways unfortunately taking advantage of some difficult times I've been through over the past six months, and I think they see me as an easy mark," Matt said. Referring to the circumstances of his dismissal, he added, ". . . I will tell people they don't know the circumstances of that situation. I promise you, people don't know. And I'm not at liberty to talk, nor would I want to talk about that."

In the eight months since he'd been fired, Matt had now spoken publicly four separate times. I'd said nothing. Depending on the day, I was portrayed in the press either as Matt Lauer's mistress or his victim, and depending on what you'd heard, I deserved either scorn or compassion, public humiliation or privacy. I was no longer a person but a story, a blank canvas onto which Matt's narrative could be projected by strangers. And even though Matt's accuser had been identified as Meredith's assistant in Sochi—and there were pictures online of me in Sochi, named as Meredith's assistant—to refute anything that was said would allow the press to claim I was outing myself, playing into the attention-seeking trope and forfeiting whatever privacy and dignity I had left.

It took a toll. I was functioning, but barely, and not at all without alcohol. I wasn't anything close to a partner, sister, daughter, or friend to anyone. Without my mother, my father seemed to have given up. When he stopped answering his phone—which I hadn't even noticed—my brother called the police, who found him delirious and dehydrated on his floor after a fall. He developed a MRSA infection that spread to the valves of his heart. He struggled after open-heart surgery and was never the same. It fell to my brother to clean out my parents' house and put it up for sale, while managing my father's hospitalization and taking care of a new baby. I flew out to help him for one weekend, and I drank the entire time.

Secrets spill from one part of your life to another, contaminating what you think you are protecting until you no longer know where the truth ends and the lies begin. I could not keep the past from contaminating the present, the lies from staining the truth, the hate I felt for myself from tainting the love I felt for the few people left in my life. I could never go back to being the person I had been, and I did not recognize the person I had become. I was not safe to love and impossible to fully know. I couldn't do it anymore.

I finished my final story and asked for a leave of absence from NBC, but without the structure and routine of going to work every day and having some semblance of a purpose, I fell apart. My mother was gone, and my father appeared to be following her. In the year since I'd met and fallen in love with my boyfriend, I'd watched as his hair turned gray and his life was consumed by my secrets and my pain. Now that I wasn't going to work, I watched the look of relief on his face every time he came home and found that I hadn't hurt myself or drunk myself to death. I could see that being with me was slowly ruining his life and I tried to push him away, but he would not go. I felt as though all I'd ever done was hurt and shame and humiliate the people I loved. I didn't want to live anymore. I was done. But the people around me intervened and got me to a hospital. Because of them, I am here.

To tell this story is to conjure, again and again, the memories and images of the past that I tried for years to bury and forget. But in all these years, there is still no image more painful to me than the memory of myself sitting blankly in the back of a cab, indifferent to where I was being taken, as the cabdriver put his hand through the small window into the back seat to hold mine. Then he asked to pray with me.

Had those people not helped me, my beautiful children would not be here. I would never have known the incomparable moments with them to come—each so happy, so precious, and so beautiful that every day I wonder how the very same world that put me in that cab could behold such pure, unbridled, miraculous joy. My mother had tried to tell me of those moments. *This is gold*, she wrote in the letter on pink stationery—then, in a final act of mothering, saved those words for nearly thirty years, when I would most need to hear them.

# SIXTEEN.

# Getting Out of Survival Mode

*Why Textbook Signs of Trauma Are Confused for Character Flaws*

Six months earlier, a friend had casually asked how I was dealing with all the "trauma."

I had no idea what she was talking about.

*Fine*, I said, relieved. Apparently "trauma" was one of the few problems I didn't have. Even the word annoyed me: It rhymed with "drama" and it sounded precious. Whenever I heard doctors say "contusion" instead of bruise or "laceration" instead of cut, I would shout in my mind, *Just use normal words!* This was no different. Bad things happened in life. That was it.

Now I was in a psych ward, and though I knew I needed to be there, I didn't see how anyone could possibly help.* There was

---

* Journalistic housekeeping: The personal narrative portions of this chapter describing my extremely humbling time in the psych ward are—clearly—not intended as an exhaustive clinical analysis of my psychiatric state but as an account of my struggle to overcome avoidance and accept help. While I referenced my own notes and records, I did not attempt to interview my clinicians, and I intentionally limited narrative

nothing wrong with me. What was wrong *was* me. There was no diagnosis or cure for a ruined life or being a bad person. Sure, I drank too much, but practically everyone I knew drank too much to some degree. It wasn't as though I was physically dependent on alcohol, either, because I didn't have withdrawal symptoms. I was just screwed up.

It was not as though I did not want help. At home was the man I wanted to marry and the dream of the children I wanted to have, but I still thought that ship had sailed in Sochi. Now I was broken, defective, ruined. The only decent thing to do was to get out of his life, since no amount of cruel, self-destructive behavior could convince him to see me as worthless as I felt. The more he loved me, the more I felt like a fraud. It was the same with my brother. The damage was done, there was no changing the past, and even if I could undo what had happened, I'd probably just find some other way to ruin everything again. There was no point. I thought I'd be discharged in time for happy hour.

But I wasn't sent home. I gave example after example of how horrible I was—all the inexplicable, inexcusable things I'd done over the past three years—and the staff looked oddly unsurprised. It wasn't like I was *crazy* crazy. I still didn't see why I was there. I wasn't hearing voices or having delusions. I just couldn't keep pretending. I'd been flailing frantically for years to keep my head above water and instead I pulled everyone under who'd tried to pull me out. I was ready to let myself sink.

Eventually I found myself in a tiny room sitting against a cinder-block wall, trying to figure out what else I could say to get

details to avoid violating the privacy of others. I will forever be grateful for the care and support I received during this time. Though I have deliberately avoided any identifying information here, to those who helped me: Thank you for saving my life.

the doctors to understand that they could stop looking for a diagnosis. Then I realized that no exhaustive search for one appeared to be underway. The more I argued, the more confident they seemed: It was, among other things, textbook post-traumatic stress disorder. Those other things—feeling suicidal, anxious, depressed, unable to cope without alcohol and endlessly devastating paroxysms of grief—were not small problems, but neither were they surprising nor difficult to accept. The mere suggestion of PTSD was another story entirely.

I wasn't having it. A bruise was a bruise, a cut was a cut, I absolutely did not have PTSD. Soldiers had PTSD. I'd read *Mrs. Dalloway*. I'd watched *Platoon* dozens of times with my former-Marine, Vietnam-vet father. PTSD was what happened when bad things happened to good people, and while it was a generous thought, I was the only common denominator in all my problems. Thanks, but no thanks. The staff seemed nonplussed, and I saw that I was about to be told something that I did not want to hear. *You've been doing it your way, and how's that working out for you?*

Well, I was in a damn psych ward, wearing bright yellow sticky socks and showering with Johnson's baby wash. Not great.

Yet apparently PTSD was highly treatable. I did drink too much, but abusing alcohol was common alongside PTSD, and that was treatable, too. I was not irredeemable. It was only *after* Sochi that I'd gone off the rails, doing things I didn't understand, becoming someone I didn't know, drinking while I was awake and taking pills to sleep. Any reasonable person could see that there was some clear cause and effect at work, and that my way of dealing with it—namely, drinking and saying I was fine—was not working. If I couldn't acknowledge that, okay, but they suggested I stay there until I could.

I stayed for ten days.

TRAUMA HAS BECOME SUCH a buzzword that it feels almost disingenuous to use it. If everything is traumatic, then nothing is traumatic. But even for those who study it, it's difficult to define.

"For most people it means a really bad event or experience, usually one that 'sticks,' that you don't forget, and that can have an enduring impact on you," wrote Bruce Perry, MD, PhD, in his book, *What Happened to You? Conversations on Trauma, Resilience, and Healing*, coauthored with Oprah Winfrey. ". . . Yet trauma has been hard for the academic world to define and therefore understand in its full scope. Part of the challenge is that the 'bad event' is subjective."

How can that be? His example: During a fire at an elementary school, a veteran firefighter puts out the fire as a matter of routine, while a child who witnesses his classroom burst into flames experiences feelings of intense fear, confusion, and helplessness. The trauma here is not the fire itself but the way the individual experiences it, and whether and how their stress response is activated. For the firefighter, the fire feels predictable and controllable, and so is not traumatic. For the child, it is the opposite—unpredictable and beyond his control—so it is. How can the same event be traumatic for one person but not the other? The answer comes down to what the Substance Abuse and Mental Health Services Administration (SAMHSA) calls its "Three E's" definition of trauma: the Event, how that event is Experienced, and the Effects.

"Not very simple or satisfying, I know," continued Dr. Perry. "The dilemma of defining trauma is not completely solved, and that leads to continued confusing use of the term."

At least it's not just me.

But there is something incredibly simple and satisfying about thinking about trauma this way, and that's understanding that our reactions to traumatic events are not moral or rational choices we make, but biological responses we experience. We think our reactions in high-stakes moments tell us who we are. Are we brave? Are we cowards? Are we trustworthy? We might then look at the firefighter and wonder what kind of a human being could walk into a burning elementary school *without* having an intense emotional response. After all, this is a fire threatening the lives of hundreds of helpless children. Or the child might look back and wonder if his terrified reaction means he is a coward. Otherwise, why didn't he try to fight the fire himself?

But if we recognize our reactions to trauma for what they are—biological stress responses—we can understand that the two wildly different reactions of the firefighter and the little boy to the exact same threat are not reflections of their characters but their experiences. The firefighter has encountered fires before and was expecting to encounter this one, so he saw the fire as predictable and not that much of a threat. The child went to school to learn and play, so experienced the fire as both an unexpected shock and a totally unpredictable, life-threatening danger. But his traumatized reaction to it says nothing about his integrity or courage. It just says that his body's stress response system didn't have nearly as much experience responding to fires as the firefighter's.

Yet, too often, we take our reactions in these moments to be definitive revelations of who and what we really are, and when we're disappointed, we can carry the shame of it for the rest of our lives. A person who's being sexually assaulted freezes due to tonic immobility and then blames themselves for not screaming, or they "wait it out" instead of fighting someone they can't overpower and then blame themselves for being weak. But, again, often these are not conscious choices. The brain registers a threat, the reacting part of the brain overwhelms the thinking part, and we react without really thinking. Our conscious selves take a back seat to our survival mechanisms and our ideas of character and courage go out the window. If you survive long enough to second-guess your responses, then your brain did its job perfectly.

"I think that the fundamental thing that's important to understand is that your body has all of these incredible coping mechanisms that help you make it through life," says Dr. Perry. "Stress is an essential element of healthy development. What we know is that the pattern of stress makes a big difference in how your body makes long-term adaptations.* Predictable, moderate stressors help you learn to regulate and build your stress response, almost like weight lifting builds muscle. But when stress occurs that is completely unpredictable or prolonged and we're always walking on eggshells, that will lead to atypical responses. You'll become more reactive and more hypervigilant. You'll have difficulties sleeping. A whole cascade of problems can occur."

Over time, our bodies hone and develop those responses until they become so subconscious and ubiquitous that we mistake them for personality quirks and character flaws.

"I love to unpack common behaviors that people dismiss as idiosyncrasies and explain them in terms of what is happening within the nervous system," says Louise Godbold, executive director of the nonprofit Echo, which provides training on trauma and resilience. "Once you realize that what's happening is perfectly normal, it's such a relief, because people think they're going crazy when they're

---

* Scientists conceptualize stress in three distinct patterns: positive (short-lived, adverse experiences, such as meeting new people or getting a shot), tolerable (more intense but still short-lived adverse experiences, such as the death of a family member, a car accident, or a family disruption such as a separation or divorce), and toxic (intense adverse experiences sustained over a long period of time, such as abuse or neglect). Our level of exposure to these stress patterns during childhood development can impact how we react to stress for the rest of our lives: a 1997 CDC/Kaiser Permanente

not. Things like startling easily or always waiting for the other shoe to drop, those are forms of hypervigilance—being hyper alert to potential threats."

"People protect themselves by starting to do these maladaptive things, and often they don't understand what's going on," says Dr. Perry. "They say something's wrong with me. When somebody's drinking too much and acting like a jerk, you're not going to really understand what's happening by going, 'Hey, what's wrong with you?' The best way to understand them is to say, 'Was there something that happened to you that led to this change in behavior? What happened, that all of a sudden you're like this?' When you start to do that, you realize that a person likely would not act that way unless there was some reason for it."

Whatever those changes—whether it's drinking all the time, acting erratically, or finding ways to push people away or alienate them—they do not make you a bad person. Nor do they mean that you've become forever alienated from who you once were. They mean only that you became the person you needed to be to get through a given situation at a given time.

"Once you understand that those circumstances are over," says Dr. Perry, "instead of asking yourself, 'What's wrong with me?' you can ask, 'How do I get back to who I really am, and what's core to me? And is there a way to actually grow from what happened?'"

---

study found that exposure to toxic stress, or Adverse Childhood Experiences (ACEs), leads to permanent changes in the development of the brain, including a low threshold for stress throughout life, a suppressed immune response, chronic health problems, and cognitive deficits that continue into adulthood. About 64 percent of American adults reported experiencing at least one type of ACE and nearly one in six reported experiencing four or more. To better understand the impact of trauma, ACEs are a helpful place to start. Visit the CDC's website (cdc.gov) for more information on ACEs, or take the ACEs quiz at acesaware.org.

That is post-traumatic growth, which can make us stronger and more resilient. But sometimes, even when you understand the threatening circumstances are over, your stress responses continue to kick in and the same subconscious survival mechanisms that helped you survive in the past start to jeopardize your ability to function in the present. That's PTSD. The kind of traumatic event that can lead to it will usually involve an injury or the possibility of an injury, fearing for your survival or the survival of someone you care about, or a threat to your physical integrity. The overarching characteristic shared by all traumatic events is a feeling of power- lessness, fear, and loss of control that results from being unable to prevent or change its outcome. Most of us will experience a trau- matic event in our lives—about 70 percent—but only 6 to 8 percent will ever develop post-traumatic stress disorder. When the trau- matic event is rape, though, that number climbs to almost half, making it an order of magnitude more likely to cause PTSD than other kinds of traumatic events.

Why? One reason—among many—is because so many victims understand right away that they're never going to be believed over their abuser.

"That makes you feel even more helpless," says Dr. Perry. "There's a certain degree of helplessness and paralysis from the be- ginning. That's what chronic abusers exploit."

PTSD is now the fourth most commonly diagnosed psychiatric disorder in America, and given the way it is diagnosed—for more than one month, patients must display a certain number of symptoms in each of four symptom clusters that contain a total of twenty pos- sible symptoms—it's a diagnosis that can seem like something of a catchall. A *New Yorker* analysis pointed out that, with 636,120 pos- sible symptom combinations, 636,120 different people could con- ceivably have a unique set of symptoms and yet share the same diagnosis. But it's important to keep these numbers in perspective. While PTSD is the fourth most diagnosed psychiatric disorder, it represents only 3.5 percent of adults overall, a tiny fraction of the nearly 70 percent of people who experience traumatic events and nowhere near the numbers of people who experience anxiety or depression.

Why do some people develop PTSD and not others? Most people who experience traumatic events compartmentalize what happened only as long as they need to. Eventually, they allow themselves to think about and process what happened. When they're reminded of what happened, they can recognize that it's no longer happening and that it's not likely to happen again. They can be reminded of the past without constantly reliving it or flashing back to it. For a person with PTSD, it's different. Instead of processing what happened, they bury it. The fear and pain they experienced festers and grows larger and larger in their minds instead of being put into perspective. The same psychological defense mechanisms that worked so well in the short term—avoiding, numbing, burying, compartmentalizing—become a way of life. They get stuck in survival mode and can't get out of it, long after the danger has passed.

"I always like to take things back to, and forgive the big word, our phylogenetic roots—we're animals and we live in a dangerous world," says clinical psychologist Dr. Barbara Rothbaum, the director of the Trauma and Anxiety Recovery Program at Emory University School of Medicine as well as the Emory Healthcare Veterans Program. "It is important to remember where the danger was, and what we did to survive. The events that can lead to PTSD are so big and so important that it's kind of like they're stamped on our brain indelibly. It doesn't mean anything is wrong or broken. It doesn't mean people are weak or not coping or they're wimps. It's not that way at all. It's the opposite of that."

In other words, it is not the weak who develop PTSD, but the people who hold out the longest without getting help or even acknowledging that something is wrong. It's those who hide their suffering so well that they find ways to function indefinitely despite it, even if those ways are ultimately self-destructive. Again, *if you are still here, then your brain did its job perfectly.*

But surviving and living are not the same thing, and it is a cruel irony that the same mechanisms that enabled a person with PTSD to survive and function for so long will become the cause of so much suffering in the end. They work so well that when the time comes for survival to stop and living to begin again, they can't *stop* working. Eventually they become second nature, seemingly indistinguishable from our personalities, even when they no longer make sense. Without even realizing it, avoiding the reality of what happened becomes a central tenet of our ability to function. Even those who don't develop full-blown PTSD after a traumatic event can still struggle with this.

"There's nothing wrong with the way you responded to danger," says Godbold. "It's just that now, those responses are no longer life-serving."

But even though PTSD is a serious and complex psychiatric disorder, that still doesn't mean that there is something wrong with you or that you are crazy. It just means that you need some support.

---

EVEN I HAD TO ADMIT that the cause-and-effect rationale was difficult to deny. Before Sochi, had I depended on alcohol to function? Hated myself, behaved with an almost compulsive recklessness, needed prescriptions to sleep, struggled with nightmares? No; no, no, no, and no.

One by one, I went through each of the seemingly inexplicable new personality traits I'd brought home from Sochi. Drinking to get through the day was a numbing behavior, which falls under the avoidance symptom cluster for PTSD. My ironclad insistence that I was fine, that I could just bury what happened and move on because good quarterbacks have short memories—all that was avoidance, too. My erratic, reckless choices, the recurrent nightmares—these were forms of reexperiencing, part of the intrusive symptom cluster. The years of constant paranoia that Matt might reinsert himself into my life and destroy it on a whim, my compulsive need to make sure he was "okay" with me, the insomnia and self-destructive behavior, even changing my appearance and becoming more sexually assertive so that I'd never get caught off guard by a man's sexual advances again—these were forms of hypervigilance, another symptom cluster (also called hyperarousal).

The fourth symptom cluster—negative mood symptoms or, as the DSM-5 describes it, "negative alterations in cognitions and mood associated with the traumatic event(s), beginning or worsening after the traumatic event(s) occurred"—sounds like utter gobbledygook. In plain English, it's viewing and understanding the world differently after the trauma, seeing it as a more dangerous, frightening, and hopeless place. Moreover, it's viewing and understanding yourself differently. It might be believing that you're a bad person because of what happened to you or how you reacted to it, or that these things could only have happened *because* you were a bad person all along. It's that voice in your head that tells you there is something deeply, profoundly wrong with you, that you're to blame because of what you did or did not do to survive. It's hating yourself.

Viewed this way, it's not hard to see how seamlessly these behaviors lend themselves to judgment from others, too—and why they make victims so easy to discredit in the public eye and in court. To react in utterly predictable ways to sexual assault is to also inhabit exactly the kinds of behaviors that are often used to discredit a victim's character and paint them as unreliable witnesses to their own experiences.

One by one, I saw how my train wreck of self-destructive behaviors could be translated into concrete, clinical terms. They weren't inexplicable at all; they were about power and control. The pattern was undeniable. Whenever I went out drinking and no man took advantage of me, or when I told a man 'no' or that something 'wasn't my thing' and I was listened to and respected, I'd felt a small part of my power return. My reckless choices were a way of proving to myself that I could still be vulnerable in a world of men without being preyed upon by men, and despite the undeniable risks, I then felt a little bit safer in the world. That was why I kept doing it. I'd lost power and control in Sochi, and it was a void I was still trying to fill, all these years later. I had not come back from Sochi a different person, but a different version of myself: the person I had to be to cope with an impossible situation. That didn't mean I was a terrible person. It meant I was a person who'd been through something terrible and now needed some help.

That changed everything.

MeToo had showed me that all the hideous, confusing, messy circumstances of what happened in Sochi were not weird aberrations but extremely common characteristics of sexual harassment and assault, that all the seemingly incomprehensible ways I had felt and reacted to them were not incomprehensible at all but almost textbook reactions to sexual assault. In the psych ward, learning about trauma, I was discovering that all those incomprehensible things which felt for years like someone else's compulsions I was powerless to stop—these, too, were textbook. More than that, they were easily diagnosed symptoms of a highly treatable disorder that was very common after sexual assault.

For years, I'd felt so alone and beyond help, when I had never

been even remotely alone or beyond help. The signs were there all
along. I'd just been too ashamed to see them.

———

I WAS STILL IN THE PSYCH WARD, and still mostly convinced that
all this trauma stuff was bullshit, when I learned of Barbara Rothbaum's work. She's published hundreds of scientific papers and
eleven books on the treatment of PTSD, including (with Edna
Foa, PhD) *Treating the Trauma of Rape: Cognitive-Behavioral Therapy for PTSD*, a seminal guide for clinicians. One of the doctors
mentioned that I should check out her work and, clueless to the
fact that she was one of the world's leading researchers on the treatment of PTSD, I'd casually called her from the psych ward. She
called me back and patiently answered my questions, then referred
me to a trauma specialist in New York.

It was a surreal experience, then, to send her an interview request years later while reporting this book and realize I'd actually
already talked to her—from the psych ward, in my sticky socks.
When I mentioned this to her, she laughed. It seems I was not the
first skeptical patient she'd encountered.

The first and hardest obstacle, she explained, was avoidance—
the insistence that we're "fine" and "handling it" and don't need help.

"People have a natural tendency to avoid what scares them and
makes them feel terrible," she says. "To push it away and keep going through. But if you do that, then you don't process it and it can
fester, and that's where I think it can haunt people . . . We begin to
believe our stories of what happened to us, rather than understanding what really happened. There's so much guilt involved, and
shame, in the events that lead to PTSD. I think there's something
so healing about saying your most embarrassing, shameful, scary

moments out loud to a person trying to be helpful. The more we can do that, the distress decreases."

That process is known as prolonged exposure therapy (PET)—slowly reexposing yourself to the trauma in a controlled, safe environment, sort of like getting back on the horse after a fall. But though exposure therapy is considered the first-line treatment for PTSD and has more empirical support than any other treatment method, it also has a very high dropout rate in an outpatient setting. Symptoms can even be intensified for those who drop out prematurely.

"Exposure therapy can sometimes make the patient feel worse, at least initially," says Rothbaum. "It's a good worse, like when you work out and your muscles are tired, but that's frightening, especially without the right support. And it's still the nature of PTSD that people are avoidant, especially if it's hard to get to an appointment every week and you don't really want to go through it. But if you stay with the therapy, it works. And people have to be ready for it at the right time."

I was ready for it. For me, the psych ward was rock bottom, and I wanted the most direct route out, even if that route was the steepest. Prolonged exposure therapy—which was readily available in New York and covered by my insurance—was that way out. But it is not easy. At the time, I often described it as torture. It is no small thing, to walk into a room and functionally rip open a wound, then have to walk right back out into the world forty-five minutes later feeling as vulnerable as you've ever felt in your life. Getting myself to those sessions every week was one of the hardest things I've ever done. Sometimes I would leave a session, go home, and stay in bed for the rest of the day. Or I'd go straight to the gym and stay there for hours, working out until I could barely walk home. But I was only able to do whatever I needed to do to get back to those sessions every week because I wasn't working, had a support-ive partner, and didn't yet have children who needed me to come home and be their loving, responsive mother as soon as I walked in the door. It helped that I understood that the therapy was intense because it wasn't meant to last forever, and it gradually got easier. Each week, I felt better and stronger, and more my old self. In the end, it gave me back my life.

But I would never judge anyone for dropping out, especially if they don't have adequate support as I did. Rothbaum is continuing to develop treatment approaches to address these issues.

If exposure therapy is not a fit for you for whatever reason—and it is not a fit for everyone—there are other options. A gentler, empirically supported alternative is cognitive processing therapy (CPT), which provides specific techniques for evaluating and chang-ing upsetting thoughts without having to repeatedly reexperience the traumatic event. Other effective treatment options include eye movement desensitization and reprocessing therapy (EMDR) and the emotional freedom technique, also known as tapping, which draws from both exposure therapy and CPT. None are easy, though some are easier than others. But it's only through accepting and processing what happened in the past, rather than trying to bury it altogether, that you can truly move on.*

"There are different camps within the trauma world of what works, but the message that is most important to me is that

---

* One caveat here that I would be remiss not to share: Seeking treatment can be a double-edged sword. Without the psych ward or trauma therapy, I know that I would not have the life I have today. Thanks to the therapy, I was able to heal and move on. Three years after I left the psych ward, my daughter was born and my husband and I applied for life insurance. He was approved immediately, while I was denied by multiple companies due to my documented history of suicidal episodes, depression, PTSD, and the alcohol abuse that accompanied it. It is impossible to describe how

whichever treatment makes sense to you, the treatment works," says Rothbaum.*

From choosing a treatment method to choosing to seek treatment at all, that element of choice is critical, and is itself a source of healing and empowerment. Since the overarching characteristic of a traumatic event is a feeling of powerlessness, the act of making the decision to face it—and choosing how to do so—is critical to how well the treatment works. If you feel cornered or forced, if the treatment doesn't make sense to you or you're not ready for it, not only will it not work, but it can backfire and set you back further.

"It is a bit of trial and error," says Godbold. "Remember again, the cornerstone of any trauma recovery is giving back power and control to the survivor. The more control you can give people over their own healing, the more they realize how clever their bodies and brains are. Just as trauma rewires our brains, we can rewire our brains back. We can rebuild."

---

devastating those rejection letters were to a new mother. The shame of those denials, and the guilt of what they potentially meant for my child, left me catatonic for days. It's a cruel Catch-22: Had I never gotten treatment, I would likely have no life to insure and no reason to insure it, but I'd have no trouble getting approved for a life insurance policy. Beyond life insurance, certain jobs may also require you to disclose your mental health history, psychiatric hospitalizations, or past issues with substance abuse, and those disclosures can disqualify you from consideration, even though the employer may acknowledge that the traumatic event was not your fault and that seeking treatment for it was the responsible course of action. It is unfair. I have no redeeming lesson to offer here. It's just one more painful reality that would be dishonest to leave unacknowledged.

* Her 2020 book with Sheila A. M. Rauch, *PTSD: What Everyone Needs to Know*, offers an overview of different treatment options and is a helpful, accessible place to start, and for those not ready or able to begin therapy, their 2023 book *Making Meaning of Difficult Experiences: A Self-Guided Program* is a step-by-step workbook that can be done privately and at your own pace.

YEARS AFTER THE PSYCH WARD, this is my definition of trauma: It's the unspeakable part of your past that you will do just about anything to hide from the people you love. For me, it was the moment in Sochi when I just gave up, or later when I saw the towels and froze in submission and shame, or when Matt first pushed me to my knees in his office and I stayed there; it was that I'd allowed such degrading, humiliating things to happen at all, and all the reckless, self-destructive things I felt I had to do to live with them.

It can feel like saying these things aloud will literally kill you, as though no one who hears them could ever accept or love you, and that you'll be alone forever. One day, you might rationally understand that what happened wasn't your fault, that you didn't deserve it, and that how you reacted didn't make you a bad person but a human being—but only if you confront what happened and get the help you need to process it. I promise you, no one—even if they don't understand or can't forgive—will ever be as cruel as the voices in your head, and nothing will ever be as terrifying as the moment you begin speaking these unspeakable things aloud.

I have been there, sitting in the psych ward in my sticky socks, saying these things—and worse—to my own brother and to the man I loved, fully believing I would never see either of them again afterward. You can't change the past, but it will not always hurt so much, and you do not have to be alone because of it. When you're ready, you can have your life back. You can have yourself back. You can be truly known and still love and be loved in return.

You can do this.

SEVENTEEN.

# A Survivor Mission

*Choosing Between Healing and Justice*

Textbook sexual harassment, textbook sexual misconduct, textbook acquaintance rape, textbook sexual trauma, textbook post-traumatic stress disorder: Where the hell was this textbook, and why hadn't I read it?

Clearly, I wasn't the only one to have missed it. Since MeToo, I've been hearing the same story again and again. *Something like that happened to me, and I became a completely different person after that.* Women—and a few men—have told me that it happened to them in high school, in college, and at their first jobs. It happened with their bosses, with a teacher or a coach or someone else they trusted that they couldn't afford to alienate. They went back, too, and then they blamed themselves, and for years thought they were the only ones. All along I thought I was the exception, when really I was more like the rule.

I thought back to Mimi Alford and Elizabeth Smart and all the questions about their stories that I'd never bothered to ask because

I thought I already knew the answers. I thought about the years since Sochi when I'd known the truth about the rumors about Matt and still said and done nothing. First I'd allowed him to take advantage of my ignorance, then I'd enabled him to hide behind my shame. Even after he was fired, I'd said nothing and tried to move on with my life, but he certainly hadn't been silent. He'd gone from being "truly sorry" and "ashamed" to "an easy mark," and it felt as though his increasingly self-serving version of events was becoming the accepted narrative by default. He was *still* benefitting from my silence and shame, while those who'd been through the same thing, who were facing the same kinds of impossible choices I'd faced in 2014 and 2017, would continue to feel just as alone and crazy as I had.

I'd been silent and complicit long enough.

What did I have to lose, anyway? My career had already been destroyed by the *National Enquirer* and I was in a damn psych ward. There was nothing I could do to fix the past, but at least I could do something to better the future. In an instant, my train wreck of a life was imbued with the possibility of usefulness and purpose. I saw a path forward when only a week earlier I could imagine no future for myself at all. On some level, I knew that it was just one more attempt to recover some meaning from the senseless, to finally be the person that my mother had wanted me to be—but I couldn't *not* do it. I had to do it. It felt like the only way to truly heal.

This, too, I would later learn, was textbook.

---

"WE BECAME ACCIDENTAL ACTIVISTS," says Louise Godbold, director of the nonprofit Echo, of her experience talking publicly about her allegations against Harvey Weinstein. "That was the salvation for many of us, a place to channel your energies and not just be some pathetic creature who this thing was done to, who wasn't able to protect herself. That's an exaggeration, but it gave a sense of agency, which again, goes back to power and control, and of there being a bigger and greater meaning to all of this."

Power, control, and meaning—the voids left behind in the aftermath of trauma, which we are forever seeking to make whole.

Why is that?

The power and control part is easy enough to understand. "Trauma robs the victim of a sense of power and control over her own life," wrote Harvard professor of psychiatry Judith Herman, MD. "Therefore, the guiding principle of recovery is to restore power and control to the survivor. She must be the author and arbiter of her own recovery."

Recovery, according to Dr. Herman, unfolds in three broad stages. First, and most importantly, safety must be established and maintained. Since survivors often feel unsafe within their own bodies, this begins with the body itself and then moves outward to relationships and environment. No other recovery can take place unless safety has been established, and as recovery moves into the second phase—remembrance and mourning—the need to preserve safety must be constantly balanced against the need to face the past. During this second phase, the survivor is empowered by making the choice to confront the past. "The survivor can revisit the past in order to grieve and make meaning of the trauma," wrote Dr. Herman. "She will never be the same person she was before the traumatic events in her life, but out of her grief she can forge a new identity that neither denies her past nor allows it define her entirely." Life can begin to go on.

The third stage of recovery, then, is reconnection with ordinary life. "The core experiences of psychological trauma are disempowerment and disconnection from others," wrote Dr. Herman, so recovery cannot take place in isolation but instead within the context of relationships. While most will seek the resolution of their traumatic experience in their personal lives alone, some do it on a larger scale by sharing it and becoming a force for social change. They might seek justice directly, support the recovery of others, or raise awareness to try to prevent future abuses.

"While there is no way to compensate for an atrocity, there is a way to transcend it, by making it a gift to others," wrote Dr. Herman. "The trauma is redeemed only when it becomes the source of a survivor mission."

---

THE BOOK YOU ARE HOLDING in your hands is my survivor mission. It's an attempt at restitution for my failures as a journalist. It's an act of atonement for my complicity in Matt's abuses, and to those I hurt. More than all of that, it is a mother's desperate, determined effort to do all that she can to ensure that none of this ever happens to her children, or anyone else's. It has consumed years of my life, and just for the mere possibility of change, it has already been worth it.

But however healing it has been, it still terrifies me.

With speaking out comes the inevitable consequences, and these must be weighed against Dr. Herman's first rule of recovery—establishing safety. To tell one side of a story is to invite the telling of the other, which means that some degree of power and control will necessarily be lost. We can never have complete narrative ownership over the past, and the first step in avoiding accountability for perpetrators will almost always be attacking the credibility and motives of their accusers. No matter how seemingly open-and-shut the case, naming or even alluding to the identity of the abuser invites repercussions. Put bluntly, their only way out will be through you.

CONSIDER BROCK TURNER, WHO was caught in the act of sexually assaulting his unconscious victim, Chanel Miller, by two bystanders, both of whom later testified against Turner in court. Rarely is a sexual assault case ever as open-and-shut as Miller's. She was provably intoxicated. Two bystanders witnessed her assault, intervened to stop it, noted she was unconscious, and remained with Turner until the police arrived. The police collected evidence and Miller underwent a rape kit. Still, Turner denied it all anyway, saying that Miller "seemed to enjoy" the assault before he was "suddenly tackled by a group of guys." Even in a rape case as unusually straightforward as Miller's, Turner gambled that he could attack her credibility so severely that his version of events would be believed over hers.

"It was like watching wolves being clipped off their leashes while someone whispered in your ear that meat has been sewn into your pockets," Miller wrote in her memoir, *Know My Name*. Turner was convicted and sentenced to three years' probation and lifetime sex offender registration, but only six months in jail, because the judge felt that a longer prison sentence "would have a severe impact on him." Infuriating as that is, Miller's case serves as a baseline, best-case scenario for anyone who makes a sexual assault allegation.

Another example: In November 2023, R&B singer Casandra Ventura—known professionally as Cassie—filed a lawsuit against hip-hop and fashion mogul Sean Combs under New York's Adult Survivors Act, alleging Combs had physically abused and sexually coerced her for more than a decade, including rape. The suit included a detailed description of an incident in a Los Angeles hotel in 2016 in which Combs punched her in the face, followed her into the hallway after she tried to leave the room, and threw glass vases at her, which shattered; she claimed the incident had been captured by hotel surveillance cameras but that Combs had paid $50,000 to obtain it. In response to the suit, Combs "vehemently denie[d] these offensive and outrageous allegations" and claimed that Ventura's lawsuit was "riddled with baseless and outrageous lies, aiming to tarnish [his] reputation and seeking a payday." The next day, though, the suit was settled for an undisclosed sum, later revealed to be $20 million. Six months later, surveillance video of the 2016 assault in the hotel hallway surfaced publicly, substantiating Ventura's allegations; a hotel security worker would later testify that Combs had actually paid $100,000 to obtain what he thought was the only copy.

"I take full responsibility for my actions in that video," Combs said in a statement released in May 2024—quite a departure from calling Ventura's accusations baseless and outrageous lies she'd told for money.*

In the face of serious allegations, a denial is to be expected—but not all denials are created equal. Victims can also face a disproportionate, outsized denial that is less concerned with asserting innocence and more concerned with threatening and blaming the accuser. This is known as a DARVO response, first identified by psychologist Dr. Jennifer Freyd, professor emeritus of psychology at the University of Oregon. DARVO is an acronym for Deny, Attack, Reverse Victim and Offender. In a DARVO response, the accused offender creates the impression that he is the true victim by

---

* Combs was arrested by federal agents in September 2024 and charged in a three-count indictment with racketeering conspiracy, sex trafficking, and transportation to engage in prostitution. In July 2025, he was convicted on two counts of transportation to engage in prostitution but acquitted of racketeering conspiracy and sex trafficking. In October 2025, he was sentenced to four years and two months in prison and a $500,000 fine.

portraying those seeking to hold him accountable as malicious aggressors, loudly accusing them of defamation, false accusations, and smearing. A DARVO denial goes beyond an assertion of innocence to an overstated, disproportionate response to being accused at all.

"I have observed that actual abusers threaten, bully and make a nightmare for anyone who holds them accountable or asks them to change their abusive behavior," Freyd wrote in her 1997 paper coining the term. "This attack, intended to chill and terrify, typically includes threats of lawsuits, overt and covert attacks on the whistleblower's credibility, and . . . will often take the form of focusing on ridiculing the person who attempts to hold [them] accountable."

Just as intended, these types of denials can be devastating.

"When a victim receives a DARVO response, they're more likely to blame themselves for what happened, which is a testament to its effectiveness," Freyd says. "And when third parties hear a DARVO response, it works for the perpetrator in the sense that people tend to find the perpetrator more innocent and the victim more guilty—and that is really bad, because it shows that it works. The only good news is that if we educate people in advance, and they know what a DARVO is, they're not going to be as swayed by it. They can recognize it and put it into perspective."

But there is no sugarcoating the reality that any sexual abuse victim who chooses to speak out or seek justice must be prepared for devastating and destabilizing consequences—and for the low likelihood of any kind of resolution, let alone healing or justice. We've seen the uphill battle faced by victims when they try to report sexual harassment and assault to their schools, employers, and other institutions in positions of authority. Going to the police is often worse.

"Survivors who have had encounters with the justice system often speak of them as a 'second rape,'" wrote Dr. Herman in her 2023 book, *Truth and Repair*. "Police often interrogate them as though they were suspects rather than victims. Prosecutors don't want to be bothered with cases that might be difficult to win because of common prejudices that juries might share. Judges often share these prejudices as well."

Even when the system works—and remember that, in my case, the system technically worked perfectly—the stigma, shame, and isolation is shattering. Your life will never be the same. No matter the circumstances, to claim to be a victim of sexual assault is, unfortunately, to invite a lifetime of suspicion and disbelief. It is to lose countless relationships, and to pay a terrible price.

And I can tell you, years after being outed in the press, that walking through the world knowing that a substantial portion of it will always see you as a liar takes a strange and exacting toll. You come to expect constant and automatic disbelief, even in the most mundane parts of life. When I first learned I was pregnant with my daughter, I carried a positive pregnancy test with me for months because I assumed no one would believe that I was pregnant since I wasn't showing. Once I called to order takeout from a mom-and-pop restaurant and offered to pay over the phone, but they insisted that I could just pay when I came to pick up the food. I was shocked. *We trust you*, they said, and it nearly brought me to tears. Years later, when my toddler bumped her head on a doorframe, I immediately dialed the on-call pediatrician. Halfway through describing the bruise on her forehead, I froze. *They're not going to believe me that I didn't hit her*, I thought; *they're going to take my daughter away*.

We take for granted that people take us at our word in day-to-day life—until you ask to be believed. Then they don't. Over the years, when women have told me that they want to speak out but can't, they always say variations of the same thing. They don't want to let down "the movement," to let other women suffer alone, to be complicit in allowing their abusers to continue abusing. They want to help. They want to be a force for change. They want it to have meant something, to set an example for their daughters. But what happens to our daughters when we lose our jobs and can't get another one? We want to be brave but cannot afford to be irresponsible. If we speak out because it's the right thing to do, we blame ourselves for the consequences. If we stay silent out of a sense of responsibility, we blame ourselves for failing to stop our abusers. Once again, there are no good options.

In those conversations, I say the same thing that my flight attendant mother used to say to me. When the cabin pressure drops suddenly—which, don't be fooled, means that everyone around you is slowly suffocating—you must first secure your own oxygen mask before anyone else's, even your child's. If you don't help yourself, you can't help anyone else, period. More than that, when you sacrifice your own well-being, you force those you love to bear the burden of your suffering. "The movement" isn't going to pay your bills, give you health insurance, or cover the cost of the therapy you need. It's not going to put a roof over your head or provide for your children. We all want to be brave, but bravery can be as selfish as it is selfless. When others love and depend on you, survival in itself is heroic. I don't say this to discourage anyone from speaking out or following their conscience. I say it so that we stop blaming those who cannot, and in the hope that they stop blaming themselves.

"The survivor who undertakes public action also needs to come to terms with the fact that not every battle will be won," wrote Dr. Herman. ". . . She must be secure in the knowledge that simply in her willingness to tell the truth in public, she has taken the action that perpetrators fear the most."

And to those who have spoken out, and to those who will—thank you.

# EIGHTEEN.

# Redefining Risk

*Believing Women, False Allegations, and*
*"Celebrity Victimhood Status"*

B y the time I left NBC, I'd worked around celebrities for more than a decade. I'd seen what happened when people read about themselves in the tabloids. They lose their minds. They become reflections of their public images rather than the other way around, until even private life feels like a public performance. Fame damages people, disconnects them, warps their sense of reality irrevocably—and these are famous people who are being *celebrated* by the media. That's why we call them celebrities.

I was never going to be a celebrity—and, for what it's worth, thank God—but I could not have fathomed what it was to be harassed, humiliated, and threatened by the media. Again, thank God. If I'd known when I made the complaint to NBC that anyone would ever know what was in it or who made it, I don't know if I would have had the courage to do it—but I do know I wouldn't have been able to live with myself if I didn't. By April 2019, having been outed by the tabloids in everything but name, I was at another breaking point. I could not go back to my old life and I could not start a new one. I was trapped.

The idea of writing a book had given me hope and purpose for the first time in years, but it landed me in the tabloids all over again, now characterized as a disgruntled ex-mistress shopping a tell-all. "Accuser who got Matt Lauer fired is shopping tell-all book," alleged *Page Six*. The piece, which identified me as Meredith Vieira's former assistant, reported that "the woman who precipitated Matt Lauer's downfall—and the loss of his $25 million NBC job—is shopping around a tell-all book. . . . A source tells us Lauer and the aide—who subsequently rose to the role of a *Today* producer— embarked on a long-term affair starting in Sochi. . . . A source said, 'This was not a fling; it was an affair. She went and complained and Matt was fired.'" The *Daily Mail* headline: MATT LAUER PUTS ON A BRAVE FACE AMID REPORTS OF A TELL-ALL BOOK BY MEREDITH VIEIRA'S FORMER ASSISTANT, WHOSE AFFAIR LED TO NBC TERMINATING TODAY ANCHOR'S $25M CONTRACT. To the media, I was either a coward if I chose to stay silent or an opportunist if I chose to speak for myself. I could not do anything right, and I felt more voiceless and powerless than ever. I was never going to hire a ghostwriter and pump out a tell-all, but I knew the only kind of book I was willing to write could take years to report. Yet the longer I said nothing, the bolder and more shameless Matt became, and the more likely it was that some press outlet would just go ahead and publish my name and picture. At any moment, I could wake up to find a mob of paparazzi at our door.

I'd already been followed home from 30 Rock at least once, and that was chilling in itself—but then details began to emerge about how Harvey Weinstein had used high-powered lawyers and the Israeli private intelligence firm Black Cube to try to silence his accusers. The man who'd followed me home, filming me on his phone for the last three blocks . . . had that been a reporter, or some private security contractor working for Matt? I couldn't know. I couldn't really even know if he'd been following me at all. Maybe I was losing my mind. But from that moment onward, whenever anyone was remotely kind to me—from the person next to me on a flight to the regulars at the coffee shop and the dog run—I wondered if they were tabloid reporters or private investigators that Matt had hired to befriend me, as Weinstein had done with one of his accusers. I was living in constant fear that was not totally irrational, and because it wasn't entirely beyond the realm of possibility, I couldn't let down my guard.

But for all my anger at the media scrutiny, I understood it. The press was just doing its job. Matt had wielded unbelievable power as anchor of *Today* and the public had a legitimate right to know how he'd abused it—which meant I was collateral damage. That was no doubt one of the reasons why he must have felt so confident the women he targeted would keep silent: What woman in her right mind would ever subject herself to this? His fame as anchor of *Today* was just one more power he'd abused. My only options now were to continue living in constant fear or to accept that public exposure and humiliation were inevitable and get it over with. Horrible as the thought was, there was something to be said for that.

I was thirty-four years old. Put bluntly, my childbearing years were not infinite, the clock was ticking, and I knew I couldn't possibly get pregnant—let alone sustain a healthy pregnancy—when the world felt so threatening and out of control. I'd already lost four years to Matt Lauer, and I would never again make the mistake of assuming I had time. *If you can't let this go, you might as well just jump off the George Washington Bridge, because you're throwing away your life.* You always think you have time—and then your mom goes out to check the mail one morning and never comes back. The future is never guaranteed. Every moment I spent hiding from the past was a moment lost with the children I so desperately hoped I would be able to have. At least if I outed myself, I could have some degree of control over when it happened, and how. It would be awful, but some degree of control seemed better than none.

I knew my allegations would need to be vetted and scrutinized by a respected reporter so Matt could not dismiss them out of hand as gossip, as he'd been doing for years with the tabloids. Ronan Farrow had just won the Pulitzer Prize for his investigative reporting in *The New Yorker*, and he'd discovered my identity months earlier, while I was still working at NBC. At the time, I'd ignored his overtures, but now I'd heard that he was writing a book about NBC and Weinstein and I was worried my story might already be in it. But though it would have been an undeniable boon for his book, Farrow made no elaborate pitch to get me to go on the record. Instead, he made it abundantly clear from the beginning that putting my name to my allegations would have a devastating impact on my life, and that he would be seeking Matt's side of the story.

That was only fair. My biggest worry about MeToo from its beginning was not the inevitable backlash it sparked, but the sudden popularity of silencing unpopular people it enabled. Speaking out against Matt Lauer would mean—and was always going to mean—that he would speak out against me, the nobody from nowhere. That was just the cost of being heard. Farrow warned that the fact-checking process would be painful and that I would have no control over what he published—that his book would contain my story but not *be* my story. It would be his reporting, his analysis, his conclusions, his narrative of events. Neither I nor Matt but Farrow would have the final word.

Terrifying and disempowering as that was, it was the safest and most empowering choice available to me at the time.

Farrow's book, *Catch and Kill*, was slated for release on October 15, 2019. I booked a room at a hotel upstate for that entire week, thinking I could escape the tabloids—and because I had some idea what was coming. Matt's response to my allegations was simple enough: I'd wanted it all along. I'd thrown myself at him and then seen the hysteria of MeToo as an opportunity to pass myself off as a victim. As we would see a few months later during Harvey Weinstein's first New York trial, it would become one of the go-to defense arguments for powerful men accused of misconduct.

"We have created a society of celebrity victimhood status," said Donna Rotunno, Weinstein's lead defense attorney in his first New York trial, in an interview with reporter Megan Twohey of *The New York Times.* "We have created a society where women don't have to take any responsibility for their actions. And we have created a society where if we say believe all women, that means we're not supposed to question anyone at all. So there is absolutely no risk for a woman to come forward now and make a claim—zero."

———

THE INITIAL "BELIEVE WOMEN" slogan that arose from MeToo was never "believe all women, all the time"—an obvious absurdity. To say "believe women" is only to acknowledge how often we disbelieve women when it comes to sexual harassment and assault, especially compared to other types of crime. When I saw that my stockpile of quarters had been stolen from my car, I wasn't worried about being accused of spending them and then lying to pass myself off as a victim. No one questioned whether the quarters were taken by accident or suggested that I left the door unlocked because I secretly wanted my money stolen and was too embarrassed to admit it. The title of the original campaign was "Start by Believing" from the nonprofit End Violence Against Women International, where psychologist Dr. Kimberly Lonsway is director of research.

"'Start by Believing' doesn't mean 'believe everything,'" Lonsway says. "It's an orientation to begin an effective interview and an effective investigation. We believe in due process, we believe in innocent until proven guilty, but when somebody comes to the police department and says that their bike was stolen, the police start from the assumption that the bike was stolen because otherwise, nobody would ever bother going to the police. If you start by not believing someone who comes in to report a crime, you're not going to do a successful interview and you're not going to get the information you need."

To that end, the reason we must better understand seemingly "counterintuitive" victim behavior is not because it always indicates that a sexual assault has occurred, but because too often we wrongly interpret it as proof that a sexual assault could never have occurred. Every victim reacts differently, but our misconceptions surrounding victim behavior mislead us into seeing common reactions to sexual trauma as suspect when they are perfectly normal. When allegations fail to conform to the myths and stereotypes surrounding sexual harassment and assault, we tend to disbelieve them— even though we know that most incidents of sexual harassment and assault do not resemble the stereotypes at all. As Lonsway says, "When you go down the list of characteristics that cause people to question whether or not this was really a sexual assault, in many cases those are the common, typical dynamics of actual sexual assault." But none of this is to say that we should always believe. It is to say that we should *stop* disbelieving for the wrong reasons.

Our constant focus on victim behavior rather than offender behavior is just as backward. Sexual abuses do not occur in a vacuum. The behaviors and characteristics of sex offenders are well documented. Research has shown that there are two principal factors that facilitate sex offenders: certain aberrant character traits (a disregard for rules and the rights of others, a willingness to exploit others, and a lack of empathy) and deviant sexual arousal. This is not to say that every person with those character traits or deviant sexual urges will commit a sex crime—most, actually, do not.

"What is different for those who commit sexual offenses is that they allow deviant urges and problematic personality traits to combine to engage in self-gratifying behavior that harms others," wrote forensic psychologist Veronique Valliere, PhD, in *Unmasking the Sexual Offender.* In her experience, it is the individual's character, rather than their specific sexual preferences, that is the determinant factor in whether they commit sex crimes.

This is why it is the alleged offender's character and behavior, and not the alleged victim's, that should bear the most scrutiny. That is common sense. But, again, that does not mean that accusers should be unequivocally believed. It is just as nonsensical and offensive to suggest they never lie as it is to assume that they always lie. There is no denying that false allegations occur. Though rare, the possibility should never be discounted, just as it should never be assumed.

"There's research on false allegations and the nature of them," says Valliere. "When you are going to make a false allegation, you want to be the victim, right? You want to be believed, and you want whatever gain there is in the victimization. Typically the false allegation will have a clear perpetrator and a clear victim. . . . You're not going to engage in all this self-doubt, self-blame, hesitation. . . . There are often certain characteristics in a false allegation that tend to meet our stereotypes of assault, like, he held me down, he strangled me. That's not always the case—I mean, children can be coached—but there are elements that you look for, where credibility breaks down."

Forensic psychiatrist Dr. Barbara Ziv played a role in the vacated conviction of William Arnold Jr., a Nashville man who spent nearly seven years in prison after being wrongly convicted of sexually assaulting a boy he mentored through the Big Brothers Big Sisters program. As an expert in both offender and victim behavior, Dr. Ziv assessed that Arnold's behavior "in no way, shape or form conforms to the patterns of behavior of a child molester or pedophile, even in [the victim's] accounting" and that the victim never told "the same story twice," which was "the hallmark of a non-credible witness." Arnold's conviction was vacated on appeal.

"I know what the discrepancies are, I know how to interview, I know what patterns of behavior are, I know how people talk about sexual assault, I know when there are conflating situations," Dr. Ziv says. "It is not that difficult to get to the truth when someone knows what they're doing."

In the most egregious false accusation cases, whole systems break down. The Duke lacrosse case, for example, was the result of a combination of a false allegation, prosecutorial misconduct, and reckless, irresponsible media coverage. Author Alice Sebold wrote a bestselling memoir about her rape, only to learn years later that she'd misidentified an innocent man in a police lineup. That man, Anthony Broadwater, was unjustly incarcerated for sixteen and a half years. Sebold's allegation was not false—there is ample evidence that she was sexually assaulted—but the wrong man was falsely convicted, and to this day, her actual rapist remains unidentified.

We must also better distinguish between a false allegation and a credible one that is unprovable—an area encompassing many, if not most, allegations of acquaintance rape. Without being in the room and reading the minds of everyone involved, how can we distinguish between a person who regrets a consensual sexual encounter and one who legitimately did not consent?

"I get those questions in every single training and they're absolutely important to answer," says Valliere. "When you regret something, do you bring all this public attention to it? To report an offense is to completely expose what happened. Whenever I hear,

'Oh, they were afraid they were going to get caught cheating so they said it was rape,' I point out that the best way to get caught cheating is to freaking report it as a rape. Most people who don't want to get caught keep their mouth shut and pretend nothing happened. I'm not saying it's impossible, but you know what, if you drive through Pennsylvania and see an animal with four legs, it's probably not going to be a giraffe. I'm not saying there are no giraffes in Pennsylvania, but it's mostly horses and cows, so let's be realistic."

I've heard enough palpable fear in the voices of reasonable men terrified of being falsely accused that I would never deny how important these questions are. And even though most credible rape allegations are never reported in any capacity, the social and professional consequences of an allegation alone can be enough to devastate a life. I would be dishonest not to admit that I think there is good reason for men to be afraid of false allegations. This is, emphatically, not because of an epidemic of false rape allegations, but because everything about the way we handle sexual assault is a recipe for disaster.

We have generations of men who have been taught that they need only listen specifically for the word "no" when it comes to sex, and that as long as they never hear it, then they're good to go. Or they've been taught that, even if they do get a no, they can just keep pushing until their partner stops saying it. Is that consent? Without a legal definition that applies to everyone, it's anybody's guess. As long as consent remains an undefined, moving target, it virtually guarantees that there will be confusion, misunderstanding, and disagreement, which makes sex almost categorically unsafe. Then along came MeToo, and suddenly those generations of men feel, perhaps rightly, that the goalposts on consent have been moved retroactively—and continue to move. Those who raised perfectly reasonable questions during the height of the movement's frenzy

were often cast as part of the problem. Men who legitimately believed they were following the "rules" of consent were left to question whether their honestly well-intentioned sexual behavior might
have been predatory all along. Imagine the fear and shame that
accompanies living with those kinds of unanswered questions in
our new, post-MeToo reality. Think of what that does to a sense of
self-worth, or decency, or even the most basic concept of what it is
to be a good man in the world. Our failure to talk about this openly
in the wake of MeToo is among the myriad ways we are not only
failing and alienating young men today, but setting them up to fail
in the future.

Then layer on top that generation upon generation of women
have been raised never to be difficult, not to make a fuss, not to
embarrass men by rejecting them, to "be nice" and go along to get
along whenever possible. Women learn that it is practically unforgivable to lead men on and then, God forbid, change our minds.
There are reasons that we've been socialized this way, not least the
need to survive. But combine all that with the moving target that is
consent and the emotional confusion endemic to acquaintance
rape, and it should be no surprise that unacknowledged and unreported sexual assaults are so common.

Then, when we factor in an inconsistent, seemingly impossible-
to-pin-down definition of rape that is dependent upon both the
victim's location and our nonexistent definition of consent, we are
left with the dangerous and uncomfortable possibility that a traumatized, vulnerable, or simply confused person might ask "Was I
raped?" and decide the answer is yes when it may very well be no.
I know exactly how it feels to be surrounded by a chorus of well-
meaning people pressuring you to say the word "rape" when you
are unsure or unready. I know how easily a vulnerable person in
obvious emotional distress can be manipulated or exploited by others. The boundaries surrounding consent and acquaintance rape

are profoundly confusing. People who are forced to navigate them often find themselves alone and afraid, with little guidance to be found and false assumptions—and ulterior motives—everywhere.

An example from my own life: I went to a fraternity formal in college, and as I was leaving, was invited to an after-party by one of the fraternity brothers. My date hadn't made a move and I was still wide awake, so I went home, changed into jeans, and headed to the party. The university ran a free shuttle that would take us door to door at night—this was Baltimore in the mid-2000s—and it took a full half hour to arrive, then pulled away before I'd even gotten to the door. The fraternity brother who'd invited me opened the door happily and then locked it behind me. The house was empty. There was no party. I felt like an idiot. He proudly explained that he'd known for months that I'd wanted to hook up with him, which was why he'd invited me over. I hadn't, and didn't. But I was so mortified that I played along, as though I'd been in on the plan all along. In truth, I felt cornered and tricked, and while he was perfectly nice, I never wanted to have sex with him that night. I went along anyway, if only because I was too embarrassed to tell him that he had misread the situation.

I talked about that night to friends for years as though it were a date rape, when in truth there was nothing to stop me from walking out the door but my own pride, and potentially the awkwardness of having to spend a half hour with a man I'd just rejected while I waited for the shuttle to return. Had I felt cornered and tricked? Yes, but then I made a choice, and that choice was entirely mine to make. I regretted it, but it did not haunt me for years. I never had nightmares. My personality did not change. I got over it. I learned from it. But these situations are fraught with shame, unspoken rules, societal expectations, and, more often than not, a great deal of alcohol.

It's a recipe for disaster.

At the same time, consider all the people who drink and have sex, or work together and have sex, and yet don't commit or get accused of sexual assault. There's a reason that organizations almost universally prohibit sexual activity between superiors and subordinates, and one surefire way to avoid destroying your career is just *not to do it*. But people will often do risky and stupid things. Sex is an inherently risky act, and always has been. Women know this. We are never allowed to forget. If MeToo raised awareness that sex is risky for men, too, then all the better. It is.

# NINETEEN

# He Said / She Said

W e owe it to our viewers to pause for a moment. This is shocking and appalling, and I honestly don't even know what to say about it," said *Today* anchor Savannah Guthrie on the morning of October 9, 2019. "It's very painful for all of us at NBC and who are at the *Today* show. It's very, very difficult."

". . . We don't know all the facts in this, but there are not allegations of an affair," said Hoda Kotb, openly acknowledging what had long been the accepted version of events in the building. "There are allegations of a crime. And I think that's shocking to all of us here who have sat with Matt for many, many years."

Farrow's book did not go on sale for another six days, but the night before, *Variety* had published an excerpt—specifically, the portion of my interview describing that night in Sochi—at 9:56 p.m. Pacific time. This was 1:00 a.m. in New York, where I was already asleep. RONAN FARROW BOOK ALLEGES MATT LAUER RAPED NBC NEWS COLLEAGUE, read the headline. The first paragraph summarizes the book's other 400-plus pages, while the second says that "Farrow's most explosive interview in the book is with Brooke Nevils, the former NBC News employee whose complaint about Matt Lauer led to the co-anchor's firing from the 'Today' show in 2017." The next morning, my name and photo had already been aired on national television as, once again, I'd slept through it all.

NBC had also released a statement: "Matt Lauer's conduct was appalling, horrific and reprehensible, as we said at the time. That's why he was fired within 24 hours of us first learning of the complaint. Our hearts break again for our colleague."

Reporters were camped outside our apartment, buzzing the door, calling, and texting. What could I possibly say? I hadn't even read the book, and when I read the article in *Variety* summarizing my interview in the most salacious way possible, I found it nearly impossible to believe that the woman they were talking about could possibly have anything to do with me. It felt like I was reading about someone else entirely, and I felt terrible for her. But all this? This wasn't *my* story. While Matt was anchor of *Today*, it felt as though every story had been his to tell, including what he did to my body. Once I made the complaint to NBC, its contents became NBC's to characterize, and thus what Matt did to my body became "inappropriate sexual behavior in the workplace." Now it was Farrow's turn; it was his story now. I was still just a nobody from nowhere—a tiny, massless, meaningless object being tossed about, the plaything of larger people and powers.

I was on the floor of our bedroom, curled in a ball, staring at the place where the floor met the baseboard, when I felt my then fiancé's hand at the base of my spine. He was touching me cautiously, as though I were a wounded, dying animal who might lash out at him.

Matt had released an open letter, he said, and it was not short.

An Open Letter:

Over the past two years people have asked why I have not spoken out to defend myself more vigorously against some of the false and salacious allegations leveled at me. It is a fair question and the answer is deeply personal. Despite my desire to set the record straight and confront the individuals making false allegations, I wanted nothing less than to create more headlines my kids would read and a new gathering of photographers at the end of our driveway. So I decided to just stay quiet and work on repairing my relationship with the people I love. It has been the most important full-time job I have ever had.

But my silence has been a mistake.

Today, nearly two years after I was fired by NBC, old stories are being recycled, titillating details are being added, and a dangerous and defamatory new allegation is being made. All are being spread as part of a promotional effort to sell a book. It's outrageous. So, after not speaking out to protect my children, it is now with their full support I say "enough."

In a new book, it is alleged that an extramarital, but consensual, sexual encounter I have previously admitted having, was in fact an assault. It is categorically false, ignores the facts, and defies common sense.

I had an extramarital affair with Brooke Nevils in 2014. It began when she came to my hotel room very late one night in Sochi, Russia. We engaged in a variety of sexual acts. We performed oral sex on each other, we had vaginal sex, and we had anal sex. Each act was mutual and completely consensual.

The story Brooke tells is filled with false details intended only to create the impression this was an abusive encounter. Nothing could be further from the truth. There was absolutely nothing aggressive about that encounter. Brooke did not do or say anything to object. She certainly did not cry. She was a fully enthusiastic and willing partner. At no time did she behave in a way that made it appear she was incapable of consent. She seemed to know exactly what she wanted to do. The only concern she expressed was that someone might see her leaving my room. She embraced me at the door as she left.

This encounter, which she now falsely claims was an assault, was the beginning of our affair. It was the first of many sexual encounters between us over the next several months. After we returned to New York, we both communicated by text and by phone. We met for drinks, and she met me at my apartment on multiple occasions to continue our affair. Our meetings were arranged mutually. At no time, during or after her multiple visits to my apartment, did she express in words or actions any discomfort with being there, or with our affair.

She also went out of her way to see me several times in my dressing room at work, and on one of those occasions we had a sexual encounter. It showed terrible judgment on my part, but it was completely mutual and consensual.

Brooke now says that she was terrified about the control I had over her career and felt pressure to agree to our encounters after Sochi. But at no time during our relationship did Brooke work for me, the Today Show, or NBC News. She worked for Meredith Vieira (who had not worked for the Today Show in several years) in a completely different part of the network, and I had no role in reviewing Brooke's work.

I admit, I ended the affair poorly. I simply stopped communicating with her. Brooke continued to reach out. She admitted to NBC at the time she filed her complaint that she called me late at night while I was home with my family in an effort to rekindle the affair. But I attempted to go back to my life and pretend as if nothing had happened. I understand how that must have made her feel. However, being upset or having second thoughts does not give anyone the right to make false accusations years later about an affair in which they fully and willingly participated.

Between February 2014 and November 2017, Brooke and I saw each other more than a dozen times at professional gatherings, both large and small. Despite the fact that our affair was over, she always went out of her way to greet me warmly and engage in conversation. It was not until I was called in to speak to an NBC attorney on November 28, 2017 that I first learned Brooke had any complaint. I answered all questions openly and honestly for more than an hour. At that meeting I was **never** told that Brooke claimed our encounter in Sochi was non-consensual. Had I been, I would have defended myself immediately.

After Brooke filed her complaint in late 2017, her attorney publicly insisted she wanted to remain anonymous. He said she just wanted NBC to "do the right thing." But within a year she was reportedly out trying to sell a book. And it appears that she also sought a monetary payment from NBC. Now she is making outrageous and false accusations to help sell a different book and stepping into the spotlight to cause as much damage as she can.

But Brooke's story is filled with contradictions. Which Brooke is to be believed?

- She claims our first encounter was an assault, yet she actively participated in arranging future meetings and met me at my apartment on multiple occasions to continue the affair.

- She says I was the one pursuing the relationship, yet once it was over, she was the one calling me asking to rekindle it.

- She says she felt pressure to continue the affair because I had control over her career, but she did not work for me, the Today Show, or NBC News.

- She said she wanted to remain anonymous, yet she was reportedly trying to sell a book within year [*sic*] after filing her complaint.

- She said she just wanted NBC to "do the right thing," yet she sought a monetary payment, and two years after I was fired, she is stepping forward to do more damage.

There are people who fully understand the actual dynamic that existed between Brooke and me. They have reluctantly and quietly reached out in the past two years and shared what they know. They have accurately described Brooke and her role in this affair. I hope those people will understand that these allegations cross a serious line, and what they can share is a vital truth, even if it may seem unpopular.

Because of my infidelity, I have brought more pain and embarrassment to my family than most people can ever begin to understand. They've been through hell. I have asked for their forgiveness, taken responsibility for what I **did** do wrong, and accepted the consequences. But by not speaking out I also emboldened those who continue to do me harm with false stories.

One such story I should have confronted a long time ago is an example of why I believe my silence was a mistake. Despite numerous erroneous reports in the past, there was **not** a button in my office that could lock the door from the inside. There was no such locking mechanism. It didn't exist. NBC confirmed this fact publicly following my termination.

It would have been impossible to confine anyone in my office, for any purpose, and I have never attempted to make anyone feel as if they were confined in my office. I have never assaulted anyone or forced anyone to have sex. Period.

Anyone who knows me will tell you I am a very private person. I had no desire to write this, but I had no choice. The details I have written about here open deep wounds for my family. But they also lead to the truth. For two years, the women with whom I had extramarital relationships have abandoned shared responsibility, and instead, shielded themselves from blame behind false allegations. They have avoided having to look a boyfriend, husband, or a child in the eye and say, "I cheated." They have done enormous damage in the process. And I will no longer provide them the shelter of my silence.

Matt Lauer

———

I WATCHED SILENTLY AS my fiancé read the letter, waiting for the horror and revulsion—and the inevitable regret that he'd stayed with me—to appear on his face. But they didn't.

"I can't believe they put this monster on television for twenty years," he said. "I can't believe you were alone in a room with this guy in Russia."

It was as though he'd finally met the Matt Lauer I had been describing for all these years.

Then I understood: Since Matt was fired in 2017, most people had only the image of the charismatic, carefully polished news anchor they'd been watching on *Today* for twenty years. No allegation against him—or any number of allegations against him—could have outweighed such a perfectly produced image, decades in the making by the best broadcasters in the business. Now Matt had let the mask drop. This was the real Matt, in his own words—his real voice, his real thoughts, his real character—for all the world to see.

Matt's open letter is worth more than any apology. It relieves me of the need to convince anyone who Matt really is.

It hardly matters that most people who read it will never hear a word I say or ever learn the other side of the story. They don't need to. Instead they can read his words and recognize some version of the man who wrote it from their own lives—whether that's their own abuser, the bully who terrorized them at school, or the boss who made their lives a living hell—and know instantly that anyone who proudly signs his name to such a letter has no business in a position of power over other human beings. Matt's words, clearly meant to make me regret exposing him, are instead a testament to exactly why I did. Reporting him was the right thing to do. It had to be done.

I would do it again.

But that does not change the fact that Matt's open letter is still what is found when anyone searches the internet for my name, which he repeats fifteen separate times. There is no hiding it when I apply for jobs or try to hire a caregiver for my children, who will one day be taunted with Matt's words at the bus stop and in the school locker room. I am a living cautionary tale for any woman who might dare to speak out against a powerful abuser. It is humiliating, dehumanizing, and strewn with obvious, defamatory falsehoods that can never be scrubbed from the internet. I could refute Matt's letter, line by line and bullet by bullet, but to what end? I have lived with it for more than half a decade. When a man with so much power and fame goes to such lengths to shame and silence someone with neither, he succeeds only in shaming himself.

This is not to say, though, that Matt's letter was unsuccessful. Instead, it powerfully illustrates how persuasive the false stereotypes and myths surrounding sexual harassment and assault can be. When he declares that my allegation defies common sense, Matt's open letter even appeals to those false stereotypes directly before relying on one trope after another. In that sense, sure, my allegations indeed defy the stereotypes often conflated for "common sense," but then again, Matt's open letter blatantly defies reason. To respond to an allegation that he anally raped an intoxicated subordinate in his corporate hotel room after personally supplying her with alcohol by *putting in writing and then releasing to the press* an admission that, as a principal of a Fortune 50 corporation, he in fact "engaged in a variety of sexual acts" with that intoxicated subordinate is in itself astounding.

But such extreme confidence underlines a crucial point. Because the burden of proof is on the accuser, a denial needs only to cast doubt. While we must scrutinize and question every detail of an accusation, a denial need not be proven to be true, but merely accepted as *feasible*. Discrepancies and contradictions quickly render allegations and their accusers unbelievable and uncredible, but often go unnoticed and unchallenged in denials. That's a much, much lower bar.

Matt, then, can issue a denial filled with easily refutable claims because he can comfortably assume that they will be taken at face value by the same press that is so appalled by the suggestion to "start by believing." For the accuser, details matter. Matt's open letter, though, makes sweeping assertions with no detail or evidence whatsoever, but can apparently assume, correctly, that these will never be scrutinized. One example: He falsely asserts that we "met for drinks" as part of some romantic extramarital affair, despite the fact that he is one of the most famous and recognizable broadcast journalists in the country and certainly in New York. Where did we go? What did I drink? Did he pay with his NBC credit card? Surely Matt can produce a witness to such a public extramarital outing with an obviously younger, supposedly infatuated young woman, or his assistant or driver can corroborate his claim. For me to make any such assertion about Matt, I'd be expected to provide, at minimum, a date, time, and location so that Matt could refute it by providing an alibi. But for Matt, there is apparently no need. Even though Matt is a disgraced journalist who—at the very least—lied for decades about his sexual misconduct, *he* is taken at his word.

"At no time during our relationship did Brooke work for me, the *Today* show, or NBC News," he wrote, which is easily proven false by my employment records. It also highlights another sinister reality common to workplaces dominated by high-performing, "superstar" types—that these organizations are often structured to protect their most valuable employees. For all the years that I worked directly for Meredith as her assistant or producer, I was never her direct report and she was never technically my supervisor. Instead I worked for a production manager or line producer, who then assigned me to assist Meredith, freeing the on-air talent from the time-consuming administrative and managerial responsibilities of a direct report. Because the time and energy of superstar employees is so valuable, this is a perfectly justifiable business practice for any organization. It also carries the undeniable bonus of providing another layer of organizational insulation between high performers and potential liability so that, should any superstar be accused of abusing a subordinate, they can technically claim that they *had* no subordinates.

In Matt's case, this is a moot point, as even NBC doesn't dispute his professional power over me: "Some of [Matt's inappropriate sexual] behavior took place in the workplace, and Matt Lauer is Matt Lauer," NBC News president Noah Oppenheim told employees on November 29, 2017, when asked about the nature of my complaint. "And this person was an employee of NBC. So obviously there's a power differential there." But Matt tries to exploit the technicality anyway.

In fairness, because Matt released his open letter before *Catch and Kill* was published, reporters did not have access to Farrow's full accounting of events and could not interrogate how they differed from Matt's. In the meantime, though, the press obligingly lent Matt their platforms, leaving his assertions unchallenged. But when *Catch and Kill* was released a week later, Matt's open letter remained unscrutinized while every detail of *my* story was interrogated, debated, and criticized at length, even though it had already been corroborated by both NBC and Farrow—two parties that agree on practically nothing else. Matt had every right to defend himself, but certainly a denial that asserts unverified facts deserves at least the same level of scrutiny, if not more, as an allegation that has already been vetted by two independent parties in direct opposition to each other and found credible by both.

Yet, calculating and manipulative as it is, I don't believe Matt's letter is completely disingenuous. I think Matt probably believes every word. We all engage in some degree of protective self-delusion about our pasts; I discovered plenty of my own as I reported this book. I think Matt, like many people, also probably believes the rape myths to be true—and so likely believes they exonerate him. From his assertion that my allegation is "categorically false" (except for the sexual harassment and misconduct to which he admits, and for which he was fired) to that it "ignores the facts" (except for all those that he openly acknowledges, including that he anally penetrated a drunk subordinate) to his argument that it "defies common sense," the foundation of Matt's defense is the rape myth itself. In other words, since I did not behave as a stereotypical rape victim would, then it's only common sense that I cannot possibly be a real one. Who am I to judge him for that? I made the same mistake for years.

But Sochi was a singularly life-altering incident in my life, one that I have spent more than ten full years trying to understand. For

Matt, it may have been just another Olympics. He may genuinely no longer remember the details of the specific sexual acts he perpetrated in Sochi, whether we went for drinks or where I worked at NBC. Or he could have me confused with any number of female underlings over the years, whereas for me—and for that matter, any other subordinate at NBC—there was only one Matt Lauer, vaunted anchor of *Today*.

Matt's letter is most convincing and effective in the explicit threat he issues to his other, still-unnamed victims: "For two years, the women with whom I had extramarital relationships have abandoned shared responsibility, and instead, shielded themselves from blame behind false allegations. They have avoided having to look a boyfriend, husband, or a child in the eye and say, 'I cheated.' They have done enormous damage in the process. And I will no longer provide them the shelter of my silence."

How coolly and shamelessly he invokes *their children* to threaten them, in yet another way, into submission and silence.

It is so chilling that it is easy to ignore that, like most of Matt's arguments, it neither makes sense nor is true. In 2014, I *did* look my boyfriend in the eye and say "I cheated," and I accepted the consequences—which were devastating. My choice to report Matt three years later in no way shielded me from blame but forced me to endure far more than my fair share of it, and I endure it still. It meant walking away from a career I loved and being subjected to national scrutiny and ridicule for a chapter of my past that, believe me, I would have far preferred to remain private. That Matt, who admittedly lied for years about his "cheating," would think he can discredit anyone by calling them liars or cheaters is laughable.

But nonetheless, his threat worked. In the years since he released his open letter, no other women have come forward to discuss their allegations against Matt publicly. Then again, neither is there any need. Matt has no power anymore.

I REMEMBER BEING ASKED that day whether I would be "issuing a statement" in response, and how hilarious and surreal that seemed. I was a woman losing her mind, holed up in her apartment, slouched over an iPad in her pajamas. I did not "issue statements" any more than I made proclamations, declared war, or bestowed knighthoods upon my subjects. The last thing I wanted to do that day was offer any more of myself for public condemnation and judgment.

Yet that open letter was so overawing in its viciousness that to say nothing would have only helped Matt to justify it. For twenty years, Matt—a self-described "very private person"—had inserted himself into the center of the national spotlight, where he was perennially entitled to the last word in every conversation as anchor of *Today*. This was no ordinary man casually lashing out at his abuser on Facebook; Matt's words had extraordinary power. Anyone who'd experienced sexual abuse and read his open letter would be made to feel more alone, more afraid, and more powerless— and if those words were left unanswered, they would feel there was little reason to hope and every reason to be ashamed.

I gave my a response to Stephanie Gosk—the NBC News investigative reporter who'd protected my identity for nearly two years.

"I knew what kind of person Matt Lauer was when I made the decision to report him to NBC in November 2017, and I knew what kind of a person he was when I made the decision to tell my story to Ronan Farrow," it read. "In both of those cases, I asked that my allegations be thoroughly investigated, and that Matt be given the opportunity to defend himself. I provided dates, times, evidence of communications, and corroborating accounts. Both NBC and Farrow found me credible. As his open letter clearly reveals, there may be more than one Matt Lauer. There's the Matt Lauer that millions of Americans watched on TV every morning for two decades, and there is the Matt Lauer who this morning attempted to bully a former colleague into silence. His open letter was a case study in victim blaming and concluded by threatening any other woman who might dare to speak out against him. This is the Matt Lauer, then the most powerful asset at NBC News, who I feared when I continued to engage with him, as many victims of acquaintance rape do, particularly in the workplace. This is the Matt Lauer I reported in November 2017. I was not afraid of him then, and I am not afraid of him now, regardless of his threats, bullying, and the shaming and predatory tactics I knew he would—and now has—tried to use against me. The shame in this story belongs to him."

It was a statement of how I wanted to feel rather than how I actually felt. I was very much afraid of him, and I still am. It would be foolish not to fear a shameless man who demonstrates no remorse and has $80 million and extremely powerful friends. If *Catch and Kill* proved anything conclusively—with its terrifying descriptions of the tactics used by the private intelligence contractors and powerhouse attorneys employed by Harvey Weinstein—it was that the rest of us have little defense against extremely rich, powerful people. Money buys silence, and if it doesn't, it can buy threats, stalking, harassment, and suffering. And Matt has a great deal of money. That is reality, and it is a terrifying one in which to live the rest of my life, and for my children to begin theirs.

I have no choice but to accept it. I know that nothing I say will ever have any real impact on Matt Lauer. But if my words cause one manager, one executive, one coach, one pastor, one staff sergeant, one professor, one abuser in a position of power to reconsider his assumption that those who are vulnerable have no choice but silence, then that is impact enough.

FOR ABOUT TWO WEEKS, I learned what it was to have an image of my face be worth money on the open market, to walk down the street and be hunted, ambushed, and harassed by a pack of men, knowing that they had every right to do so. I read things about myself in the national press that were in no way true, and then comforted myself by remembering that I was so profoundly unimportant that it didn't really matter. I realized that everyone I'd ever trusted in my life now had the ability to sell stories about me to the tabloids, that photos of me and screen grabs of my idiotic or intimate texts were now marketable to the *Daily Mail*. I understood what it was to feel as though, simply by existing, I was not safe and never would be again. My fiancé walked down the street with me and within hours was the subject of a *Page Six* article. A random photo of me as a guest of a guest at a book party was all over the newspapers and on television. I was a liability, a burden, a problem, a human blight—an embarrassment to everyone who knew me, who probably now wished they'd never known me at all. It nearly broke me.

Those two weeks, though, allowed me to understand something about fame that I never would have otherwise: For someone like Matt, it was both a power to be wielded and an inconvenient restraint on his impulses. Female subordinates, with their guaranteed deference and discretion, provided a safe outlet for those impulses. My mother was right. We were conveniences.

*Catch and Kill*, Farrow's book, is more than four hundred pages long. Years of shame and suffering, hours of questions and fact-checking calls, became about seven of those pages. The book was never meant to be about me, nor was it ever meant to be an exhaustive account of my story. Gone were my repeated recriminations and endless self-blaming, along with much of the emotional confusion underlying them. Are there characterizations in Farrow's telling of my story that I would have made differently? Narrative simplifications that I might not have made or sources that I wish he had spoken to directly? Absolutely, but that's how it goes when you give a journalist your story. There is still no other reporter I could have trusted more.

But by the time the book was released, versions of my story had been so widely circulated in the media that I was soon besieged by reporters who took issue with Farrow's telling of it. By streamlining my endless recriminations and self-blaming, had Farrow made me seem more sympathetic than I really was, and Matt more of a monster than he really was? Wasn't that changing my story?

When I spoke with Farrow—more than a year after making the complaint to NBC but only a few months out of the psych ward and into trauma therapy—I was, in many ways, just beginning to come to terms with what had happened in Sochi. I look back at it now and it is painfully obvious that I was nowhere near ready to talk to any journalist about what had happened. As much as I believed that telling my story would help others, I was doing it in no small part because I felt I had little choice if I were ever to regain some semblance of control over my life. But I was not nearly as strong or as "okay" as I thought I was. It has taken me years to fully understand and articulate Sochi and its aftermath, but even just in the months between my interview with Farrow and the book coming out, I'd been able to let go of some of the shame. I could see that being flattered by Matt's advances when I walked into that hotel room didn't necessarily mean that I must have wanted to comply with them, as I'd believed—and blamed myself for—for years. I understood that even though Matt's advances had not been violent, what happened in that hotel room had *never* begun as a "normal sexual encounter," as I'd so often described it. I could articulate that even though I hadn't overtly objected to oral sex that night the way I had to anal sex, it was neither "normal" nor consensual, either.

Now I was stuck in another trap: If the way I told the story evolved at all, I was "inconsistent"—but if I told it exactly the same way every time, then I was "rehearsed." Another impossible situation. And then there was the fact that I wanted to write this book. I'd earned my living as a journalist for the entirety of my career, but now seeking a platform to tell my own story was seen as greedy and suspicious—just as Matt had implied in his open letter. Was I exactly the opportunist that Matt claimed? Was I using Farrow's book to tee up sales for the salacious tell-all I was going to write? I had no way of proving otherwise.

I thought that after a career in journalism, I knew how to navigate the media. Instead I was hopelessly naive about the way the press treats ordinary people who don't have powerful publicists and expensive defamation attorneys to issue legal threats on demand. Now I found myself in the crosshairs of the very institutions I'd trusted and revered since I was a kid, believing they were heroic for speaking truth to power. But I had no power. I just felt bullied, alone, and hopeless, unable to do anything right. The brutality of life under the press's microscope would be a nightmare for anyone, but for someone still processing and attempting to heal from prolonged sexual trauma and its messy aftermath, it was a form of psychological torture that I truthfully did not know if I would survive. Frankly, I don't know how I did.

But it wasn't over.

Two weeks after releasing his open letter—on October 23, 2019—Matt released a photo of himself giving an off-the-record interview with John Ziegler, a media personality widely known for arguing that Jerry Sandusky, convicted of forty-five separate counts of sexual abuse of young boys over a fifteen-year period, is actually innocent. In that Matt was a well-connected media insider who would have had practically every journalist in the world clamoring for an interview with him, Ziegler was an odd choice. Then, a few days later, my former executive producer—whose firsthand account of events I have already included here—got a call from a former NBC executive beseeching her to help Matt clear his name. She refused.

Eventually the *Catch and Kill* craze died down. Harvey Weinstein was convicted by a New York jury and sentenced to twenty-three years in prison.* The pandemic hit. People were dying. The world moved on. I'd heard that Matt was planning to attack Farrow's reporting directly but that was beyond my control and anyway, I wasn't particularly concerned. The obvious hypocrisy and absurdity of Matt—the same disgraced journalist who'd lectured Brian Williams on personal honesty and Bill O'Reilly on sexual harassment—going after anyone's journalistic integrity, let alone Farrow's, was just too ridiculous.

But in May 2020, then *New York Times* media reporter Ben Smith published a column headlined IS RONAN FARROW TOO GOOD TO BE TRUE? Two days later, Matt released his 4,800-word companion piece, WHY RONAN FARROW IS INDEED TOO GOOD TO BE TRUE, which was published online as an op-ed on a media gossip site and comically dubbed in media circles as "The Mattifesto."† It purports to seriously examine Farrow's integrity as a journalist and reveal critical new insights gleaned from sources close to the events, including the former NBC executive who'd called my former boss on Matt's behalf in late 2019. Though my former boss specifically refused to help Matt or have anything to do with him, Matt presents

---

* This conviction was later overturned by a New York appeals court and retried in 2025, resulting in a split verdict.

† Matt's opinion piece remains available online and I encourage readers to consider it for themselves.

a secondhand version of their conversation as reported fact in support of his claims. He also "interviews" two of my ex-boyfriends, who Matt allows to remain unnamed (one, fairly enough, disputes an imprecisely worded passage in *Catch and Kill* and the other asserts that he felt Matt had no power over his career, while ignoring that Matt directly employed his brother for more than a decade; both point out that Farrow never contacted them directly). Matt argues that another of his accusers cannot be taken seriously because he considers her a disgruntled ex-NBC employee, as though Matt himself is not the ultimate disgruntled ex-NBC employee. Even I can admit, though, that not all his points are so absurd, and some—however disingenuously—ask fair questions.

But while he goes to great lengths to criticize and cast doubt on Farrow's telling of events, nowhere does Matt bother to deny, explain, or try to justify his role in any of them—which no one seemed to notice. There we were, locked in our apartment during the pandemic, trying to get disinfectant wipes and face masks like everybody else, and then suddenly the national press gives Matt Lauer, disgraced journalist whose multimillion-dollar contract was famously terminated for cause, a platform to self-servingly attack a Pulitzer Prize–winning reporter by anonymously interviewing my ex-boyfriends. Had the world gone insane? Had I?

This is why understanding Matt's point of view, considering his arguments, and recognizing how effectively he appeals to tropes and false assumptions to cast doubt is so instructive—and important. Again and again, Matt's argument is not an assertion of innocence, but a deflection of blame. On the other hand, compare Matt's words to those of *other* men accused of sexual assault, who demonstrate their own humanity in light of accusations against them rather than seeking to destroy the humanity of their accusers.

"First, I want to apologize directly to the young woman involved in this incident," said Kobe Bryant in 2004, after the criminal sexual assault charges against him were dropped. "I want to apologize to her for my behavior that night and for the consequences she has suffered in the past year. Although this year has been incredibly difficult for me personally, I can only imagine the pain she has had to endure. I want to apologize to her parents and family members, and to my family and friends and supporters, and to the citizens of Eagle, Colorado. I also want to make it clear that I do not question the motives of this young woman. No money has been paid to this woman. She has agreed that this statement will not be used against me in the civil case. Although I truly believe this encounter between us was consensual, I recognize now that she did not and does not view this incident the same way I did. After months of reviewing discovery, listening to her attorney, and even her testimony in person, I now understand how she feels that she did not consent to this encounter."

Or Aziz Ansari, accused in the press of sexual misconduct at the height of MeToo in January 2018: "In September of last year, I met a woman at a party. We exchanged numbers. We texted back and forth and eventually went on a date. We went out to dinner, and afterward we ended up engaging in sexual activity, which by all indications was completely consensual. The next day, I got a text from her saying that although 'it may have seemed okay,' upon further reflection, she felt uncomfortable. It was true that everything did seem okay to me, so when I heard that it was not the case for her, I was surprised and concerned. I took her words to heart and responded privately after taking the time to process what she had said. I continue to support the movement that is happening in our culture. It is necessary and long overdue."

# TWENTY.

# "She Has Changed Her Memories, and Now She Was Raped"

*Alcohol, Trauma, and Remembering Sexual Assault*

Aften the excerpt of *Catch and Kill* leaked, I hid from the world for nearly two months. Life changes irrevocably when you are too embarrassed and ashamed to say your name when you check in at the doctor's office or pick up your laundry. By the time the tabloid frenzy was over, I had shingles and the flu, and there went another month.

Then came the fear and claustrophobia of the pandemic in New York City. Sirens echoed down eerily deserted streets. Life compressed into monotony, punctuated only by the nightly ritual of moving, trancelike, to the window of our apartment to clap for the city's health-care workers.

Amid all that, I quietly began reporting this book, knowing that the first thing anyone I might want to interview would find when they googled me was not my long body of work as a journalist but Matt's open letter and op-ed. Each day, I forced myself to my desk, the present and the future on hold as I painstakingly relived a past that I wanted only to forget. I thought of Matt's "interviews" with my ex-boyfriends and wondered, with his seemingly infinite time and resources, would Matt devote the rest of his life to interrogating everyone who'd ever known me, every bad breakup, every one-night stand, every embarrassing thing I'd ever done? Would I ever be safe? Would the world doubt and disbelieve me for the rest of my life? For months, multiple Reddit threads had actively debated whether I was a liar, and the more I read, the more hopeless and afraid I felt.

"Report it as a sexual assault to the police. If you don't, it sounds more like regret than assault, as in this case."

"unfortunately she destroyed her own credibility by willingly going to a married man's hotel room after a night of drinking? Pathetic to cry wolf for attention. Especially after she admitted to having sex with him again after the so called 'Rape.'"

"He says they carried on an affair and she never worked for him. I mean that's a pretty good defense against someone selling a book unless they can deny that with proof."

"They carried on a long affair and he says she was begging him to get back together with her after he broke it off, aka the implication being that someone who was raped would not be actively seeking out and begging to be with her rapist."

"I wonder what will happen when it comes out he was innocent and the bitch made it all up. Oh that is right he will still be guilty and the bitch will not be punished in any way."

These were some of the nice ones, to say nothing of the emails my fiancé received at work about specific parts of my body, asking if he enjoyed Matt's leftover garbage (this is a gentle paraphrasing). I know how tempting it is to look at those comments and say, *Oh, don't worry, those are just bored people on the internet that don't matter.* They do matter. They are the jury pool.

I wanted to check myself back into the psych ward, but with every available hospital bed in the city needed for COVID patients, that wasn't an option. I buried myself in this book, interrogating everything I didn't understand about my own past, trying to see why I hadn't understood it at the time. I looked again and again at the comments online and asked myself—had none of this happened to me and I read these allegations, would I have believed me? I knew that the answer was no. Even now, with everything I've learned, I still understand the hesitation. Unless you were there, can you ever really know what happened in a room between two people?

Perhaps the better question is, can they?

"She has changed her memories, and now she was raped," Weinstein's lead defense attorney, Donna Rotunno, told the jury during her closing argument in his first New York criminal trial that February, referring to prosecution witness Annabella Sciorra. "Now she is the darling of a movement."

The idea haunted me. Who has not revisited memories only to discover that the stories we've come to tell ourselves about our pasts are not true? Memories are rarely the exact truth, but what remains between what we cannot forget and what we can live with remembering. I understood from trauma therapy that this was not always an intentional self-deception, that the evolution of memory is a reality of surviving trauma. To keep the secrets that endanger our survival, the mind tells its own lies that let us function when the truth makes the world too terrifying. Eventually we come to believe the stories we tell ourselves about what happened rather than the truth of what happened. To heal is to do the painful work of untangling the two. But how can we know which parts of our memories are the stories, and which parts are the truth? Is that truth—not your truth or the other person's truth but *the* truth—even knowable?

———

*SHE HAS CHANGED HER MEMORIES, and now she was raped.* Rotunno's argument relied upon the expert testimony of Professor Elizabeth Loftus, PhD, a memory researcher at the University of California, Irvine. Loftus, who was named the most influential female psychologist of the twentieth century by the *Review of General Psychology*, has published more than twenty books and six hundred papers. In one famous experiment, she convinced adults that they had been lost in the mall as young children when they had not. But Loftus is best known in the press for the "Memory Wars" of the 1990s, when she questioned the reliability of "repressed memories" recovered through psychotherapy. Her later work delves into the possibility that memories can become tainted, or corrupted, over time. Her conclusions might make you question everything you think you know about your own past.

"Truth and reality, when seen through the filter of our memories, are not objective facts but subjective, interpretive realities," Loftus wrote in her 1991 book, *Witness for the Defense*. "We interpret the past, correcting ourselves, adding bits and pieces, deleting uncomplimentary or disturbing recollections, sweeping, dusting, tidying things up. Thus our representation of the past takes on a living, shifting reality; it is not fixed and immutable, not a place way back there that is preserved in stone, but a living thing that changes shape, expands, shrinks, expands again, an amoebalike creature with powers to make us laugh, and cry, and clench our fists. . . . We perceive the blending of fact and fiction that constitutes a memory as completely and utterly truthful. We are innocent victims of our mind's manipulations."

Rotunno's argument insists that reinterpretation of events is invalid, that our understanding of the past must remain static for it to be true. If you didn't think it was rape when it happened, you cannot say it was rape now. But this flies in the face of how we understand the world. I remember when I was seven years old and discovered that the tooth fairy had exchanged the lost tooth under my pillow for a five-dollar bill. Later, I learned that it was my mother. *She has changed her memories, and now her mother is the tooth fairy?* Well, fine, guilty as charged. I remember in 2013 when I met a world-renowned super surgeon, celebrated on the front page of *The New York Times* and hailed as the future of regenerative medicine. Eventually I learned otherwise. *She has changed her memories, and now she met a con man.* Guilty again! For years, I remembered being drunk and alone in the Russian hotel room of the most powerful man I knew, who'd demanded anal sex until I relented. Back then I thought that was consent; later I became better informed. *She has changed her memories, and now she was raped.* Guilty again?

Loftus's work is more nuanced than Rotunno's argument suggests: After learning that my mother was the tooth fairy, did she then *seem* more like the tooth fairy in my memories of her? Might I remember her with wings? I spent weeks with Paolo Macchiarini in 2013 and thought he was a charming, brilliant doctor. Could later revelations that he was a fraud now bias my memories of him, causing me to remember him as more creepy and suspicious than he actually was? Or could it be that, now that I know he was a fraud, I better recognize aspects of his character I missed at the time? How do I know if I'm inventing or embellishing memories versus reevaluating accurate memories in light of new information?

*We perceive the blending of fact and fiction that constitutes a memory as completely and utterly truthful. We are innocent victims of our mind's manipulations.* In other words, Loftus's research suggests my honest attempts to seek the truth of what happened could have led me to believe another lie. That prospect made my blood run cold. I thought of the lame, deferential phrases I'd said as I'd tried to say no to Matt's demands for anal sex, phrases that had echoed in my mind for years on end, haunting me. Before MeToo, I saw them as so weak and pathetic that the pain that followed could only have been my fault. After MeToo, I saw them as earnest attempts to thwart the intentions of someone I couldn't afford to anger or embarrass. The same phrases, first interpreted as consent, struck me three years later as the opposite. Was this a "tainted" memory, corrupted by MeToo?

That wasn't my only question about memory. I'd had a lot to drink, yet I could remember certain aspects of that night so well and others barely at all. How was it, for example, that I could remember what happened in Matt's hotel room, but hardly anything about what I'd done in my own hotel room only minutes before? Traumatic memories, I'd always heard, are seared into your brain indelibly. That was the case with the headboard, coming toward me and receding, coming toward me and receding. Yet, for all the years of flashbacks, I could not, and still cannot, tell you what that headboard looked like. I could not pick it out of a headboard lineup. It's a patch on the wall, as clear and real as any memory that I have, but I can't tell you if the edges are round or square. I can't remember, but there is no question that I was on my hands and knees in that hotel room, staring at the headboard as Matt anally penetrated my body. At the core of these questions are the central issues of how alcohol and trauma effect memory. But did I really want to know the answers? By asking, wasn't I undermining my own credibility?

Just as any lawyer will tell a client never to say anything that could potentially be construed as accepting responsibility or admitting guilt, most lawyers will tell sexual abuse victims never to admit that they are unsure of their memories. In legal terms, accepting responsibility is seen as admitting liability; similarly, admitting that your memory isn't perfect hands the defense reasonable doubt.

But nobody has a perfect memory. Some degree of reasonable doubt is built into most sexual assaults. Alcohol, trauma, even the years upon years that can precede a delayed disclosure—all are common characteristics of acquaintance rape, and all negatively affect memory. In court, memory is evidence, but there's no chain of custody for the contents of someone's mind. To rely on memory evidence at all is inevitably to insert reasonable doubt into the equation.

Victims of sexual harassment and assault, then, face a daunting task whenever they try to seek justice: They must first be believed to even be treated as victims at all. A break-in leaves a broken window. A murder leaves a dead body. With an acquaintance rape, corroborating evidence can establish that sexual contact took place, but the victim must still effectively prove a negative—the absence of consent—beyond a reasonable doubt. We know that both alcohol intoxication and trauma—characteristics common to sexual assaults—change how memory is acquired, retained, and retrieved, but how and exactly to what extent remain open questions. Researchers cannot bring subjects into a lab and traumatize them to see what they remember; they can only rely on self-reporting and simulation, which obviously have their limits. Nor can researchers get their subjects blackout drunk in the lab because to do so would be, effectively, to give them alcohol poisoning. And asking subjects to accurately remember what they *don't* remember is clearly problematic, too.

But if you drink, you already know the broad strokes of what alcohol does to memory: It makes us not remember. (If any of us actually remembered how we looked and behaved while drunk, it's hard to imagine we'd ever drink twice.) It also lowers our inhibitions, diminishes our ability to read and respond to social cues, and makes us comparatively indifferent to the consequences of our actions. Put a bunch of drunk people together and you get a heady mix of people with their guards down who are increasingly oblivious both to the boundaries of others and the consequences of crossing them. When it comes to consent—not the clearest and most well-understood of boundaries under the best of circumstances—it's a perfect storm.

"There are research studies that ask men about past experiences when they coerced or forced a resisting partner to have sex," says Professor Heather D. Flowe, PhD, a memory researcher and co-director of the Applied Memory Lab at the University of Birmingham in the United Kingdom. "They found that they focused on the cues that implied to them that the victim wanted to have sex, and missed the signals that indicated that these were nonconsensual encounters. Essentially, they saw what they wanted to see and ignored the protestations, especially when they're drinking."

"Beer goggles," if you will, don't so much make our potential sexual partners look better but make them look more interested and willing to have sex than they actually might be. Even for well-intentioned sexual partners, this makes intoxicated sex risky. Sure, plenty of drunk people have sex with each other and everything works out fine, but many other times it doesn't—and in the aftermath, memories are patchy, nonexistent, or outright conflicting. Granted, there are readily available ways to avoid this situation. If you don't trust someone enough to be sure they're not going to falsely accuse you of rape, don't have sex with them. If you're so drunk you wouldn't get behind the wheel of a car, don't get into bed with somebody—especially if they are *also* too drunk to get behind the wheel. If you get drunk on a work trip and want to have sex with an underling, don't. If an underling gets drunk and wants to have sex with you, don't do that either. If these choices don't sound fun, consider the alternative.

But not everybody is well-intentioned, and for a sexual predator, a drunk person makes an ideal target. They probably won't remember much of what happens, and even if they do, they likely won't be believed because they were drunk. Our ability to accurately remember what happens to us is our first line of defense against abuse because people know that if they hurt us, we remember and can hold them accountable. Start drinking, though, and that line of defense is quickly rendered moot, especially if you've had a lot of alcohol very quickly.

Alcohol begins to impair memory at levels even below the legal limit for intoxication—a .08 blood alcohol content (BAC). Beyond that, memory can start to become spotty. These spotty memories of what happened are called fragmentary blackouts. You have "islands" of memory that provide some insight into events, but you can't recall them in their entirety, though people can often fill in some of the gaps if cued by others. At about twice the legal limit, or a .16 BAC, it's possible to experience an en bloc blackout, in which no memory for events is encoded at all.

"A blackout is not repression and it's not ordinary forgetting, either," says Harvard clinical psychology professor Richard J. McNally, PhD. "The alcohol prevents the missing episode from getting encoded and consolidated into memory in the first place. Hence, it's not available for recall."

The memory isn't gone, because it was never there; you can't forget what you have no capacity to remember. But how and when someone will black out varies greatly from person to person in unpredictable ways. Some people say they have never blacked out, while others seem to start to lose memory as soon as they start drinking. Women, in particular, appear to be more prone to blacking out than men. It's not BAC alone that tells us whether or when someone will black out, but the way in which a drinker drinks—their individual level of alcohol tolerance, what and how much they've eaten, the concentration of the alcohol, but most importantly, how quickly their BAC rises. The faster you drink, the more likely you are to black out. And while it's possible to build up a tolerance to other effects of alcohol such as speech and balance, the brain does not appear to develop much if any tolerance to the effects of alcohol on memory.

"That helps explain why longtime, heavy drinkers can keep functioning without appearing highly intoxicated, even while in a blackout," says Aaron White, PhD, a senior scientific adviser at the National Institute on Alcohol Abuse and Alcoholism at the National Institutes of Health and a leading expert on blackouts. "Basically, a person can do anything during a blackout that they could do while equally intoxicated and not in a blackout."

Think about that, though: This means that blackouts and cognitive impairment do not necessarily go hand in hand, which raises all sorts of questions about the relationship between memory loss and the capacity to consent. For some people—typically heavy binge drinkers or alcoholics, but it varies—the part of the brain that records memory can shut down and cause a blackout, but their high tolerance to alcohol allows other parts to continue working relatively normally, so they can function for prolonged periods while remembering nothing. Yet when we say a person is "blackout drunk," we typically assume they are so cognitively impaired from alcohol that consent is impossible. Scientifically, though, it's a gray area, and with gray areas come reasonable doubt.

During the Brock Turner trial, for example, the defense called alcohol and memory expert Kim Fromme, PhD, then a professor of clinical psychology at the University of Texas at Austin and the director of the Studies on Alcohol, Health and Risky Activities

Laboratory, where she'd studied how alcohol affects the brain and behavior for more than twenty-three years. (Fromme declined to be interviewed.)

"About the only thing that is impaired during an alcohol-induced blackout is memory," Fromme told the jury. "It's the failure to transfer information from short-term to long-term memory. So while in a blackout, you're able to carry on conversations, engage in voluntary actions, make conscious decisions, anything in the moment, because you're using your short-term memory to do that. It's only the failure to transfer that information from short-term memory to long-term memory that leads to an inability to remember it."

This suggests that it's possible to be drunk enough that you are not recording memory but have such a high alcohol tolerance otherwise that you are not too cognitively impaired to consent.

In the Turner trial, this got ugly. Even though, again, Turner was interrupted by bystanders while visibly sexually assaulting his unconscious victim, Chanel Miller, here's how she was cross-examined by his attorneys on the stand: "You drank the quantity of vodka in the red cup. You drank it all down at once, right? Like chugged it? And that was a decision you made, right? And you did a lot of partying in college, right?" To prove she was cognitively impaired, the prosecution offered an incoherent voicemail Miller left minutes before she was found behind the dumpster unconscious with Turner on top of her. Fromme testified that, since cognition is governed by another part of the brain than speech, "you can't infer from slurred speech that cognition, behavior, decision-making, are necessarily impaired beyond the level at which you could engage in voluntary actions . . . having slurred speech has never stopped somebody from making a stupid eBay purchase, for example."

But "voluntary" and "consenting" are not synonymous, and the law has much higher standards for consenting to sex than it does for shopping on eBay. Take the sex out of it altogether, and the absurdity of his defense's argument becomes glaring: had Turner found a stumbling, slurring Miller behind a dumpster and gotten her to "voluntarily" transfer the contents of her savings account into his or "consciously choose" to sell him her car for $1, the jury would have laughed them of the room. Drunk people voluntarily, consciously choose to do all sorts of stupid things; that's why laws exist to prevent them from being victimized and from victimizing others.

And while alcohol impacts everyone's memory differently, by the point of intoxication at which en bloc blackouts tend to occur— at around twice the legal limit and above—most drinkers' cognitive abilities could already be significantly impaired.*

"It really depends on how intoxicated the person is during the blackout, as well as how sensitive they happen to be to the other effects of alcohol," says White. "Impairments in things like decision-making and impulsive control begin after just a few drinks. As the BAC goes up, the severity of the blackout goes up, but so does the level of impairment in impulse control, decision-making, balance, speech, et cetera."

Victims who experience fragmentary blackouts remember some of what happened, but tend to either question the accuracy of their memories and discount them, or they assume they won't be considered credible unless they can give a seamless narrative of events. When they do disclose or report what they remember, they are often pressured to reconstruct what happened into a complete narrative— but because memories were never recorded in the first place, they

---

* At the conclusion of her testimony in the Turner trial, Fromme was asked by a juror whether she had ever "personally talked with a person while they're having a blackout and found them to be acting normally and able to make rational decisions." She answered no.

can't. When victims are pressured to fill the gaps, they often guess and undermine their credibility.

"There's a double standard for how memory is supposed to work in sexual assault cases because the stakes are so high and in the back of everybody's minds, there's the question of false allegations," says Flowe. "That's why we need to work together to create evidence-based procedures to ensure that due process is met on both sides and we're building the best cases we can."

An American who lives and works in the UK, Flowe is a co-editor of *Alcohol and Remembering Rape: New Evidence for Practice*, which combines current memory research with guidance from law enforcement, prosecutors, defense attorneys, judges, and victims' organizations to offer real-world recommendations. One of her research's key findings: Though alcohol intoxication decreases the quantity of information recalled, it does not necessarily impact the accuracy of the information recalled.

"In other words, a victim who was drunk during an assault may remember less about what happened, but what they do remember is likely to be just as accurate as someone who was sober," she says. "This is important for investigators and legal professionals to understand, as it means that a victim's fragmented or incomplete memory should not be seen as a reason to doubt their credibility. Instead, interview techniques should be adapted to support victims in providing as much accurate information as they can remember, without pressure to fill in gaps or provide a 'perfect' narrative."

Victims often fear that to say "I don't know" or "I don't remember" undermines their credibility, but Flowe advises investigators that this is more a demonstration *of* credibility rather than a strike against it, as it suggests victims are being honest about the limitations of their memories. She cautions that pushing victims to remember more, or to try to connect the dots, can potentially do more harm than good. Her research shows that even if they were intoxicated while their memories were encoded, people are more than 90 percent accurate when they are allowed to freely report them—but when they are subject to focused and repeated questioning about details they do not know, accuracy drops.

"When people have weak memories of an event and are pressured by the police to remember more details, they might feel compelled to try to fill in the gaps, which can lead to inaccuracies in their reporting," says Flowe.

She advises investigators to prioritize questions that are critical to the investigation, and to carefully consider the costs and benefits when they ask follow-up questions. But Flowe has also seen how well-intentioned scientific recommendations like hers can be used against victims in the courtroom, as she did while consulting with the Crown Prosecution Service on its rape and serious sexual offenses (RASSO) trainings.*

"I was talking about alcohol myopia—how intoxicated people focus on details that are central and salient, and for victims, that will likely be the perpetrator and what the perpetrator is doing," says Flowe. "Nevertheless, victims are asked, what color were the curtains? From a forensic standpoint, the curtains aren't all that important anyway, and the empirical data tells us to ask about things that are central and salient, because that's what victims are most likely to accurately remember. Here in the UK, lawyers serve both as prosecutors and defense [attorneys], so somebody raised their hand and said, 'This is great, when I'm working for a defendant, I'll just focus on the peripheral details.' That's the danger when you bring science into an adversarial system like a courtroom."

---

* The Crown Prosecution Service is an independent government body that prosecutes criminal cases in England and Wales. It decides which cases should be prosecuted, advises police during the early stages of investigation, determines the appropriate charges, prepares cases, and presents them in court, similar to a district attorney or attorney general in the United States.

Consider defense attorney Jennifer Bonjean's cross-examination of Miriam Haley in Weinstein's second New York criminal trial, in which she tried to cast doubt on Haley's memory by asking whether she'd worn jeans on the night in question.

"It's possible, but I don't remember him ripping jeans off," Haley answered. ". . . I didn't take my clothes off. He raped me. I didn't arrive naked."

The emotionally salient detail was the removal of her clothes, not the specific items of clothing, so Haley's inability to remember exactly what she wore nearly nineteen years earlier aligns with what we know about memory. Yet, it was used by Weinstein's defense in an effort to discredit her.

Traumatic memory can lead to similar problems. As Flowe describes, alcohol myopia focuses an intoxicated person's attention on what is central and salient, losing peripheral details in the process. During a traumatic experience, the same thing occurs: Attention is typically focused on the central and salient details of what is occurring, and peripheral details are often lost. If you're held up at gunpoint, you might remember the gun but not your assailant's face. If you're running from a collapsing building, you might remember the sound of falling debris and breaking glass, but have no idea when or where you lost your shoes. You remember the danger, not the details.

"The peripheral details get scrambled, but you remember the gist of what happened," explains McNally, a preeminent scholar in the study of traumatic memory and the author of *Remembering Trauma*. "Traumatic memories are typically associated with quite a bit of negative emotion—often fear, but it can be guilt, shame, anger—and emotion tends to strengthen the memory, so people will remember the trauma especially well."

From a survival standpoint, this makes perfect sense. We need to remember close calls and dangerous situations so that we can avoid them in the future. But McNally cautions that, though they may come close, traumatic memories are not as indelibly imprinted on our memories as is often suggested.

"The vividness of a memory does not guarantee its authenticity," he says. "Memory does not operate like a videotape machine that records things with flawless fidelity. Every time you recall a memory, you're reassembling it from elements distributed throughout the brain. There is always a possibility that some things get distorted, left out, or inserted inadvertently. The most likely accurate characterization of the memory will be the one closest in time, but it's not a question of whether traumatic memory is either indelible or totally malleable. The truth lies somewhere in between."

It's another gray area, and it means more reasonable doubt—especially when we layer on the effects of alcohol, as often happens in a sexual assault. Even the most traumatic and emotionally salient memories may not be recorded once the brain's hippocampus is impaired by alcohol, and there appears to be no recognizable rhyme or reason to which memories will be retained during a fragmentary blackout. In theory, according to White, you could go to a party and remember having a drink, not remember something traumatic happening, but then remember the taxi ride home. Alcohol can override even the most primal of our brain's survival mechanisms: Our ability to remember the dangers we have survived, and how we survived them. The good news is that, according to Flowe, what is remembered will be just as accurate as any other memory.

But how accurate is that, over years and years and years?

*We are innocent victims of our mind's manipulations.*

*She has changed her memories, and now she was raped.*

If I really wanted those answers, I'd have to ask Professor Elizabeth Loftus myself—star witness for Harvey Weinstein, Ghislaine Maxwell, Bill Cosby, and Jerry Sandusky—*if* she'd even talk to me. With Matt's open letter and op-ed at the top of my online résumé, I couldn't imagine why she would.

# TWENTY-ONE.

# Believing Beyond a
# Reasonable Doubt

## *Honest Liars, Different Truths*

P rofessor Elizabeth Loftus, PhD, has testified or consulted
in hundreds of cases beyond Harvey Weinstein's, plenty of
them equally high-profile. Some of the even more unpopular
defendants for whom she's testified include Robert Durst, O. J.
Simpson, and Ted Bundy. Whoever the defendant, challenging
witness testimony is an inevitable part of due process, and since her
research can establish reasonable doubt over pretty much anyone's
memory—and thus, testimony—Loftus is in high demand. She is
also highly controversial.

"Child sexual abuse victims, in her view, never have a clear
memory, never have a good memory, should never be believed," attorney Lisa Bloom, who represented several Jeffrey Epstein accusers, told *Rolling Stone* during the Ghislaine Maxwell trial. (In 1985,

during a child sex abuse trial, Loftus testified that she had been sexually abused herself at age six, by a babysitter.)

"If the MeToo movement had an office, Beth's picture would be on the ten-most-wanted list," her brother Robert told reporter Rachel Aviv in her National Magazine Award–winning 2021 profile of Loftus in *The New Yorker*. Her brother David added, "Here these women are blossoming into a world in which people are finally going to listen to them, and then they're going to have some professor on the stand—someone they've never met before—tell the jury that they can't be believed."

Then there was the letter sent by students to the dean of her university's law school, demanding that she be removed from the faculty: "We are terrified that she is a professor for future psychologists and lawyers and is training them to further traumatize and disenfranchise survivors."

For months, I avoided reading Loftus's testimony in the first Weinstein trial—it is only human to avoid what is painful—not least because after hearing Rotunno's "changed her memories and now she was raped" closing arguments, I figured I got the gist. But when I finally read the trial transcript, I was confused. Loftus had not discussed sexual assault or harassment, consent, MeToo, Weinstein, or his accusers. Rather than questioning the validity of any specific victim's memories, she gave general teaching testimony on the malleability of memory in general. That was exactly what I wanted to understand.

"I would think that I might be the last person you would want to talk to," she says, at the beginning of our first interview.

Loftus understands why her research is so threatening to people. "I think that's the fear, that somehow if you question some memories, it's going to be questioning all memories, but nobody's saying that," she says. "I'm not calling anybody a liar. These are people who really believe in what they're saying. That's what I study. But that is, I think, part of the motivation for wanting to reject this line of work and reject that it has any applicability. It's threatening."

More than that, Loftus often testifies for unpopular people accused of indefensible crimes and does not apologize for it. I'm not sure that she should. A bedrock principle of our justice system is that everyone, no matter how reviled, is entitled to a defense.

"I would like to send people the Weinstein testimony and say, tell me exactly what you disagree with," she says. "When the media says, 'Loftus is there to say that these memories, in this case, were fake and not real,' that contributes to the extreme reaction people have to me. I was once giving a talk in which I overheard someone say, 'Wow, she's really toned down her message.' I haven't toned down anything, but they have this image of me as a madwoman. When they actually hear what I have to say, it sounds toned down."

While her testimony did not address or challenge the memories of Weinstein's victims—or even rape victims generally—Loftus's published work delves into thornier issues. She is the coauthor of articles that directly examine how memory distortion might lead to false accusations of sexual assault that rely on some fairly problematic notions of consent. One published in 2015 suggests that "information relevant to the likelihood that the accuser consented to sex" includes whether the accuser was "a virgin versus experienced" or "usually open to casual hookups." Another from 2023 examines how memories of "sexual compliance"—defined as sexual encounters in which a person prefers not to have sex, but chooses to do so for reasons other than sexual desire—can be distorted into false accusations of rape. While conciliatory sex may well be consensual, left unaddressed is the reality that some of the reasons someone might comply with sex—such as feeling they can't say no—preclude the possibility of consent altogether. Might papers like these contribute to her anti-MeToo reputation?

"I don't think it's coming from those articles, really," says Loftus, who points out that she is neither the lead author of those papers nor a social psychologist who studies consent, but a cognitive psychologist who studies memory. "Most people are just reading what the media says. . . . The MeToo movement has had some enormous benefits for bringing attention to the abuse of people who take advantage of situations, and that's a good thing. But the downside is that it has closed off attention to the problem of false accusations and wrongful convictions. Maybe as time goes on, the pendulum will swing back to the middle and we could care about both sides."

On the one hand, Loftus is right. At the height of MeToo, the reigning concern over false allegations became decidedly less important in the public consciousness, yet there is no question false allegations do occur. On the other hand, false allegations are rare and our legal system is specifically designed to protect the innocent from wrongful conviction. That's why it places the burden of proof on the accuser. If distortions in memory can lead to false allegations, they can also lead to false denials. Is a false denial any less unjust than a false accusation? When it comes to sexual assault, has the pendulum ever been in the middle?

"This reminds me of when I was glued to the television over Clarence Thomas and Anita Hill and those hearings," Loftus says. ". . . The next day *The New York Times* asked for my opinion about who was lying and who was telling the truth, and essentially I said, they could both be telling the truth. They just have a different truth."

To her point, Loftus's work raises the possibility that both the victim and the accused are "honest liars," who believe earnestly in their accounting of events but fail to understand how their own distorted memories could be deceiving them.

"Can you explain the concept of tainted memory to me?" I ask Loftus. "Because you can have a memory and change the way you view it."

"Yes, in light of new information that comes along," Loftus

says. "The main thing I have studied over the years is how new information, usually it's misleading information—or it could just be biased or suggestive information—can distort or contaminate somebody's memory. When I make people believe the car went through a yield sign instead of a stop sign because I asked a leading question that suggests the wrong sign, that's an example of something we call the 'misinformation effect.'"

"You're talking about changing factual memories, versus perception of a fact," I say.

"Yes," answers Loftus. "Usually we're adding objects to people's memories, or changing their memory for an object, making them believe the bad guy had a brown jacket instead of a green jacket, but sometimes in these studies, you can distort people's memories for how aggressive somebody was, and that kind of change might connect more closely to some of the sexual abuse cases where there's a dispute about whether it's assault or consent."

Here is how Dr. Loftus explained a tainted memory to me. Let's say I go to the doctor for an eye exam, and during the exam, the doctor leans over me and his elbow brushes against my breast. I don't feel violated or assaulted because, at the time, I don't perceive it as intentional. I believe he's just leaning over to look at my retinas.

"If I were then to read in the paper a month or two later that this doctor has now been arrested for assaulting female patients, I could start to reconstruct that experience," she explains. "That new information could bias the way I reconstruct the experience I actually had, shifting it toward assault."

"I think Donna Rotunno, when she describes 'changing' and 'relabeling' memories, it sounds like she is saying that people are intentionally choosing to do this," I say. "In terms of assault or sexual misconduct cases, it can take a while to recognize behavior as abusive. That's not changing a memory, that's changing a view of the memory, or an understanding of the memory."

"Right, that's true," she says.

"So in those cases, that's not a person reconstructing a memory, or lying, that's just a person changing their perception of what happened, because the underlying facts aren't changing. In a tainted memory, someone's reconstruction of the facts would change."

"Exactly," she says. "In principle, you could remember something accurately, but now have a new view of it, but not change the factual memory."

But Loftus's research shows that the reverse can also be true.

"You can have an interaction with another person and later learn that the person is bad or has been accused of bad things," she says, "and it's going to change the way you remember what you thought were lovely interactions with that person."

"So, for example, someone might have viewed a sexual encounter as consensual, but once they better understand what is required for consent, that might change their understanding of what happened," I say. "That can happen. But at the same time, relabeling that event as nonconsensual could also lead them to remember what happened as more coercive than it actually was."

"Right," she says.

". . . Is there any way to know which it is?"

"No," says Loftus. "Not without some sort of independent corroboration."

Which, especially in cases of acquaintance rape, we know there rarely will be. Where does that leave us?

I lay out a scenario: A woman has been sexually assaulted and is trying to come to terms with what happened. Thinking aloud, I begin to walk through all the ways that memories of sexual assault can be discounted.

If the victim was so drunk she has no memory at all, then there's nothing to believe, and the perpetrator can argue that she consented but just doesn't remember. On the other hand, if she wasn't so drunk that she blacked out but has *some* fragmented memories, the perpetrator can argue that she's not credible because her memory is spotty and that the memories she does have could have been corrupted. Or, if alcohol didn't impact her memory at all and she has vivid, traumatic memories of the assault, well, even traumatic memories aren't indelible. If she wasn't traumatized and her memory is crystal clear, then her memories could have been distorted during the many conversations she's had while trying to process the assault. The more time she takes to process it and decide to report it, the less accurate her memory is likely to be. There were some witnesses the night of the assault, but they were likely drinking, too, and who's to say that their memories will be any more reliable than hers? At the same time, the same can be said of the perpetrator, who may honestly believe the incident was consensual—but his memory could be distorted, too. How can the victim be believed?

How can *anyone* be believed?

"That's the dilemma," says Loftus. "What do you do? But I'm just a memory person. That's up to society to figure out: Given what we know about the human mind, what should be our policies? But that's beyond my pay grade."

IT SEEMS TO ME THAT society is not especially concerned with this particular dilemma. It's only human to avoid what is painful, and this is too painful to think or talk about, especially when odds are it's never going to happen to us.

That's what I used to think, anyway.

In the meantime, we have a system in which innocent men are terrified of being falsely accused and wrongly convicted, and victims of sex crimes have little to no hope of justice, even when evidence of their abusers' guilt is overwhelming. Bill Cosby has been accused of sexual misconduct or assault by at least sixty women in incidents dating back to 1965. He admitted under oath in a 2005 deposition that he had obtained seven prescriptions for quaaludes to give to women he wanted to have sex with. In Pennsylvania, he was tried twice, convicted once, and sentenced to three to ten years in prison for sexual assault in 2018, only to have his conviction overturned in 2021 for due process violations. He remains a free man. Harvey Weinstein has been accused of sexual harassment or assault by nearly a hundred women in incidents dating back to the 1970s. The New York City Police department had an audio recording of him seemingly admitting to sexually assaulting a woman in 2015, but nothing was done. He was tried for sexual assault in 2020 based on charges made by three women, but one of those women's charges had to be dropped due to allegations of police misconduct. Weinstein was convicted anyway, but that conviction was overturned in 2024, citing due process errors made by the trial judge. When Weinstein was retried in 2025 for sex crimes against three women, the verdict was returned split: one conviction, one acquittal, and one mistrial on the final charge after the jury foreman refused to continue deliberating. As of this writing, New York is planning to retry Weinstein on the mistried charge a *third* time, while Weinstein's attorneys are also appealing his 2022 conviction in California and have said they plan to appeal his New York retrial as well.

Yet these cases are exceptional, not because their defendants are famous but because they were reported, investigated, and tried at all. Our most reliable source of data about sexual assaults is the National Crime Victimization Survey (NCVS), administered by the Bureau of Justice Statistics. Those numbers reveal the degree to which the system is failing everyone but perpetrators: Out of every 1,000 sexual assaults perpetrated in the United States, 310 are reported, 50 will lead to an arrest, and only 25 perpetrators will be incarcerated. For the 950 rapists out of 1,000 who will face zero consequences, the system is working great. But would a system with fewer protections work any better? For as much as memory research muddies the water, it's ultimately telling us what we already know: Neither we nor the law can definitively know exactly what happened in a room between two people based on their accounts alone. It's not a question of believing his truth or her truth because, to Loftus's point, both may honestly believe they are telling it. Memory may not be perfectly reliable, but that is not to say that it is totally unreliable, either.

There is plenty we can do to give jurors better options than either believing victims on blind faith or disbelieving them based on misinformed "common sense." We can, and should, insist on a legal definition of consent that distinguishes between different forms of agreement. We can, and should, educate ourselves so that our "common sense" about sexual abuse reflects reality rather than stereotypes. We can stop blaming sexual abuse victims for their humanity and start by believing them, as we do victims of other crimes, and then properly investigate their claims. We can question the actions of the accused rather than the reactions of their victims. We can stop normalizing exploitative sexual behavior and hold accountable those who abuse their power over others, regardless of what we stand to lose when they fall from grace. We can stop avoiding what is painful and ask ourselves the hard questions that we would rather avoid.

Many people saw MeToo as an attempt by women to avoid being accountable for their desires, confusing desirability and attractiveness with desire and attraction themselves. A man might be attractive because he's handsome, charismatic, powerful, or rich. He might be desirable as an institutional figure, a leader, a celebrity, a person in a position of tremendous power. It does not follow that because a man is desirable and attractive that every woman at any given time will desire or be attracted to that man, nor does it follow that, even if she is, she will necessarily act on either feeling. But when such a man believes he knows otherwise, and acts on that belief with impunity at the expense of women who are not in a position to refuse him precisely *because* of his power or authority, he is abusing that power. MeToo, at least at the outset, was not about women fleeing the consequences of their desires. It was about women finally refusing to be held accountable for what they did not desire at all.

MeToo was, in that sense, about accountability. Women are accountable for performing as the economic equals of men, while ignoring the fact that the economy relies on them unequally to bear and raise children, then rewards them unequally for doing so. Men are reproductively fertile 365 days a year, every single year of their adult lives, while women are reproductively fertile a few days a month for about half their lives—yet women bear sole accountability for contraception and pregnancy. Working mothers are accountable for doing their jobs as if they have no children and accountable for mothering their children as if they have no jobs. This is what it is to be a woman, and reconciling these roles is accountability enough. Anyone who chooses to hold a position of power is accountable for not abusing those who have less power, period. Desire and attraction have nothing to do with it.

But as it stands today, we leave victims alone and ashamed, left in impossible situations, struggling to come to terms with truths that likely can never be proven, even to themselves. To heal is to restore the power and control to the present that was lost in the past, but when your past is a minefield of unanswerable questions, what then?

Is healing even possible?

# Epilogue

t is, but it is not easy.

    We got married during the height of the pandemic, in the front yard of my husband's childhood home in Kansas, before twenty-one people and amid an ungodly number of mosquitoes. Two months later, I was pregnant with my daughter. Three months after that, we left New York and moved to Baltimore, where I went to college and still feel at home.

    The day we met our new neighbors, I was heavily pregnant and awkward as ever. *What brings you to Baltimore? Well, we were chased out of New York by the tabloids!* I barely spoke. What could I say about the past twelve years of my life that would not lead to pain and humiliation? I could say I was a producer, but then would have to answer the requisite polite questions about what I produced, which would lead back to NBC News. Sometimes I would say "freelance media stuff," because I did do one freelance producing job after leaving NBC, but I knew there were no more on the horizon and the last thing I wanted to do at the beginning of a new life was tell more lies. Sometimes my husband's pride would get the better of him and he'd mention that I was writing a book, and inevitably questions would follow. *What's it about? When can we read it?*

The most truthful answer I have ever managed is to say *It's not a happy book*, and then make a joke about something I would rather be writing about, like bunnies or poodles or the space race. But this, too, is a bit of a lie. It is true that this is not a happy book, and that my dream of a career in journalism is now a cautionary tale. There is no denying that the reality of sexual harassment and assault is ugly, and that the cost of reporting them is too high. But in the end, I know the most important story of my life is not one of abuse but hope, faith, and resilience. My life is a love story. A miraculous one.

Then there are the times that people see my maiden name on a piece of mail or hear through the grapevine that Matt Lauer, if you remember that guy, has written some hideous stuff about me on the internet. Or sometimes I can't help myself, and I joke about how I was once in a psych ward for ten days and that, yes, I'd be happy to lend you some hospital-grade sticky socks. Inevitable as they are, these are the conversations I dread the most.

The temptation is there, every single day, to try to bury all this once more, to pretend it happened to someone else—not because I am afraid of the past, but because I am so enthralled by the present. Every moment with my husband and children is a piece of a life I once thought I could never have. My family is a living reminder of all that I nearly lost to shame. It is always easier to avoid difficult conversations, to spare those we love from painful truths, to hide in the face of shame rather than to confront it. But to be a parent is not to shield your children from the world but to prepare them for it. To rob them of the chance to learn from their mother's mistakes would be to fail them as a parent. I owe my children every opportunity to make better choices. I am their mother. Someday, they will understand.

Lives carry on. There is no burying the past. There are no fresh starts. We are who we are, and that will always include who we once were.

When those dreaded conversations about the past begin—just as my self-defense mechanisms kick in and my walls reflexively shoot upward—I often realize that the people before me are simply trying to shed their *own* defenses. They did not find the courage to bring up my past because they want to judge or be cruel. What they want, desperately, is to be seen and heard and more truly known. They see in me a momentary opportunity to put down the weight of their secrets, and their shame.

*That happened to me when I was seventeen and I've never been the same.*

Or, *I should have done more to stop it.*

Or, *I've never told anyone.*

Or, *I still can't forgive myself for not reporting what happened.*

A great many more people than you would expect have been in psych wards and know what it is to live with secrets and shame. Everyone has a past, a secret self that terrifies them. People make mistakes. They disappoint. They fall apart. They are terrified of being found out, but they see that my secrets and shame are known to the world and yet I am still here. My past means I have no choice but to be vulnerable, and it turns out that vulnerability opens more doors than power, money, or fame ever could. Matt's attempt to isolate and shame me into silence has succeeded only in freeing me from the burden of pretense. Now my memories of the past, and all the pain that comes with them, are as precious to me as the future.

Since my father's descent into Alzheimer's, I understand that we are guaranteed neither.

When he first held my daughter, my father cried inconsolably because he knew how much my mother would have loved to hold one of her grandchildren, yet never would. Two weeks later, he called crying again, because he so wanted to meet my daughter before he died. He'd already forgotten her.

First I watched as my mother's death robbed my father of a cherished future with his beloved wife, then I listened as Alzheimer's robbed him of his ability to treasure their past. Some days, he remembered my daughter perfectly. On the days that he didn't, he would find pictures of her and ask me to send a few more. They don't have to be good ones, he'd say, he just wanted to remember her a little bit longer, to know what she looked like today, right now. Knowing he would forget his past made the present all the more meaningful to him. Eventually, it seemed to free him from the burden of his grief.

But it also meant that he would "discover" what had happened to his daughter over and over again. He must have kept some tab open on his phone—it was a *People* article published years earlier, "Everything to Know About Brooke Nevils, the Emmy-Nominated Producer Accusing Matt Lauer of Rape"—and every time he would find it, he would call me crying, as devastated as the first time he read it. The last time, he did not call but texted because it was so early. It was a few weeks before he died.

> *6:30am, I read all this, yet again, for maybe the fifth or sixth time. No matter how many times, I must nonetheless accept the reality that this happened to my precious, sweet, loving, brilliant daughter. The facts will not change. I am devastated that this actually happened to MY Brookie. The passing of time can work both for and against us. YOU are MY daughter for whom I have always been—and always will be—*

*eternally proud. Please know that Mom and I will both always be there, smiling, because we are so proud of you. Love, Dad.*

If I bury the past, I will lose these memories, too, and my mother, all over again. When one door closes, another opens.

Worse were the days that he was conscious of what having Alzheimer's meant: that one day he would have no idea who I was, or my daughter, or his own name. On those days, I'd try to comfort him and say that there were things in my past that I wished I could forget, that those memories still haunted me and would probably haunt me forever.

"Were they my fault?" he'd say, horrified.

No, Dad, they were not your fault.

"Whatever they are, let them go," he finally said. "Don't let your past ruin your life. Let it go."

We can allow the past to mean everything or to mean nothing, but, however painful, it is more a friend than an enemy. I would never say to anyone that this kind of story has a happy ending, a redemptive arc, or some intrinsic meaning or value. Bad things happen, and we make those who are brave enough to tell terrible truths pay a terrible price. It will not always be okay. It may never be all right. Any happiness I have found in the aftermath is not because the world is fair, but because I have been loved.

Bullies and abusers hide behind our shame, use it to keep us silent and make us feel alone, but only if we give them that power.

You are not alone. You can never be worthless.

You matter.

# In Memory

---

**KAREN HAYNES NEVILS**
*August 22, 1949–August 19, 2017*

**RANDALL CRAIG NEVILS**
*January 19, 1945–April 8, 2022*

## *Acknowledgments*

Several years into writing this book, I was having lunch with a mom friend in Baltimore—an attorney for a large corporation—when she looked at me, leaned back from her soup, and said, *If I'd made a complaint against anyone in my office, nobody would ever know about it.* My mind reeled at the thought. I imagined an alternate ending for the dream-filled young woman from St. Louis who set out for New York to become Nora Ephron and became a cautionary tale instead. Maybe she'd still be writing and producing news documentaries, or maybe she'd have written the kind of book she always wanted to write rather than this one. The answer, like so many in this story, is unknowable. It just is what it is.

Then I remember another conversation, one I'd had back in New York a few months after leaving the psych ward, when a friend asked if I'd talk to someone about trauma therapy. I met them for coffee, and I remember staring silently down into my mug as this relative stranger poured out one horrific story of child sexual abuse after another. Their raw vulnerability was disarming, and in a misguided effort to make them feel less alone, I spoke of my own shame. I talked about how it was compounded by the constant fear of waking up to find my face on the cover of a tabloid alongside a stranger's sensationalized version of what happened to my body.

A blank, stone-cold look suddenly appeared across the table.

*At least the person you reported is famous, otherwise no one would care what happened to you.*

Whenever I've been tempted to give up on this book, I think of that conversation. I remind myself that, most of the time, when these ugly stories are told, no one listens—and that it has been the honor and privilege of my professional life to write this book. Very, very few people in my position have ever been afforded such an opportunity.

I have worked on the book you now hold in your hands for longer than I have ever worked on anything in my life, beginning it alone in my sticky socks all those years ago and now finishing it surrounded by a warm, loving family of my very own. As this long chapter finally comes to a close, I still sometimes think of those two conversations, and my feelings swing dramatically between all-consuming rage and an overwhelming sense of gratitude.

In the end, gratitude always prevails.

---

TO MY TIRELESS and aspirational agent, Yfat Reiss Gendell: Thank you for saving me from myself too many times to count, for being the calm voice in the chaos, and for your indefatigable strength and courage. Telling a story about vulnerability and shame required a powerful shield, and you have been that for me. Thank you.

To my editor, Emily Wunderlich of Viking: When I asked for ruthless honesty, you gave it with kindness and grace. When I felt hopelessly out of my depth, you helped me find a way forward. When the task of editing this book required you to confront and challenge my blind spots and deepest fears, you never took the path of least resistance. Instead, you did an extremely difficult job with more honor and decency than I thought possible. I could not have done this without you. Thank you.

To my equally ruthless and relentless fact-checker, Hilary McClellan, to whom I have referred for years as my book therapist: It takes a rare person to do the intellectually exhausting, emotionally fraught, and yet necessarily merciless work you have done on this book. As ever, thank you.

To Brian Tart and Andrea Schulz: By giving voice to this topic and illuminating its gray areas rather than avoiding them, you are making the world a safer and more understanding place for anyone who lives with a terrible truth to tell. Thank you.

To Carlos Zayas-Pons: There are few things more professionally embarrassing and personally humbling as a fully grown adult than having to write another email explaining why you are once again incapable of meeting a perfectly reasonable deadline. Your constancy and kindness were lifesaving for an exhausted, frazzled mom always at the end of her rope. Bless you, Carlos! Thank you.

To Kate Stark, Rebecca Marsh, Carolyn Coleburn, Yuleza Negron, Bridget Gilleran, and Mary Stone: Thank you for helping this book find its way into the hands of those who need it.

To the eternally patient and exacting Gabriel Levinson, Tess Espinoza, Tricia Conley, and Madeline Rohlin: It was never my explicit intention to make your jobs impossible, but man, did I always find a way. After so many years, the thought of handing this book off to strangers was more terrifying than you can probably imagine, yet you treated this project—and me—with the utmost compassion and professionalism. Thank you.

To Christina Nguyen and Jason Ramirez: You turned a

manuscript filled with ugliness and pain into a physical object of elegance, dignity, and shared human experience. Thank you.

To the entire Viking team: Thank you for your infinite care, patience, and compassion. From the extra months of maternity leave to my endless trials in managing childcare, breastfeeding, and always inconveniently timed preschool pickups, you have allowed me to be exactly the kind of mom I wanted to be while doing the most meaningful professional work of my life. Thank you.

Thank you to the brilliant literary photographer Beowulf Sheehan, who made a self-conscious, unphotogenic mother of two toddlers with acute mommy brain (look where?) and three hours' sleep feel like Oprah for a day. I will forever aspire to be the woman you captured in your photos.

Thank you to the small army of attorneys whose diligence, caution, and counsel helped me find the courage to face the daunting task of putting these words out into the world.

Thank you to my former employer, NBC, who investigated my complaint and acted swiftly in response to it despite the considerable cost, and to the legal, human resources, and medical teams there who supported me as I navigated treatment and recovery. I have not forgotten, nor will I ever forget, your many small acts of grace and humanity during a time I genuinely feared I might not survive. Thank you.

One final time, thank you to every single person interviewed within these pages, named and unnamed, many of whom have devoted their lives to combating sexual harassment, assault, and trauma; to the pursuit of justice; and to helping others overcome the shame, fear, stigma, and misunderstanding that accompanies the heartbreaking aftermath of these situations. Thank you for your courage. Thank you for your time. Thank you for your trust. Thank you for your patience. Most of all, thank you for the work that you do so tirelessly, which has helped me and countless others when we have felt most alone and afraid.

———

NO LITTLE GIRL DREAMS of growing up to write this book, but neither does anyone dream that their wife, mother, sister, daughter, goddaughter, daughter-in-law, ex-girlfriend, ex-coworker, or friend will, either. My name alone is on its cover, but many people I love have sacrificed a great deal to support me in this yearslong effort. These are the people who saw me broken in the psych ward, who walked through paparazzi to reach my apartment door, who offered me work when I had none, who traveled across the country for my parents' funerals, and who stood for and by me in every way imaginable. To protect your privacy, I will say only this:

Without you, I very much doubt I would still be here. You helped me rebuild my life, and made it one of meaning, joy, and love. Thank you.

To my brother: There has never been a moment in my life that I have not known absolutely that I could ask for your help and that you would give it. The brother, husband, and father you have become is the best testament I can imagine to the people our parents were. They would be, as I am, so very proud of you. Thank you, my oldest and dearest friend.

To my husband: No woman could ever feel more safe, loved, or blessed than I do with you. I look at our life, our beautiful children, and the way I still feel whenever you walk into a room and I realize—every single day—the great truth of my life: *I have been so very lucky.* Thank you.

To my children: I know that this book, which lays bare so many of your mom's failures and mistakes, will sometimes make your lives more difficult. Please, please forgive me. Perhaps by seeing the foolish, flawed young woman I once was, you can truly begin to understand how long and hard I fought to become your mother, and the bottomless depths of my love for each of you.

To those men and women who have quietly shared their stories with me over the years: Thank you for your vulnerability and courage, and for believing in me. Where my efforts have fallen short, please forgive me. If this book gives you even a small fraction of the strength and hope that you have given me, it will have been well worth it. Thank you.

———

SHAME MAKES YOU FEEL like a fraud in your own life. Confronting it on these pages has meant reliving my worst and darkest years as I was living what I knew would be some of the best and most precious times of my life: getting to marry my best friend; being blessed with two pregnancies in my late thirties that each felt like miracles; and every moment of these fleeting, golden years of our children's young lives. I wake up every morning in a house with no secrets, where I am safe and loved. Then I leave all its warmth and joy behind to confine myself alone in a room with Sochi, its aftermath, and all the shame and fear that still comes with it.

This dual way of living has sometimes felt cruel, but I have come to recognize it as a blessing. It has shown me that it is not despite my past that I lead the beautiful life I have today but because of it. Every time I am forced to revisit those dark times, I more fully appreciate the present. I remember just how quickly—in the time it takes to pat a seat or walk to the mailbox—life can change forever. As the years passed, a new imperative for writing this book began to take hold.

If there is anything—*anything*—that you can do as a parent to make the world safer for your children, you do it. This book was something I could do.

It is only human to avoid what is painful, and I know these pages hold one unconscionably painful subject after another: shame; grief; trauma; sexual harassment; sexual assault; abuses of power and our shared complicity in those abuses, conscious and unconscious. Confronting these unspeakable things sparks our greatest fears—about ourselves, our pasts, and even the people we love—and yet, here you are. You have turned every page.

So, finally, to my reader: This story's defining act of courage is yours.

Thank you.

# Notes

**INTRODUCTION**

**xix** "she did not like": Jennifer Gonnerman, "The Haunted Juror," *New Yorker*, February 16, 2024, newyorker.com/news/our-local-correspondents/the-haunted-juror.

**xix** The two boys: Gonnerman, "Haunted Juror."

**PROLOGUE**

**1** In January 2015: Chai R. Feldblum and Victoria A. Lipnic, *Select Task Force on the Study of Harassment in the Workplace* (US Equal Employment Opportunity Commission, June 2016), eeoc.gov/ select- task- force- study- harassment- workplace.

**2** the profit consequences: Michael Housman and Dylan Minor, "Toxic Workers," Working Paper 16-057 (Harvard Business School, November 2015), https://www.hbs.edu/ris/Publication%20Files/16-057_d45c0b4f-fa19-49de-8f1b-4b12fe054fea.pdf.

**CHAPTER ONE: MAGIC**

**6** "And right now she": Meredith Vieira, "Meredith Vieira Reflects on Virginia Tech Shooting 10 Years Later," *Today*, April 14, 2017, today.com/news/virginia-tech-10-years-later-meredith-vieira-reflects-t110361.

**7** From the very beginning: Cara Buckley, "For NBC Pages, 'Please Follow Me' Is a Fervent Wish," *New York Times*, October 13, 2008, nytimes.com/2008/10/14/nyregion/14page.html.

**9** $3 billion in pure profit: "TODAY Streak Hits 15 Years," *Today*, December 13, 2010, today.com/news/today-streak-hits-15-years-wbna40641197.

**10** Our work went out: "Broadcasting and Localism: FCC Consumer Facts," Federal Communications Commission, accessed June 5, 2025, transition.fcc.gov/localism/Localism_Fact_Sheet.pdf.

**15** "It is sort of your job": Tavi Gevinson, "What 'Tár' Knows About the Artist as Abuser," *New Yorker*, November 24, 2022, newyorker.com/culture/cultural-comment/what-tar-knows-about-the-artist-as-abuser.

**15** "I've been there": Caroline Mimbs Nyce, "A Film-Industry Armorer on the *Rust* Shooting Charges," *Atlantic*, January 25, 2023, theatlantic.com/ideas/archive/2023

/01/alec-baldwin-rust-movie-shooting-halyna-hutchins-involuntary-manslaughter
/672829.

15   "Someone is responsible": Benjamin VanHoose, "Alec Baldwin Says He Doesn't
Feel Guilt Since Accidental 'Rust' Shooting, but Is 'Struggling Physically,'" *People*,
December 2, 2021, people.com/movies/alec-baldwin-says-he-doesnt-feel-guilt-since
-accidental-rust-shooting-struggling-physically; Julia Jacobs, "What the 'Rust' Trial
Says About the Case Against Alec Baldwin," *New York Times*, March 8, 2024, nytimes
.com/2024/03/08/arts/rust-shooting-alec-baldwin.html; Morgan Lee, "Judge Upholds
Dismissal of Involuntary Manslaughter Charge Against Alec Baldwin in On-Set
Shooting," Associated Press, October 25, 2024, apnews.com/article/alec-baldwin-rust
-shooting-halyna-hutchins-051dfa2cb09a3cbd355aee9ad6ed19c4.

17   "Lauer also was described": "NBC News Workplace Investigation," accessed June 5,
2025, media-cldnry.s-nbcnews.com/image/upload/today/z_creative/NBC%20News
%20Workplace%20Investigation.pdf.

18   One in this coterie: Marisa Guthrie, "NBC News Booker Matt Zimmerman
Fired Amid Misconduct Claims," *Hollywood Reporter*, November 14, 2017, holly-
woodreporter.com/news/general-news/nbc-news-booker-matt-zimmerman-fired
-harassment-claims-1058026.

20   "I was in that studio": Caitlin Flanagan, "Matt Lauer's Woman Problem," *Atlantic*,
November 5, 2019, theatlantic.com/ideas/archive/2019/11/lauer-had-a-problem-with-
women/601405.

## CHAPTER TWO: A BREEDING GROUND FOR HARASSMENT

24   "It was troubling, therefore": "NBC News Workplace Investigation," accessed June
5, 2025, media-cldnry.s-nbcnews.com/image/upload/today/z_creative/NBC%20News
%20Workplace%20Investigation.pdf.

25   At *60 Minutes*: Jim Windolf, "Was '60 Minutes' TV's Most Toxic Workplace?,"
*New York Times*, February 16, 2021, nytimes.com/2021/02/16/books/review/ticking
-clock-60-minutes-ira-rosen.html.

25   An external investigation: Rachel Abrams and John Koblin, "At '60 Minutes,' Inde-
pendence Led to Trouble, Investigators Say," *New York Times*, December 6, 2018,
nytimes.com/2018/12/06/business/media/60-minutes-jeff-fager-don-hewitt.html.

25   About a month before Gretchen: Chai R. Feldblum and Victoria A. Lipnic, *Select Task
Force on the Study of Harassment in the Workplace*.

26   Wherever they are, superstars: Feldblum and Lipnic, *Select Task Force*.

27   When asked whether they'd: Feldblum and Lipnic, *Select Task Force*.

28   This is exactly what: Feldblum and Lipnic, *Select Task Force*.

28   "It's been too focused": Feldblum and Lipnic, *Select Task Force*.

28   Instead, victims respond: Feldblum and Lipnic, *Select Task Force*.

32   "Upon investigation," Sepler: "Written Testimony of Fran A. Sepler, President
of Sepler & Associates," US Equal Employment Opportunity Commission, June
20, 2016, eeoc.gov/meetings/meeting-june-20-2016-rebooting-workplace-harassment
-prevention/sepler.

32   Consider Bill O'Reilly: Emily Steel and Michael S. Schmidt, "Bill O'Reilly Settled
New Harassment Claim, Then Fox Renewed His Contract," *New York Times*, Octo-

ber 21, 2017, nytimes.com/2017/10/21/business/media/bill-oreilly-sexual-harassment .html; Michael Barbaro, host, *The Daily*, podcast, season 1, episode 186, "Bill O'Reilly Goes on the Record," *New York Times*, October 23, 2017, nytimes.com/2017/10/23 /podcasts/the-daily/the-daily-bill-oreilly-sexual-harassment.html.

32    It brought in $325 million: Michelle Castillo, "Here's How Much Money Bill O'Reilly's Show Made, According to One Media Analyst," CNBC, April 19, 2017, cnbc.com /2017/04/19/heres-how-much-money-bill-oreillys-show-made-according-to-one -media-analyst.html.

33    In 2017, O'Reilly personally: Steel and Schmidt, "Bill O'Reilly Settled"; Barbaro, "Bill O'Reilly Goes."

33    Factor in the $25 million: Stephen Miller, "HR Lessons from Bill O'Reilly's $25 Million Severance Deal," Society for Human Resource Management, April 24, 2017, shrm.org/resourcesandtools/hr-topics/compensation/pages/hr-lessons-from-bill -oreillys-25-million-severance-deal.aspx.

33    Moreover, the study found: Feldblum and Lipnic, *Select Task Force*; Housman and Minor, "Toxic Workers."

33    warned the 2016 EEOC: Feldblum and Lipnic, *Select Task Force*; Housman and Minor, "Toxic Workers."

34    *Today* was the biggest: Joe Hagan, "Long Night at *Today*," *New York*, March 22, 2013, nymag.com/news/features/today-show-hosts-2013-4; Marisa Guthrie, "The Leader of the Pack," *Hollywood Reporter*, April 10, 2012, hollywoodreporter.com/tv /tv-news/leader-pack-310298.

34    In 2012, he became: Brian Stelter, "At NBC, a Struggle to Revive the Morning Magic," *New York Times*, March 13, 2013, nytimes.com/2013/03/14/business/media /at-nbc-a-struggle-to-revive-the-morning-magic.html; "Matt Lauer on His 36-Hour 'Today' Negotiation, Ann Curry and NBC's Trayvon Martin Mistake," *Hollywood Reporter*, April 11, 2012, hollywoodreporter.com/news/general-news/matt-lauer-today -salary-katie-couric-gma-ratings-ann-curry-310203.

34    *The Hollywood Reporter* named: "Matt Lauer on His 36-Hour."

35    "By the time Ann Curry": Katie Couric, *Going There* (Little, Brown, 2021), 433, Kindle.

35    They fell even further: Patrick Kevin Day, "Ann Curry Reportedly Says Last Days at 'Today' Were 'Torture,'" *Los Angeles Times*, April 18, 2013, latimes.com/entertain ment/tv/la-xpm-2013-apr-18-la-et-st-ann-curry-today-torture-20130418-story.html.

35    Even though Matt's dislike: Marisa Guthrie, "'Today' Chief: Transition Was 'Tough,' but It's Not Matt Lauer's Fault," *Hollywood Reporter*, September 26, 2012, hollywood reporter.com/news/general-news/today-jim-bell-matt-lauer-374346.

35    "We are lucky": Howard Kurtz, "Matt Lauer Gets Sliced Up as 'Today' Show's Ratings Fall," *Daily Beast*, November 26, 2012, thedailybeast.com/matt-lauer-gets -sliced-up-as-today-shows-ratings-fall.

35    Four months later, in March: Howard Kurtz, "Matt Lauer's Bruising Year After Ann Curry's Ouster Devastated the Today Show," *Daily Beast*, March 11, 2013, thedailybeast.com/matt-lauers-bruising-year-after-ann-currys-ouster-devastated -thetoday-show.

35    "the anchor connection": Stelter, "At NBC, a Struggle"; "Matt Lauer on His 36-Hour."

36    Instead, new NBC News: Bill Carter, "Despite Upheavals, NBC Extends Lauer's Contract," *New York Times*, June 13, 2014, nytimes.com/2014/06/13/business/media /despite-upheavals-nbc-extends-lauers-contract.html.

36    In 2016, Matt's contract: Mikey O'Connell, "Matt Lauer Extends 'Today' Contract Through 2018," *Hollywood Reporter*, November 29, 2016, hollywoodreporter.com /news/general-news/matt-lauer-extends-today-contract-2018-951300; Ted Johnson, "Matt Lauer Gets Pummeled Over His Questions, or Lack Thereof, at Commander-in-Chief Forum," *Variety*, September 8, 2016, variety.com/2016/biz/news/matt -lauer-forum-performance-commander-in-chief-forum-nbc-news-1201854701; Nicholas Kristof (@NickKristof), "This #NBCNewsForum feels like an embarrassment to journalism. It's about soundbites, not serious discussion of foreign policy," Twitter (now X), September 7, 2016, twitter.com/NickKristof/status /773683463803240448; Bill Grueskin (@BGrueskin), "This is a master class in bad interviewing. Like something from Leonard Pith Garnell," Twitter (now X), September 7, 2016, twitter.com/BGrueskin/status/773685941504442368.

36    "In the process, the one": "Matt Lauer on His 36-Hour."

36    "That level of fame": Couric, *Going There*, 459.

37    The manager had a similar: "NBC News Workplace Investigation."

37    Matt made overt: Elizabeth Chuck and Dartunorro Clark, "Addie Zinone: Matt Lauer Relationship Was 'an Abuse of Power,'" *NBC News*, December 18, 2017, nbcnews.com/storyline/sexual-misconduct/addie-zinone-matt-lauer-relationship -was-abuse-power-n830721.

38    One was prefaced with: David Usborne, "The Peacock Patriarchy," *Esquire*, August 5, 2018, esquire.com/news-politics/a22627827/matt-lauer-nbc-me-too.

38    The *Times* reported an account: Ellen Gabler, Jim Rutenberg, Michael M. Grynbaum, and Rachel Abrams, "NBC Fires Matt Lauer, the Face of 'Today,'" *New York Times*, November 29, 2017, nytimes.com/2017/11/29/business/media/nbc-matt-lauer.html.

38    In 2004, according to: Couric, *Going There*, 203.

38    *Variety*'s 2017 investigation: Ramin Setoodeh and Elizabeth Wagmeister, "Matt Lauer Accused of Sexual Harassment by Multiple Women," *Variety*, November 29, 2017, variety.com/2017/biz/news/matt-lauer-accused-sexual-harassment-multiple-women-1202625959.

38    In June 2023: Aarthi Rajaraman v. Michael Bass and NBC/Universal Media, LLC, Complaint, Supreme Court of the State of New York, Complaint, June 22, 2023, documentcloud.org/documents/23857459-rajaraman.

39    Couric describes how: Couric, *Going There*, 203.

39    The producer, who'd been: Tatiana Siegel, "'Cuomo-W. Trump-L.': How CNN's Jeff Zucker and His Cronies Manipulated the News," *Rolling Stone*, March 11, 2022, rollingstone.com/culture/culture-features/jeff-zucker-cnn-resign-affair-cuomo -trump-1319698.

39    Along with former *Today*: Siegel, "'Cuomo-W. Trump-L.'"

39    "It was shouted from": Brian Flood, "There Was a Top-Secret Matt Lauer 'Roast' in 2008," *Page Six*, December 6, 2017, pagesix.com/2017/12/06/there-was-a-top -secret-matt-lauer-roast-in-2008.

39    Curry said she then: Sarah Ellison, "NBC News Faces Skepticism in Remedying In-House Sexual Harassment," *Washington Post*, April 26, 2018, washingtonpost

.com/lifestyle/style/nbc-news-faces-skepticism-in-remedying-in-house-sexual
-harassment/2018/04/26/7fa8a666-4979-11e8-8b5a-3b1697adcc2a_story.html.

40    After refusing their advances: Ronan Farrow, *Catch and Kill: Lies, Spies, and a Conspiracy to Protect Predators* (Little, Brown, 2019), 375, Kindle.

40    "had hurt the show": Brian Stelter, *Top of the Morning: Inside the Cutthroat World of Morning TV* (Grand Central, 2013), 58–59, Kindle.

40    "When he took her responses": Farrow, *Catch and Kill*, 379.

40    "For Lauer, work and sex": Setoodeh and Wagmeister, "Matt Lauer Accused."

41    Three of those twelve: Ellison, "NBC News Faces Skepticism."

41    In his 2019 book: Farrow, *Catch and Kill*, 375.

41    According to these women: "NBC News Workplace Investigation."

41    "You were either able": Jodi Guglielmi, "'Today' Show Colleague Says Rejecting Matt Lauer's 'Flirting' Would 'Put a Target on Your Back,'" *People*, October 10, 2019, people .com/tv/today-show-colleague-says-rejecting-matt-lauers-flirting-create-target.

42    "And why should the onus": Couric, *Going There*, 459–60.

43    "'I don't know what's'": Farrow, *Catch and Kill*, 377.

43    Then, when she declined: Farrow, *Catch and Kill*, 376.

43    On the opposite end: Farrow, *Catch and Kill*, 374.

43    "I was so proud": Couric, *Going There*, 451.

44    "It nauseated me": Couric, *Going There*, 450.

44    Now Matt plays the talent card: Ramin Setoodeh, "Inside Matt Lauer's Secret Relationship with a 'Today' Production Assistant," *Variety*, December 14, 2017, variety .com/2017/tv/news/matt-lauer-today-secret-relationship-production-assistant-1202641040.

44    "it was a conquest": Setoodeh, "Inside Matt Lauer's."

## CHAPTER THREE: THE SCRIPT

47    In 2011, I'd gotten what: Brian Stelter, "Disappointing Fall for 'Rock Center,' a News Program with Big Ambitions," *New York Times*, June 21, 2013, nytimes.com /2013/06/22/business/media/demise-of-rock-center-shows-difficulty-of-creating -a-newsmagazine.html.

51    "Any 'abuse' came in": Monica Lewinsky, "Shame and Survival," *Vanity Fair*, May 28, 2014, vanityfair.com/style/society/2014/06/monica-lewinsky-humiliation-culture.

51    "I'm beginning to entertain": Monica Lewinsky, "Emerging from 'the House of Gaslight' in the Age of #MeToo," *Vanity Fair*, February 25, 2018, vanityfair.com /news/2018/02/monica-lewinsky-in-the-age-of-metoo.

54    Comedian Louis C.K.: Melena Ryzik, Cara Buckley, and Jodi Kantor, "Louis C.K. Is Accused by 5 Women of Sexual Misconduct," *New York Times*, November 9, 2017, nytimes.com/2017/11/09/arts/television/louis-ck-sexual-misconduct.html.

56    A senior NBC source told *Esquire*: David Usborne, "The Peacock Patriarchy," *Esquire*, August 5, 2018, esquire.com/ news- politics/ a22627827/ matt- lauer- nbc-me-too.

57    Victims of popular: Veronique N. Valliere, *Understanding Victims of Interpersonal Violence: A Guide for Investigators and Prosecutors* (Routledge, 2020), 42–44, Kindle.

64    The concept of the stereotypical: Nils Christie, "The Ideal Victim," in *From Crime Policy to Victim Policy: Reorienting the Justice System*, ed. Ezzat A. Fattah

(Macmillan, 1986), 17–30; Joke Depraetere, Christophe Vandeviver, Tom Vander Beken, and Ines Keygnaert, "Big Boys Don't Cry: A Critical Interpretive Synthesis of Male Sexual Victimization," *Trauma, Violence, & Abuse* 21, no. 5 (2020): 991–1010, doi.org/10.1177/1524838018816979.

67    "I knew I was crossing": Adam Ciralsky, "The Celebrity Surgeon Who Used Love, Money, and the Pope to Scam an NBC News Producer," *Vanity Fair*, January 5, 2016, vanityfair.com/news/2016/01/celebrity-surgeon-nbc-news-producer-scam.

67    "The trachea was never": Henry Fountain, "Young Girl Given Bioengineered Windpipe Dies," *New York Times*, July 7, 2013, nytimes.com/2013/07/08/science /young-girl-given-bioengineered-windpipe-dies.html.

68    most publicly vocal: Pierre Delaere and Dirk Van Raemdonck, "Tracheal Replacement," *Journal of Thoracic Disease* 8, supplement 2 (2016): S186–96, pmc.ncbi.nlm .nih.gov/articles/PMC4775267.

69    In 2022, a Swedish court: Michael Day, "Disgraced Tracheal Transplant Surgeon Is Handed 16 Month Prison Sentence in Italy," *BMJ*, November 25, 2019, bmj.com /content/367/bmj.l6676; "Macchiarini Scandal Is a Valuable Lesson for the Karolinska Institute," *Nature* 537 (2016), nature.com/articles/537137a; Alla Astakhova, "Superstar Surgeon Fired, Again, This Time in Russia," *Science*, May 16, 2017, science.org /content/article/superstar-surgeon-fired-again-time-russia; Martin Enserink, "Karolinska Institute Fires Fallen Star Surgeon Paolo Macchiarini," *Science*, March 23, 2016, science.org/content/article/karolinska-institute-fires-fallen-star-surgeon-paolo -macchiarini; William Kremer, "Paolo Macchiarini: A Surgeon's Downfall," *BBC News*, September 10, 2016, bbc.com/news/magazine-37311038; Leonid Schneider, "Macchiarini's Trachea Transplant Patients: The Full List," *For Better Science*, June 16, 2017, forbetterscience.com/2017/06/16/macchiarinis-trachea-transplant-patients-the-full-list; Gretchen Vogel, "Disgraced Italian Surgeon Convicted of Criminal Harm to Stem Cell Patient," *Science*, June 16, 2022, science.org/content /article/disgraced-italian-surgeon-convicted-of-criminal-harm-to-stem-cell-patient; Gretchen Vogel, "Transplant Surgeon Sentenced to Prison for Failed Stem Cell Treatments," *Science*, June 21, 2023, science.org/content/article/transplant-surgeon -gets-prison-sentence-failed-stem-cell-treatments.

69    A Vatican spokesman: Ciralsky, "The Celebrity Surgeon."

**CHAPTER FOUR: HOW IT HAPPENS**

72    Costas, who had anchored: Richard Sandomir, "Eye Infection Forces Costas to Step Aside from Olympics Coverage," *New York Times*, February 11, 2014, nytimes .com/2014/02/12/sports/costas-steps-aside-from-olympic-coverage.html; Erik Brady, "Bob Costas: On Pinkeye, How Many Olympics He Has Left," *USA Today*, August 4, 2016, usatoday.com/story/sports/olympics/rio-2016/2016/08/04/bob-costas-nbc-pinkeye /88038908.

72    The man had somehow: Brady, "Bob Costas."

73    but had already overseen: Lauren Said-Moorhouse, "Navalny May Be the Latest in a Long Line of Putin Critics Who Met an Early Death," CNN, February 16, 2024, cnn.com/2024/02/16/europe/putin-critics-dead-alexey-navalny-intl-cmd/index.html.

73    Putin responded by turning: "Timeline: Vladimir Putin—20 Tumultuous Years as

Russian President or PM," Reuters, August 9, 2019, reuters.com/article/us-russia-putin-timeline/timeline-vladimir-putin-20-tumultuous-years-as-russian-president-or-pm-idUSKCN1UZ185; Simon Shuster, "Sochi's Sixth Ring," *Time*, January 31, 2014, time.com/2849/the-sixth-ring.

74 "The trickle-down effect": Katie Couric, *Going There* (Little, Brown, 2021), 459, Kindle.

78 In 2019, when asked by: Ronan Farrow, *Catch and Kill: Lies, Spies, and a Conspiracy to Protect Predators* (Little, Brown, 2019), 385, Kindle.

78 This is a man who: Elisabeth Bumiller, "For 'Today,' New Chemistry as Lauer, with His Easy Style, Steps into a Coveted Spot," *New York Times*, February 9, 1997, nytimes.com/1997/02/09/tv/for-today-new-chemistry-as-lauer-with-his-easy-style-steps-into-a-coveted-spot.html.

78 In 2013, Brian Stelter: Brian Stelter, *Top of the Morning: Inside the Cutthroat World of Morning TV* (Grand Central, 2013), 59, Kindle.

80 Most of these "vulnerabilities": Veronique N. Valliere, *Understanding Victims of Interpersonal Violence: A Guide for Investigators and Prosecutors* (Routledge, 2020), 71, Kindle.

80 "Being with someone dangerous": Valliere, *Understanding Victims*, 71.

82 It was a ticking clock: Ramin Setoodeh, "Inside Matt Lauer's Secret Relationship with a 'Today' Production Assistant," *Variety*, December 14, 2017, variety.com/2017/tv/news/matt-lauer-today-secret-relationship-production-assistant-1202641040.

82 in 2000, when he wrote: Ramin Setoodeh, "Inside Matt Lauer's Secret Relationship with a 'Today' Production Assistant."

91 The scientific term for this: Camila Monteiro Fabricio Gama, Sérgio de Souza Junior, Raquel Menezes Gonçalves, Emmanuele da Conceição Santos, Arthur Viana Machado, Liana Catarina Lima Portugal, et al., "Tonic Immobility Is Associated with Posttraumatic Stress Symptoms in Healthcare Professionals Exposed to COVID-19-Related Trauma," special issue, *Journal of Anxiety Disorders* 90 (2022): 102829, doi.org/10.1016/j.janxdis.2022.102604.

92 Rather than fighting: Valliere, *Understanding Victims*, 129–30.

92 A few of the CDC: "Violence Prevention," U.S. Centers for Disease Control and Prevention, accessed September 2, 2025, cdc.gov/violence-prevention/?CDC_AAref_Val=https://www.cdc.gov/violenceprevention/pdf/sv_%20surveillance%20_%20definitionsl-2009%E2%80%91a.pdf.

93 "Victims do not expect": Valliere, *Understanding Victims*, 131–33.

95 "I just made some noises": Elizabeth Wagmeister, "In Tearful Testimony, Jennifer Siebel Newsom Alleges Harvey Weinstein Raped Her: 'This Is My Worst Nightmare,'" *Variety*, November 14, 2022, variety.com/2022/film/news/jennifer-siebel-newsom-harvey-weinstein-testimony-trial-1235431726.

95 During cross-examination, Weinstein's: Marjorie Hernandez, "Jennifer Siebel Newsom, Wife to California Gov, Asked to Fake an Orgasm in Court During Harvey Weinstein Trial," *New York Post*, November 15, 2022, nypost.com/2022/11/15/jennifer-siebel-newsom-wife-to-california-gov-asked-to-fake-an-orgasm-in-court-during-harvey-weinstein-trial.

95 "She's made herself a prominent": Josh Dickey, "Weinstein Trial Day 1: Defense Attacks Jennifer Siebel Newsom as 'Bimbo Who Slept with Harvey,' Jane Doe 1

Describes Attack," *Wrap*, October 24, 2022, thewrap.com/weinstein-defense-attacks
-credibility-jennifer-siebel-newsom.

95    While Weinstein was convicted: Andrew Dalton, "Harvey Weinstein Found Guilty of
Rape in Los Angeles Trial," Associated Press, December 19, 2022, apnews.com/article
/harvey-weinstein-verdict-los-angeles-rape-trial-1a3a9db4e4589a9e0fb03214bc
01fecf.

95    "We deny her natural": Kelsey Ables, "Siebel Newsom, Who Testified Against
Weinstein, Speaks Out After Sentencing," *Washington Post*, February 24, 2023,
washingtonpost.com/arts-entertainment/2023/02/24/jennifer-siebel-newsom
-harvey-weinstein.

96    Another one is depersonalization: Valliere, *Understanding Victims*, 107.

96    "'It didn't happen'": Liz McNeil, "Brooke Shields Reveals She Was Sexually Assaulted 30 Years Ago: 'I Blamed Myself,'" *People*, March 15, 2023, people.com/movies
/brooke-shields-reveals-sexually-assaulted-30-years-ago-exclusive.

### CHAPTER FIVE: "SHE DIDN'T EVEN KNOW SHE'D BEEN RAPED"

105    Objectively, it was an aberration: Patricia Tjaden and Nancy Thoennes, *Full Report of the Prevalence, Incidence, and Consequences of Violence Against Women: Findings from the National Violence Against Women Survey* (US Department of Justice
and Centers for Disease Control and Prevention, November 2000), iv, 49, ojp.gov
/pdffiles1/nij/183781.pdf.

105    Alcohol played a heavy role: "Drug-Facilitated Sexual Assault," Rape, Abuse & Incest National Network (RAINN), accessed June 6, 2025, rainn.org/articles/drug
-facilitated-sexual-assault.

107    "These are not allegations": Victoria Bekiempis, "Harvey Weinstein Attacked Polish
Model Kaja Sokola, Prosecutors Say," *Vulture*, April 23, 2025, vulture.com/article
/harvey-weinstein-retrial-kaja-sokola-named-as-accuser.html.

107    The jury's verdict: Hurubie Meko, Maria Cramer, and Anusha Bayya, "Judge Declares Mistrial on Final Weinstein Charge," *New York Times*, June 12, 2025, nytimes
.com/2025/06/12/nyregion/harvey-weinstein-sex-crimes-trial.html.

107    In California, for example: Dayna Evans, "Why Brock Turner Wasn't Technically
Convicted of Rape," *Cut*, June 7, 2016, thecut.com/2016/06/brock-turner-sexual
-assault-felony.html.

108    means that his victim: "Stanford Sexual Assault: Chanel Miller Reveals Her Identity," BBC, September 4, 2019, bbc.com/news/world-us-canada-49583310.

108    Because "the ability of": "An Updated Definition of Rape," US Department of Justice, last modified April 7, 2017, justice.gov/archives/opa/blog/updated-definition
-rape.

108    To help victims find answers: "How Does Your State Define Consent?," Rape, Abuse
& Incest National Network (RAINN), accessed June 6, 2025, rainn.org/news/how
-does-your-state-define-consent.

109    For example, under New York: New York Penal Code § 130.05 (2024), nysenate.gov
/legislation/laws/PEN/130.05.

109    Pennsylvania judge Steven O'Neill's: Maria Puente, Gene Sloan, and Jayme Deer-
wester, "Bill Cosby Retrial, Day 13: Jury Adjourns for Night After Seeking Defini-

tion of Consent," *USA Today*, April 25, 2018, usatoday.com/story/life/2018/04/25 /bill-cosby-retrial-day-13-jury-begins-deliberations/548593002.

109    In his jury instructions: Patrick Ryan and Maria Puente, "Harvey Weinstein Trial Jury Begins Deliberating, Told to Use 'Common Sense,'" *USA Today*, February 18, 2020, usatoday.com/story/entertainment/celebrities/2020/02/18/harvey-weinstein-trial -jury-instructions-before-deliberating-verdict/4786306002.

110    In her closing arguments: Shayna Jacobs, "Weinstein Lawyer Donna Rotunno's Closing Statement Argues That Prosecution's Case 'Strips Adult Women of Common Sense,'" *Washington Post*, February 13, 2020, washingtonpost.com/lifestyle/style /weinstein-lawyer-donna-rotunnos-closing-statement-argues-that-prosecutions -case-strips-adult-women-of-common-sense/2020/02/13/6359368c-4e7d-11ea-b721 -9f4cdc90bc1c_story.html.

111    Short invited the jury: Graham Bowley, "For One Bill Cosby Juror, the Work Did Not End with the Trial,'" *New York Times*, October 10, 2021, nytimes.com/2021/10 /10/arts/bill-cosby-juror-consent.html.

111    It defines both inability: Kathleen C. Basile, Sharon G. Smith, Matthew J. Breiding, Michele C. Black, and Reshma Mahendra, *Sexual Violence Surveillance: Uniform Definitions and Recommended Data Elements* (Centers for Disease Control and Prevention, 2014), 11, web.archive.org/web/20231017145235/https://www.cdc.gov /violenceprevention/pdf/sv_surveillance_definitionsl-2009-a.pdf.

112    She even asked whether Sciorra: Jan Ransom and Alan Feuer, "Annabella Sciorra Testifies in Harvey Weinstein Trial: 'He Raped Me,'" *New York Times*, January 23, 2020, nytimes.com/2020/01/23/nyregion/harvey-weinstein-annabella-sciorra-trial .html; Monica Hesse, "Harvey Weinstein's Defense Strategy Is Wretched," *Washington Post*, January 24, 2020, washingtonpost.com/lifestyle/style/harvey-weinsteins-defense -strategy-is-wretched/2020/01/24/ab8fd64e-3e20-11ea-baca-eb7ace0a3455_story.html.

112    "I felt at the time": Ransom and Feuer, "Annabella Sciorra Testifies."

112    Another prosecution witness: Jan Ransom and Alan Feuer, "Weinstein Trial: 'I'm Being Raped,' Recalls 'Project Runway' Assistant," *New York Times*, January 27, 2020, nytimes.com/2020/01/27/nyregion/harvey-weinstein-trial-mimi-haleyi.html.

113    "I felt numb," she testified: Ransom and Feuer, "Weinstein Trial."

113    "It's like I put it away": Lauren Aratani, "'I Realized I'm Being Raped': Accuser Gives Tearful Testimony at Weinstein Trial," *Guardian*, January 28, 2020, theguardian .com/film/2020/jan/27/harvey-weinstein-trial-mimi-haleyi.

**CHAPTER SIX: "THE MARK OF A PREDATOR"**

118    "I've seen this technique": Veronique N. Valliere, *Understanding Victims of Interpersonal Violence: A Guide for Investigators and Prosecutors* (Routledge, 2020), 75–78, Kindle.

118    "That's the mark of a predator": Jan Ransom and Alan Feuer, "Weinstein Has the 'Mark of a Predator,' Prosecutor Says as Trial Nears End," *New York Times*, February 14, 2020, nytimes.com/2020/02/14/nyregion/harvey-weinstein-trial.html.

119    In 2021, lawyers for former: Brian Steinberg, "ABC News Producer Accuses Former 'Good Morning America' Boss of Sexual Assault," *Variety*, August 25, 2021, variety .com/2021/tv/news/michael-corn-lawsuit-good-morning-america-abc-news -1235048782.

119   Corn argued that the emails: Oliver Darcy, "Anger and Confusion Inside ABC
      News After Former 'Good Morning America' Boss Is Sued for Alleged Sexual As-
      sault," CNN, August 26, 2021, cnn.com/2021/08/25/media/abc-news-michael-corn
      -kim-godwin/index.html.

119   Corn left ABC News: Joe Flint, "ABC News, Former Producer Settle Sexual-Mis-
      conduct Suit," *Wall Street Journal*, October 9, 2023, wsj.com/business/media/
      abc-news-former-producer-settle-sexual-misconduct-suit-54f4c309.

123   It's plain old loss aversion: Valliere, *Understanding Victims*, 20–23.

## CHAPTER SEVEN: "SOMETHING WEIRD HAPPENED"

127   "My understanding was that": Rebecca Rosenberg and Natalie Musumeci, "Anna-
      bella Sciorra Mentioned Doing 'Crazy Thing' with Harvey Weinstein, Witness
      Testifies," *Page Six*, February 6, 2020, pagesix.com/2020/02/06/annabella-sciorra
      -mentioned-doing-crazy-thing-with-harvey-weinstein-witness-testifies.

127   Weinstein's defense team attacked: Greg Evans, "Harvey Weinstein Accuser Jessica
      Mann Questioned in Court About Continued Contact with Disgraced Mogul,"
      *Deadline*, February 4, 2020, deadline.com/2020/02/harvey-weinstein-rape-trial-jessica
      -mann-panic-attack-long-friendship-with-disgraced-mogul-1202850789.

127   Two of Mann's former: Shayna Jacobs, "Weinstein Lawyer Donna Rotunno's Clos-
      ing Statement Argues That Prosecution's Case 'Strips Adult Women of Common
      Sense,'" *Washington Post*, February 13, 2020, washingtonpost.com/lifestyle/style
      /weinstein-lawyer-donna-rotunnos-closing-statement-argues-that-prosecutions
      -case-strips-adult-women-of-common-sense/2020/02/13/6359368c-4e7d-11ea-b721
      -9f4cdc90bc1c_story.html.

128   Most directly, they might: Veronique N. Valliere, *Understanding Victims of Inter-
      personal Violence: A Guide for Investigators and Prosecutors* (Routledge, 2020),
      100–102.

129   In 2013, researchers coined: Valliere, *Understanding Victims*, 100–102; Anna Mar-
      grete Flåm and Eli Haugstvedt, "Test Balloons? Small Signs of Big Events: A
      Qualitative Study on Circumstances Facilitating Adults' Awareness of Children's
      First Signs of Sexual Abuse," *Child Abuse & Neglect* 37, no. 9 (2013): 633–42, doi.org
      /10.1016/j.chiabu.2013.06.007.

131   Regardless, there is no: Chris Gilligan, "States Struggle with Rape Kit Backlogs
      Despite Funding Efforts," *U.S. News & World Report*, June 20, 2023, usnews.com
      /news/best-states/articles/2023-06-20/rape-kit-backlogs-remain-in-states-despite
      -funding.

132   In Weinstein's 2025 retrial: Hurubie Meko and Anusha Bayya, "Weinstein's Retrial
      Begins, Testing Legacy of #MeToo Movement," *New York Times*, April 23, 2025,
      nytimes.com/2025/04/23/nyregion/weinstein-retrial-opening-statements.html;
      Hurubie Meko, "Weinstein Accuser Testifies About Coerced Sex for a Second
      Time," *New York Times*, April 29, 2025, nytimes.com/2025/04/29/nyregion/weinstein
      -haley-sex-abuse-testimony.html.

133   When accuser Kaja Sokola: Hurubie Meko, "Takeaways from the Weinstein Trial,
      and a Look Ahead at Week 6," *New York Times*, May 19, 2025, nytimes.com/2025
      /05/19/nyregion/harvey-weinstein-trial-what-to-know-week-six.html.

133    Prosecutors don't pursue cases: "The Criminal Justice System: Statistics," Rape, Abuse & Incest National Network (RAINN), accessed June 6, 2025, rainn.org /statistics/criminal-justice-system.

## CHAPTER EIGHT: SEEING WHAT WE DO NOT WANT TO SEE

143    "Victims tend to display": Veronique N. Valliere, *Understanding Victims of Interpersonal Violence: A Guide for Investigators and Prosecutors* (Routledge, 2020), 114, Kindle.

144    A 1996 study: M. J. Layman, C. A. Gidycz, and S. J. Lynn, "Unacknowledged Versus Acknowledged Rape Victims: Situational Factors and Posttraumatic Stress," *Journal of Abnormal Psychology* 105, no. 1 (1996): 124–31, doi.org/10.1037/0021-843X .105.1.124.

144    A 2022 review of existing: Katie M. Edwards and Christina M. Dardis, "Sexual Activity Between Victims and Perpetrators Following a Sexual Assault: A Systematic Literature Review and Critical Feminist Analysis," *Women's Studies International Forum* 94 (2022), doi.org/10.1016/j.wsif.2022.102631.

148    If acknowledging a truth: Pamela J. Birrell and Jennifer J. Freyd, "Betrayal Blindness: How and Why We 'Whoosh' Away Knowledge of Betrayal in Relationships," *Huffington Post*, April 26, 2013, huffpost.com/entry/betrayal-blindness-how-an_b _3146159.

149    Jennifer Siebel Newsom, who: Kelsey Ables, "Siebel Newsom, Who Testified Against Weinstein, Speaks Out After Sentencing," *Washington Post*, February 24, 2023, washingtonpost.com/arts-entertainment/2023/02/24/jennifer-siebel-newsom -harvey-weinstein.

149    "That is her survival": Ables, "Siebel Newsom."

154    Moreover, victims of sexual: Valliere, *Understanding Victims*, 39–40, 71–72; Judith L. Herman, *Trauma and Recovery: The Aftermath of Violence—from Domestic Abuse to Political Terror* (Basic, 1997), 60–62, 377, Kindle.

155    "And so, even more than": Herman, *Trauma and Recovery*, 39–41.

155    Victims may offer sex: Herman, *Trauma and Recovery*, 190.

162    She repeated that version: Joseph Gamp, "Harvey Weinstein Accuser Jessica Mann Bragged to Friends He Gave Her 'the Best Orgasm,'" *U.S. Sun*, February 11, 2020, the-sun.com/news/386990/harvey-weinstein-accuser-bragged-jessica-mann-best -orgasm.

162    "She thought it was pretty": Patrick Reilly, "Ghislaine Maxwell Victim Says Virginia Giuffre Told Her About Sleeping with Prince Andrew," *New York Post*, January 7, 2022, nypost.com/2022/01/07/ghislaine-maxwell-victim-virginia-giuffre-told-me -about-sex-with-prince-andrew.

## CHAPTER NINE: WHO WE BELIEVE WE ARE

170    Four doctors at the Karolinska: Henry Fountain, "Leading Surgeon Is Accused of Misconduct in Experimental Transplant Operations," *New York Times*, November 24, 2014, nytimes.com/2014/11/25/world/leading-surgeon-is-accused-of-misconduct -in-experimental-transplant-operations.html.

172    She later alleged: Rebecca Keegan, "Paz de la Huerta Says Harvey Weinstein Raped

Her Twice. Will That Bring Him to Justice?," *Vanity Fair*, November 2, 2017, vanityfair.com/hollywood/2017/11/paz-de-la-huerta-harvey-weinstein-allegations.

173 "I felt so disgusted": Keegan, "Paz de la Huerta."

173 Her *Boardwalk Empire* contract: Keegan, "Paz de la Huerta."

173 By March, she had been: Tara Aquino, "Paz de la Huerta's 10 Most Scandalous Moments," *Complex*, February 13, 2012, complex.com/pop-culture/2012/02/paz-de -la-huerta-10-most-scandalous-moments.

173 The Weinstein Company won: David A. Graham, "How Will Democrats Respond to the Harvey Weinstein Allegations?," *Atlantic*, October 5, 2017, theatlantic.com /politics/archive/2017/10/weinstein-democratic-bankroller/542202.

174 Harvey Weinstein presented: Carla Cantor, "Rutgers Fulfills Endowment for Gloria Steinem Chair in Media, Culture, and Feminist Studies," Rutgers University, June 15, 2017, rutgers.edu/news/rutgers-fulfills-endowment-gloria-steinem-chair-media -culture-and-feminist-studies.

174 When the abuser has: Veronique N. Valliere, *Understanding Victims of Interpersonal Violence: A Guide for Investigators and Prosecutors* (Routledge, 2020), 79–80, Kindle.

174 At the same time, abusers: Valliere, *Understanding Victims*, 81–82.

174 Her high school drama: William Claiborne, "Lewinsky's Former Teacher Discloses Affair," *Washington Post*, January 28, 1998, washingtonpost.com/wp-srv/politics /special/clinton/stories/drama012898.htm.

174 Jake Tapper, now an anchor: Jake Tapper, "I Dated Monica Lewinsky," *Washington City Paper*, January 30, 1998, washingtoncitypaper.com/article/279465/i-dated -monica-lewinsky.

175 "a steady call to silence": Harriet Lerner, *The Dance of Fear: Rising Above Anxiety, Fear, and Shame to Be Your Best and Bravest Self* (Perennial Currents, 2005), 117–18, Kindle.

### CHAPTER TEN: A TURNING POINT

180 As NBC News president: John Koblin, "Andrew Lack Returns to NBC News Amid Turmoil," *New York Times*, June 9, 2015, nytimes.com/2015/06/10/business/media /andrew-lack-circling-back-to-news-and-nbc.html.

180 "Did you not deal": Brian Steinberg, "Brian Williams Apologizes: 'I Said Things That Weren't True,'" *Variety*, June 19, 2015, variety.com/2015/tv/news/brian-williams -nbc-news-matt-lauer-today-1201523737.

185 I continued trying to get: Brian Steinberg, "Jeff Fager Out at '60 Minutes' Amid Sexual Harassment Allegations," *Variety*, September 12, 2018, variety.com/2018/tv /news/jeff-fager-out-at-60-minutes-1202938409.

### CHAPTER TWELVE: ME, TOO

200 On the left we have: Madeline Berg, "The World's Highest-Paid TV Show Hosts 2016," *Forbes*, October 6, 2016, forbes.com/pictures/gjdm45elfi/5-matt-lauer/?sh= 4afa44b861da, forbes.com/pictures/gjdm45elfi/7-bill-oreilly/?sh=5856e37f691e.

**201**  About a month before his: Andrea Suozzo, Alec Glassford, Ash Ngu, and Brandon Roberts, "The Lauer Family Foundation," ProPublica, last modified May 28, 2025, projects.propublica.org/nonprofits/organizations/822034311.

**201**  He wasn't starting: "Bill O'Reilly's World: Books, Philanthropy and Speaking Engagements," *New York Times*, April 13, 2017, nytimes.com/2017/04/13/business /media/bill-oreilly-books-philanthropy-speaking-engagements.html.

**202**  By early that afternoon: Erik Wemple, "Bill O'Reilly Unrepentant on Fox News Firing: 'My Conscience Is Clear,'" *Washington Post*, September 19, 2017, washington post.com/blogs/erik-wemple/wp/2017/09/19/bill-oreilly-the-maximal-denialist.

**202**  "'How do I get out'": Jodi Kantor and Megan Twohey, "Harvey Weinstein Paid Off Sexual Harassment Accusers for Decades," *New York Times*, October 5, 2017, nytimes.com/2017/10/05/us/harvey-weinstein-harassment-allegations.html.

**203**  Their story's allegations: Kantor and Twohey, "Harvey Weinstein."

**204**  There were no messy: Emily Steel and Michael S. Schmidt, "Fox News Settled Sexual Harassment Allegations Against Bill O'Reilly, Documents Show," *New York Times*, January 10, 2017, nytimes.com/2017/01/10/business/media/bill-oreilly -sexual-harassment-fox-news-juliet-huddy.html; Emily Steel and Michael S. Schmidt, "Bill O'Reilly Thrives at Fox News, Even as Harassment Settlements Add Up," *New York Times*, April 1, 2017, nytimes.com/2017/04/01/business/media/bill-oreilly -sexual-harassment-fox-news.html.

**204**  That scale alone served: Emily Steel and Michael S. Schmidt, "Bill O'Reilly Settled New Harassment Claim, Then Fox Renewed His Contract," *New York Times*, October 21, 2017, nytimes.com/2017/10/21/business/media/bill-oreilly-sexual -harassment.html; Paul Farhi, "Bill O'Reilly's Gone—with $25 Million in Severance. Now the Hard Work Really Starts for Fox News," *Washington Post*, April 20, 2017, washingtonpost.com/lifestyle/style/bill-oreillys-gone-now-the-hard-work-really -starts-for-fox-news/2017/04/20/3ddc8f1c-25d6-11e7-b503-9d616bd5a305_story .html.

**205**  Here was a wholly: Ronan Farrow, "From Aggressive Overtures to Sexual Assault: Harvey Weinstein's Accusers Tell Their Stories," *New Yorker*, October 10, 2017, newyorker.com/news/news-desk/from-aggressive-overtures-to-sexual-assault -harvey-weinsteins-accusers-tell-their-stories; "Harvey Weinstein, Caught on Tape," *New Yorker*, October 10, 2017, newyorker.com/video/watch/harvey-weinstein-caught -on-tape.

**205**  Afterward, Weinstein "acted": Farrow, "From Aggressive Overtures."

**206**  "After the rape": Farrow, "From Aggressive Overtures."

**207**  "This looks like weakness": Jia Tolentino, "How Men Like Harvey Weinstein Implicate Their Victims in Their Acts," *New Yorker*, October 11, 2017, newyorker .com/culture/jia-tolentino/how-men-like-harvey-weinstein-implicate-their-victims -in-their-acts.

**209**  Thirty-five had their stories: Noreen Malone, "'I'm No Longer Afraid': 35 Women Tell Their Stories About Being Assaulted by Bill Cosby, and the Culture That Wouldn't Listen," *Cut*, July 26, 2015, thecut.com/2015/07/bill-cosbys-accusers-speak -out.html.

**CHAPTER THIRTEEN: NO GOOD OPTIONS**

215 When she mentioned Andrew: Katie Couric, *Going There* (Little, Brown, 2021), 435–36, Kindle.

215 He was promptly suspended: Irin Carmon and Amy Brittain, "Eight Women Say Charlie Rose Sexually Harassed Them—with Nudity, Groping and Lewd Calls," *Washington Post*, November 20, 2017, washingtonpost.com/investigations/eight -women-say-charlie-rose-sexually-harassed-them--with-nudity-groping-and -lewd-calls/2017/11/20/9b168de8-caec-11e7-8321-481fd63f174d_story.html.

220 "Going to human resources": Margaret Sullivan, "Culture of Misogyny Makes O'Reilly's Hotline Defense Nothing Short of Ridiculous," *Washington Post*, April 5, 2017, washingtonpost.com/lifestyle/style/culture-of-misogyny-makes-oreillys-hotline -defense-nothing-short-of-ridiculous/2017/04/05/671acdd0-1a0a-11e7-855e -4824bbb5d748_story.html.

222 File a discrimination charge: "Timeliness," US Equal Employment Opportunity Commission, accessed June 9, 2025, eeoc.gov/field-office/losangeles/timeliness.

222 If they don't, you will: "What You Can Expect After a Charge Is Filed," US Equal Employment Opportunity Commission, accessed June 9, 2025, eeoc.gov/employers /what-you-can-expect-after-charge-filed.

222 On the bright side: *2023 Annual Performance Report*, US Equal Employment Op- portunity Commission, accessed June 9, 2025, eeoc.gov/2023-annual-performance -report.

**CHAPTER FOURTEEN: "HE IS BELOVED BY MANY, MANY PEOPLE HERE"**

235 "The Company determined": "NBC News Workplace Investigation," accessed June 5, 2025, media-cldnry.s-nbcnews.com/image/upload/today/z_creative/NBC %20News%20Workplace%20Investigation.pdf.

238 That's how betrayal blindness: Pamela J. Birrell and Jennifer J. Freyd, "Betrayal Blind- ness: How and Why We 'Whoosh' Away Knowledge of Betrayal in Relationships," *Huff- ington Post*, April 26, 2013, huffpost.com/entry/betrayal-blindness-how-an_b_3146159.

238 "We fear risking": Jennifer Freyd and Pamela Birrell, *Blind to Betrayal: Why We Fool Ourselves We Aren't Being Fooled* (Wiley, 2013), 12–13, Kindle.

240 "They put effort": Veronique N. Valliere, *Understanding Victims of Interpersonal Violence: A Guide for Investigators and Prosecutors* (Routledge, 2020), 80, Kindle.

241 Moreover, successful abusers: Meredith Blake, "Why Phylicia Rashad's Defense of Bill Cosby Is So Infuriating," *Los Angeles Times*, June 30, 2021, latimes.com /entertainment-arts/tv/story/2021-06-30/bill-cosby-phylicia-rashad-allison-mack -james-franco-josh-duggar-britney-spears; Lisa Respers France, "Phylicia Rashad's Support of Bill Cosby Highlights Division in the Black Community," CNN, July 1, 2021, cnn.com/2021/07/01/entertainment/phylicia-rashad-bill-cosby-black-community /index.html.

241 "I learned a profound": Veronique N. Valliere, *Unmasking the Sexual Offender* (Routledge, 2022), introduction.

241 In a formal study: Valliere, *Unmasking the Sexual Offender*, 19.

242 "The victim demands action": Judith L. Herman, *Trauma and Recovery: The After- math of Violence—from Domestic Abuse to Political Terror* (Basic, 1997), 14, Kindle.

**CHAPTER FIFTEEN: THE ATTENTION**

**245** That day, *The New York*: Ellen Gabler, Jim Rutenberg, Michael M. Grynbaum, and Rachel Abrams, "NBC Fires Matt Lauer, the Face of 'Today,'" *New York Times*, November 29, 2017, nytimes.com/2017/11/29/business/media/nbc-matt-lauer.html.

**247** The allegation related: Sarah Ellison, "'Everybody Knew': Inside the Fall of *Today's* Matt Lauer," *Vanity Fair*, November 29, 2017, vanityfair.com/news/2017/11/inside-the-fall-of-todays-matt-lauer.

**248** "There are no words": Jill Disis, "Read Matt Lauer's Full Apology," CNN, November 30, 2017, money.cnn.com/2017/11/30/media/matt-lauer-full-statement/index.html.

**249** Bill O'Reilly had personally: Emily Steel and Michael S. Schmidt, "Bill O'Reilly Settled New Harassment Claim, Then Fox Renewed His Contract," *New York Times*, October 21, 2017, nytimes.com/2017/10/21/business/media/bill-oreilly-sexual-harassment.html.

**249** Gretchen Carlson received: Michael M. Grynbaum and John Koblin, "Fox Settles with Gretchen Carlson over Roger Ailes Sex Harassment Claims," *New York Times*, September 6, 2016, nytimes.com/2016/09/07/business/media/fox-news-roger-ailes-gretchen-carlson-sexual-harassment-lawsuit-settlement.html.

**252** Within hours, *US Weekly*: Dave Quinn, "Matt Lauer Sent Hoda Kotb a Congratulatory Text After 'Today' Co-Anchor Announcement," *People*, January 2, 2018, people.com/tv/matt-lauer-congratulates-hoda-kotb-on-today-coanchor-position.

**252** "You know, Matt is": Antoinette Bueno, "Hoda Kotb Reveals Matt Lauer's Text After Replacing Him as 'Today' Show Co-Anchor," *Entertainment Tonight*, January 2, 2018, etonline.com/hoda-kotb-reveals-matt-lauers-text-after-replacing-him-today-show-co-anchor-exclusive-93373.

**256** "One woman said that": Sarah Ellison, "NBC News Faces Skepticism in Remedying In-House Sexual Harassment," *Washington Post*, April 26, 2018, washingtonpost.com/lifestyle/style/nbc-news-faces-skepticism-in-remedying-in-house-sexual-harassment/2018/04/26/7fa8a666-4979-11e8-8b5a-3b1697adcc2a_story.html.

**257** Next, Matt appeared: Charlotte Graham-McLay, "Matt Lauer's New Zealand Ranch in Battle for Access over Nearby Park," *New York Times*, July 24, 2018, nytimes.com/2018/07/24/world/asia/matt-lauer-new-zealand-ranch-access.html.

**257** "And I'm not at liberty": "Matt Lauer: 'I Think They See Me as an Easy Mark,'" *Radio New Zealand*, July 24, 2018, rnz.co.nz/national/programmes/checkpoint/audio/2018655011/matt-lauer-i-think-they-see-me-as-an-easy-mark.

**CHAPTER SIXTEEN: GETTING OUT OF SURVIVAL MODE**

**264** "Part of the challenge": Bruce D. Perry and Oprah Winfrey, *What Happened to You?: Conversations on Trauma, Resilience, and Healing* (Flatiron, 2021), 105, Kindle.

**264** The answer comes down: Perry and Winfrey, *What Happened to You?*, 102–3.

**264** "The dilemma of defining": Perry and Winfrey, *What Happened to You?*, 106.

**268** The kind of traumatic: Barbara O. Rothbaum and Sheila A. M. Rauch, *PTSD: What Everyone Needs to Know* (Oxford University Press, 2020), 1, Kindle.

**268** characteristic shared by all: Rothbaum and Rauch, *PTSD*, 1.

**268** Most of us will experience: Rothbaum and Rauch, *PTSD*, 16–25.

**268** When the traumatic event: Rothbaum and Rauch, *PTSD*, 6.

268  PTSD is now: *The Diagnostic and Statistical Manual of Mental Disorders,* Fifth Edition (American Psychiatric Association, 2022), 302–13.

268  A *New Yorker* analysis: Parul Sehgal, "The Case Against the Trauma Plot," *New Yorker,* December 27, 2021, newyorker.com/magazine/2022/01/03/the-case-against-the-trauma-plot.

269  While PTSD is the fourth: "What Is Posttraumatic Stress Disorder (PTSD)?," American Psychiatric Association, last modified March 2025, psychiatry.org/patients-families/ptsd/what-is-ptsd; Rothbaum and Rauch, *PTSD,* 26–27.

269  They can be reminded: Rothbaum and Rauch, *PTSD,* 26–27.

275  A gentler, empirically supported: "Cognitive Processing Therapy (CPT) for PTSD," National Center for PTSD, US Department of Veterans Affairs, last modified March 26, 2025, ptsd.va.gov/understand_tx/cognitive_processing.asp.

275  Other effective treatment: Dawson Church, Sheri Stern, Elizabeth Boath, Antony Stewart, David Feinstein, and Morgan Clond, "Emotional Freedom Techniques to Treat Posttraumatic Stress Disorder in Veterans: Review of the Evidence, Survey of Practitioners, and Proposed Clinical Guidelines," *Permanente Journal* 21, no. 4 (2017), doi.org/10.7812/TPP/16-100.

### CHAPTER SEVENTEEN: A SURVIVOR MISSION

281  "She must be the author": Judith L. Herman, "Recovery from Psychological Trauma," *Psychiatry and Clinical Neurosciences* 52, no. S1 (1998): S98–S103, doi.org/10.1046/j.1440-1819.1998.0520s5S145.x.

281  "She will never be": Judith L. Herman, *Truth and Repair: How Trauma Survivors Envision Justice* (Basic, 2023), 4.

282  While most will seek: Judith L. Herman, *Trauma and Recovery: The Aftermath of Violence—from Domestic Abuse to Political Terror* (Basic, 1997), 190, 296.

282  "The trauma is redeemed": Herman, *Trauma and Recovery,* 296.

283  Two bystanders witnessed: People of the State of California v. Brock Allen Turner, H043709, Court of Appeals of California, Sixth District (August 8, 2018).

283  Still, Turner denied: Chanel Miller, *Know My Name: A Memoir* (Viking, 2019), 43.

283  "It was like watching": Miller, *Know My Name,* 46.

283  Turner was convicted: Jeannie Suk Gersen, "Revisiting the Brock Turner Case," *New Yorker,* March 29, 2023, newyorker.com/news/our-columnists/revisiting-the-brock-turner-case.

284  In response to the suit: Ben Sisario, "Sean Combs Is Accused by Cassie of Rape and Years of Abuse in Lawsuit," *New York Times,* November 16, 2023, nytimes.com/2023/11/16/arts/music/sean-combs-diddy-cassie-rape-lawsuit.html.

284  The next day, though: Ben Sisario, "Cassie Settles Lawsuit Accusing Sean Combs of Rape and Abuse," *New York Times,* November 17, 2023, nytimes.com/2023/11/17/arts/music/cassie-diddy-sean-combs-settlement.html.

284  a hotel security worker: "Hotel Security Worker Says Sean Combs Paid 100K for Assault Video of Cassie," *Washington Post,* June 3, 2025, washingtonpost.com/entertainment/music/2025/06/03/diddy-trial-live-updates-sean-combs-witness-testimony.

284  "I take full responsibility": Julia Jacobs, "Sean Combs Apologizes After Video Shows

Him Assaulting Cassie," *New York Times*, May 19, 2024, nytimes.com/2024/05/19 /arts/music/sean-combs-diddy-cassie-assault-video-response.html.

284 In a DARVO response: Jennifer J. Freyd, "Violations of Power, Adaptive Blindness and Betrayal Trauma Theory," *Feminism & Psychology* 7, no.1 (1997): 22–32, doi .org/10.1177/0959353597071004.

285 "This attack, intended": Freyd, "Violations of Power."

286 "Judges often share": Herman, *Truth and Repair*, 14.

287 "She must be secure": Herman, "Recovery from Psychological Trauma."


**CHAPTER EIGHTEEN: REDEFINING RISK**

290 The *Daily Mail* headline: Leah Simpson, "Matt Lauer Puts on a Brave Face Amid Reports of a Tell-All Book by Meredith Vieira's Former Assistant, Whose Affair Led to NBC Terminating Today Anchor's $25M Contract," *Daily Mail*, March 16, 2019, dailymail.co.uk/news/article-6817065/Matt-Lauer-puts-brave-face-amid -reports-tell-book-Meredith-Vieiras-former-assistant.html.

293 "So there is absolutely": Michael Barbaro, host, *The Daily*, podcast, "The Woman Defending Harvey Weinstein," *New York Times*, February 7, 2020, nytimes.com/2020 /02/07/podcasts/the-daily/weinstein-trial.html.

294 Research has shown: Veronique N. Valliere, *Unmasking the Sexual Offender* (Routledge, 2022), 59.

295 In her experience: Valliere, *Unmasking the Sexual Offender*, 59–61.

296 As an expert in both: William Edward Arnold, Jr. v. State of Tennessee, Appeal from the Criminal Court for Davidson County No. 2011-B-1778 (2019).


**CHAPTER NINETEEN: HE SAID / SHE SAID**

310 "So obviously there's": Rich McHugh, "'You Are to Stand Down': Ronan Farrow's Producer on How NBC Killed Its Weinstein Story," *Vanity Fair*, October 11, 2019, vanityfair.com/news/2019/10/how-nbc-killed-its-weinstein-story.

320 "After months of reviewing": "Kobe Bryant's Apology," Associated Press, September 1, 2004, espn.com/nba/news/story?id=1872928.

320 "It is necessary": Katie Way, "Aziz Ansari Issues Statement Denying Sexual Misconduct," *Babe*, January 15, 2018, babe.net/2018/01/15/aziz-ansari-statement-28407.


**CHAPTER TWENTY: "SHE HAS CHANGED HER MEMORIES, AND NOW SHE WAS RAPED"**

323 "Now she is the darling": Jan Ransom and Alan Feuer, "Weinstein's Lawyer Says Accusers Had a Choice in Sexual Encounters," *New York Times*, February 13, 2020, nytimes.com/2020/02/13/nyregion/harvey-weinstein-trial.html.

324 Her later work delves: Rachel Aviv, "How Elizabeth Loftus Changed the Meaning of Memory," *New Yorker*, March 29, 2021, newyorker.com/magazine/2021/04/05 /how-elizabeth-loftus-changed-the-meaning-of-memory/amp.

324 "Truth and reality": Elizabeth Loftus and Katherine Ketcham, *Witness for the Defense: The Accused, the Eyewitness, and the Expert Who Puts Memory on Trial* (St. Martin's, 1991), 19–20.

325   I remember in 2013: Henry Fountain, "A First: Organs Tailor-Made with Body's Own Cells," *New York Times*, September 15, 2012, nytimes.com/2012/09/16/health /research/scientists-make-progress-in-tailor-made-organs.html.

329   Beyond that, memory: Aaron M. White, "What Happened? Alcohol, Memory Blackouts, and the Brain," *Alcohol Research & Health* 27, no. 2 (2003): 186–96, ncbi .nlm.nih.gov/pmc/articles/PMC6668891.

329   You have "islands": White, "What Happened?"

329   At about twice the legal: "Interrupted Memories: Alcohol-Induced Blackouts," National Institute on Alcohol Abuse and Alcoholism, last modified June 2025, niaaa .nih.gov/publications/brochures-and-fact-sheets/interrupted-memories-alcohol -induced-blackouts.

329   Women, in particular, appear: Aaron M. White, "Gender Differences in the Epidemiology of Alcohol Use and Related Harms in the United States," *Alcohol Research* 40, no. 2 (2020), doi.org/10.35946/arcr.v40.2.01.

330   It's not BAC alone: "Interrupted Memories."

331   "It's only the failure": People of the State of California v. Brock Allen Turner, Reporter's Transcript of Proceedings, vol. 8, 666–67, March 22, 2016.

331   "And you did a lot": Chanel Miller, *Know My Name: A Memoir* (Viking, 2019), 176.

331   Fromme testified that: *People v. Turner*, Reporter's Transcript.

332   And while alcohol: "Interrupted Memories."

333   One of her research's: Heather D. Flowe, Theo Jores, Julie Gawrylowicz, Danielle Hett, and Graham M. Davies, "Impact of Alcohol on Memory: A Systematic Review," in *Alcohol and Remembering Rape: New Evidence for Practice*, ed. Heather D. Flowe and Anna Carline (Palgrave Macmillan, 2021), 63.

333   Her research shows: Heather D. Flowe, Melanie K. T. Takarangi, Joyce E. Humphries, and Deborah S. Wright, "Alcohol and Remembering a Hypothetical Sexual Assault: Can People Who Were Under the Influence of Alcohol During the Event Provide Accurate Testimony?," *Memory* 24, no. 8 (2016): 1042–61, doi.org/10.1080 /09658211.2015.1064536; Heather D. Flowe, Joyce E. Humphries, Melanie K. Takarangi, Kasia Zelek, Nilda Karog˘lu, Fiona Gabbert, et al., "An Experimental Examination of the Effects of Alcohol Consumption and Exposure to Misleading Postevent Information on Remembering a Hypothetical Rape Scenario," in "Alcohol: Its Impact on Memory and Cognition in Legal Contexts," special issue, *Applied Cognitive Psychology* 33, no. 3 (2019): 393–413, doi.org/10.1002/acp.3531.

335   Consider defense attorney: Hurubie Meko, "Weinstein Accuser Breaks Down in Tears During Intense Cross-Examination," *New York Times*, May 2, 2025, nytimes .com/2025/05/02/nyregion/cross-examination-harvey-weinstein-miriam-haley.html.

335   During a traumatic: Richard J. McNally, *Remembering Trauma* (Harvard University Press, 2003), chap. 2, Kindle.

335   We need to remember: McNally, *Remembering Trauma*, chap. 2.

## CHAPTER TWENTY-ONE: BELIEVING BEYOND A REASONABLE DOUBT

337   "Child sexual abuse": Andrea Marks, "Ghislaine Maxwell Defense Puts Memory Itself on Trial with First Expert Witness," *Rolling Stone*, December 16, 2021, roll

ingstone.com/culture/culture-news/ghislaine-maxwell-trial-defense-day-one
-1272648.

**338**   during a child sex abuse trial: Elizabeth Loftus and Katherine Ketcham, *Witness for the Defense: The Accused, the Eyewitness, and the Expert Who Puts Memory on Trial* (St. Martin's, 1991), 146–47.

**338**   Her brother David: Rachel Aviv, "How Elizabeth Loftus Changed the Meaning of Memory," *New Yorker*, March 29, 2021, newyorker.com/magazine/2021/04/05/how -elizabeth-loftus-changed-the-meaning-of-memory/amp.

**338**   "We are terrified": Aviv, "How Elizabeth Loftus."

**339**   One published in 2015: Deborah Davis and Elizabeth F. Loftus, "Remembering Disputed Sexual Encounters: A New Frontier for Witness Memory Research," *Journal of Criminal Law and Criminology* 105, no. 4 (2015): 811–851, scholarlycommons.law .northwestern.edu/jclc/vol105/iss4/3.

**339**   Another from 2023: Deborah Davis, Joseph Cano, Gage Miller, and Elizabeth Loftus, "The Multiple Roles of Emotion in Interpretation and Memory of Sexual Consent," *Topics in Cognitive Science* 16, no. 4 (2024): 644–60, doi.org/10.1111/tops.12691.

**340**   To her point, Loftus's: Davis and Loftus, "Remembering Disputed Sexual Encounters."

**343**   Bill Cosby has been: Patrick Ryan, Maria Puente, and Carly Mallenbaum, "A Complete List of the 60 Bill Cosby Accusers and Their Reactions to His Prison Sentence," *USA Today*, April 27, 2018, usatoday.com/story/life/people/2018/04/27 /bill-cosby-full-list-accusers/555144002.

**344**   He admitted under oath: Graham Bowley and Sydney Ember, "Bill Cosby, in Deposition, Said Drugs and Fame Helped Him Seduce Women," *New York Times*, July 18, 2015, nytimes.com/2015/07/19/arts/bill-cosby-deposition-reveals-calculated -pursuit-of-young-women-using-fame-drugs-and-deceit.html.

**344**   The New York City: Jan Ransom, "Here's a Timeline of Weinstein's New York Case," *New York Times*, April 25, 2024, nytimes.com/2024/04/25/nyregion/weinstein -new-york-case-timeline-metoo.html.

**344**   He was tried for: Ransom, "Here's a Timeline"; "NYPD Detective's Role Cited as DA Drops Part of Weinstein Sex Assault Case," CBS News, October 11, 2018, cbsnews.com/news/harvey-weinstein-lucia-evans-one-criminal-charge-dropped -today-2018-10-11.

**344**   When Weinstein was: Aaron Katersky and Meredith Deliso, "Judge Declares Mistrial on Rape Count in Harvey Weinstein's Sex Crimes Retrial After Jury Chaos," ABC News, June 12, 2025, abcnews.go.com/US/judge-declares-mistrial-rape-count -harvey-weinstein-retrial/story?id=122773350.

**344**   Those numbers reveal: "The Criminal Justice System: Statistics," Rape, Abuse & Incest National Network (RAINN), accessed June 6, 2025, rainn.org/statistics/criminal -justice-system.